MORPHOLOGY AND LEXICAL SEMANTICS

Morphology and Lexical Semantics explores the meanings of morphemes and how they combine to form the meanings of complex words, including derived words (*writer, unionize*), compounds (*dog bed, truck driver*), and words formed by conversion. Rochelle Lieber discusses the lexical semantics of word formation in a systematic way, allowing the reader to explore the nature of affixal polysemy, the reasons why there are multiple affixes with the same function, and the issues of mismatch between form and meaning in word formation. Using a series of case studies from English, this book develops and justifies the theoretical apparatus necessary for raising and answering many questions about the semantics of word formation. Distinguishing between a lexical semantic skeleton that is featural and hierarchically organized, and a lexical semantic body that is holistic, it shows how the semantics of word formation has a paradigmatic character.

ROCHELLE LIEBER is Professor of English at the University of New Hampshire. She is the author of *On the Organization of the Lexicon* (1980), *An Integrated Theory of Autosegmental Processes* (1987) and *Deconstructing Morphology* (1992), as well as numerous articles on word formation.

In this series

CAMBRIDGE STUDIES IN LINGUISTICS

General editors: P. AUSTIN, J. BRESNAN, B. COMRIE,
W. DRESSLER, C. J. EWEN, R. LASS, D. LIGHTFOOT,
I. ROBERTS, S. ROMAINE, N. V. SMITH

Morphology and Lexical Semantics

MORPHOLOGY AND
LEXICAL SEMANTICS

ROCHELLE LIEBER

CAMBRIDGE
UNIVERSITY PRESS

PUBLISHED BY THE PRESS SYNDICATE OF THE UNIVERSITY OF CAMBRIDGE
The Pitt Building, Trumpington Street, Cambridge, United Kingdom

CAMBRIDGE UNIVERSITY PRESS
The Edinburgh Building, Cambridge, CB2 2RU, UK
40 West 20th Street, New York, NY 10011–4211, USA
477 Williamstown Road, Port Melbourne, VIC 3207, Australia
Ruiz de Alarcón 13, 28014 Madrid, Spain
Dock House, The Waterfront, Cape Town 8001, South Africa

http://www.cambridge.org

First published 2004

Printed in the United Kingdom at the University Press, Cambridge

Typeface Times 10/13 pt.   *System* LATEX 2ε   [TB]

A catalogue record for this book is available from the British Library

Library of Congress Cataloguing in Publication data
Lieber, Rochelle, 1954–
Morphology and lexical semantics / Rochelle Lieber.
    p.   cm. – (Cambridge studies in linguistics; 104)
Includes bibliographical references and index.
ISBN 0 521 83171 7
1. Grammar, Comparative and general – Word formation.   2. Semantics.
I. Title.   II. Series.
P245.L54   2004
415′.92 – dc22   2003065263 CIP

ISBN 0 521 83171 7 hardback

Contents

Acknowledgments

This book was written under the best conditions imaginable. Its gestation period was prolonged by my heavy administrative duties as Chair of the English Department at UNH – ultimately a good thing, as it gave me time to discover the depths of my ignorance and to read widely while waiting for the next crisis to hit the fan. Although the book was a long time in coming, in the end I had the time to produce the manuscript in virtually one fell swoop, thanks to a full year of freedom with nothing to do but write and housetrain a puppy. I am therefore most grateful to the Center for the Humanities at UNH for a Senior Fellowship which allowed me to extend a sabbatical leave. I am grateful, as well, to the Netherlands Science Agency (NWO) for the support which allowed me to spend a month at the Free University in Amsterdam in October, 2001, and to Geert Booij for hosting me at VU. I also thank the Linguistics Department at the University of Washington for giving me Visiting Scholar status. Special thanks too go to Julia Hershensohn, Ellen Kaisse, and Fritz Newmeyer for collegiality, friendship, and hospitality during my stay in Seattle.

I also wish to thank audiences at the Free University of Amsterdam, the University of Madrid, the University of Girona, the Third Mediterranean Morphology Meeting, and the Linguistics Departments at the CUNY Graduate Center and the University of Washington, who commented on various parts of this book at various stages of its development, and contributed substantially to the honing of my ideas.

I would also like to acknowledge the help of a number of colleagues and friends. This work started some years ago in lively discussions with Harald Baayen. Our discussions resulted in several joint publications early on, before I decided to embark on an extended treatment of the subject of morphology and lexical semantics on my own. Harald will recognize some of his ideas developed here, and he'll find some ideas which he would heartily disavow. Both sets of ideas are much the better for those discussions with him. I also thank Lluisa

Gracia and Geert Booij for extensive discussion of parts of this book, and Pavol Stekauer and Julia Hershensohn for reading earlier versions of the manuscript. Thanks also to two anonymous reviewers for Cambridge University Press.

Finally, special thanks go to my husband David Hirsch for being my heart, my soul, my baseball consultant, and sometimes my most critical reader. This book is dedicated to him.

Introduction

In his comprehensive descriptive work on English word formation, Hans Marchand expressed the following opinion about the meaning of derivational suffixes (1969, 215): "Unlike a free morpheme a suffix has no meaning in itself, it acquires meaning only in conjunction with the free morpheme which it transposes." In context, what Marchand means does not seem nearly so radical. He goes on in the same passage to explain that derivational suffixes change either syntactic or semantic class, and his prime example is the suffix -er (1969, 215):

> As a word class transposer, **-er** plays an important part in deverbal derivatives, while in denominal derivatives its role as a word class transposer is not important, since basis and derivative in the majority of cases belong to the same word class "substantive" . . . ; its role as a semantic transposer, however, is different in this case. Although most combinations denote a person, more specifically a male person (types **potter, Londoner, banqueter, weekender**), many other semantically unrelated senses are possible. Derivatives with **-er** may denote a banknote, bill (*fiver, tenner*), a blow (*backhander*), a car, a bus (*two-seater, two-decker*), a collar (*eight-incher*), a gun (*six-pounder*), a gust of wind (*noser, souther*), a lecture at a certain hour (*niner* "a class at nine o'clock"), a line of poetry (*fourteener*), a ship (*three-decker, freighter*, . . .).

Marchand of course does not mean to say that -er actually means "car," "bus," "banknote," or "gust of wind" in these forms. Rather he suggests that the meaning of the affix is fluid enough to allow all of these meanings in combination with particular bases. But why should this be? What, if anything, does -er add to a base to give rise to these meanings?

This book is about the semantics of word formation. More specifically, it is about the meaning of morphemes and how they combine to form meanings of complex words, including derived words (*writer, unionize*), compounds (*dog bed, truck driver*), and words formed by conversion. To my knowledge there is no comprehensive treatment of the semantics of word formation in the

1

tradition of generative morphology. One reason for this is perhaps the late start morphology got in the history of generative grammar; generative morphology has arguably come into its own as a legitimate field of study only since the mid-1970s and has concentrated on structural and phonological issues concerning word formation to the neglect of semantic issues (see Carstairs-McCarthy 1992 for a cogent discussion of this issue).

But, another reason, a more important reason, I would argue, is that up until now a systematic way of talking about the lexical semantics of *word formation* (as opposed to words) has largely been lacking. Yet questions like the following concerning the meaning of word-formation processes have continued to be raised sporadically (see, for example, the work of Booij 1986, Corbin 1987, Szymanek 1988, Beard 1991, 1995, Lieber and Baayen 1997, Lieber 1998, Plag 1999):

- *The polysemy question*: for example, why does the affix *-ize* in English sometimes seem to mean "cause to become X" (*unionize, randomize*), sometimes "cause to go into X" (*containerize*), and sometimes "perform X" (*anthropologize*); why does the affix *-er* sometimes create agent nouns (*writer*), sometimes instrument nouns (*opener*), and sometimes patient nouns (*loaner*)? Do these affixes have any unitary core of meaning at all, and if so, what is it?
- *The multiple-affix question*: why does English often have several affixes that perform the same function or create the same kind of derived word (e.g., *-ize, -ify* for causative verbs; *-er, -ant* for agent nouns)?
- *The zero-derivation question*: how do we account for word formation in which there is semantic change without any concomitant formal change (e.g., in so-called conversion or zero derivation)?
- *The semantic mismatch question*: why is the correspondence between form and meaning in word formation sometimes not one-to-one? On the one hand, why do there sometimes seem to be morphemes that mean nothing at all (e.g., the *-in-* in *longitudinal* or the *-it-* in *repetition*)? On the other hand, why do we sometimes find "derivational redundancy," that is, cases in which the same meaning seems to be expressed more than once in a word (e.g., in *dramatical* or *musicianer*)? Finally, why does the sense of a morpheme sometimes seem to be subtracted from the overall meaning of the word (e.g., *realistic* does not mean "pertaining to a realist")?

Such questions are related: all are part of a larger question of how we characterize the meanings of complex words. The goal of this work is to develop and justify a framework in which such questions can fruitfully be raised, discussed, and answered.

I am, of course, not the first to raise these questions. They have their origins at least as far back as American Structuralist debates about the architecture of the theory of word formation. Hockett (1954) perhaps first framed the question in Structuralist theory, contrasting Item and Arrangement (IA) theories of word formation with Item and Process (IP) theories. In a classic Item and Arrangement theory, a word is built up by addition of morphemes, each of which contributes a distinct meaning to the complex word; the relationship between form and meaning is presumed most often to be one-to-one. Item and Process theorists look at word formation as the operation of processes or rules on base morphemes or words, each rule adding to or changing the form of the base, and concomitantly having some characteristic semantic or morphosyntactic effect; but again, the relationship between process and semantic or morphosyntactic effect is typically one-to-one. Contrasting with IA and IP theories are so-called Word and Paradigm (WP) theories (Matthews 1972), which map semantic and morphosyntactic properties onto words in a many to one fashion. (See Spencer 1991 for a thorough treatment of these frameworks.) IA, IP, and WP frameworks have all had their advocates within generative traditions. My own work (Lieber 1980, 1992a) has rightly been characterized as falling within the IA camp, as has been the work of Selkirk (1982), Williams (1981), and others. The theory of Aronoff (1976) falls into the IP camp, and that of Anderson (1992) into the Word and Paradigm camp.

Further, the question of form–meaning correspondence in word formation has led in recent years to the "Separation Hypothesis," most prominently advocated in Beard's *Lexeme Morpheme Base Morphology* (1995). Beard, and also Corbin (1987) and Szymanek (1988) have argued that since the form–meaning correspondence in morphology is rarely one-to-one, the semantic effects of word formation should be strictly separated from its formal effects. Word formation consists in such theories of a semantic or morphosyntactic process (for example, formation of causative verbs or agent nouns) which is strictly separated from the addition of formal morphological markers (e.g., *-ize* or *-er*). There is no expectation within such a theory that the correspondence between meaning and form should be one-to-one.

On its surface, this debate seems to be about the architecture of a morphological theory, specifically about whether morphemes – units smaller than the word – should be treated as Saussurian signs, that is, pairings of sound and meaning, and if so what we should expect about the pairing of sound and meaning. The discussion, that is, has largely been over the issue of correspondence. But at the heart of the problem is a more fundamental question: how do we talk about the meanings which can be said to be in correspondence (one-to-one, one-to-many, many-to-one) with structural units?

I argue in this book that this issue will not be resolved by looking at the architecture of a morphological theory, at least not until we have a way of talking about (describing, comparing) the semantic effects of word-formation processes in some detail and depth. We will not be able to talk about the correspondence of meaning and form until we can say in some useful way what complex words mean – what the meaning or meanings of the suffix *-ize* is (is it one or many meanings, and if many are they related meanings?), whether this meaning is the same as that of *-ify*, and so on.

I suggest that we do not yet have the theoretical apparatus to conduct such discussions. In order to talk about the semantics of word formation we need a framework of lexical semantic description which has several distinctive properties. First, it must be decompositional; it must involve some relatively small number of primitives or atoms, and the primitives or atoms it makes available should be of the right "grain size" to allow us to talk about the meanings of complex words. Further, such a descriptive framework must allow us to concentrate on *lexical* semantic properties, rather than semantic properties that manifest themselves at higher levels of syntactic structure (i.e., phrases, sentences, propositions, discourses). It must also be thoroughly cross-categorial, allowing us to discuss in equal depth the semantic characteristics of nouns, verbs, adjectives, and perhaps other categories. Finally, if we agree that word formation often creates new lexemes, our theory must allow us to talk about the meanings of complex words in the same terms that we use to talk about the meanings of simplex lexemes.

Let me start first with why such a theory of semantic description must be decompositional. This is a controversial choice in light of Fodor's extensive arguments that decompositional semantics is a waste of time. Fodor (1998) defends a position he calls *Informational Atomism*, consisting of two parts (1998, 121):

> *Informational semantics*: content is constituted by some sort of nomic, mind–world relation. Correspondingly, having a concept (concept possession) is constituted, at least in part, by *being in* some sort of nomic, mind–world relation.
> *Conceptual atomism*: most lexical concepts have no internal structure.

I have no quibble with Fodor's doctrine that nomic mind–world relations are the fundamental stuff of meanings at some level, that is, that meaning must ultimately be grounded in a lawful relation between language and the world.

I understand from the philosophers that the only game in town is to anchor meaning in truth conditions at some level. But I find Fodor's notion of conceptual atomism to be question-begging, especially if one is interested in questions concerning the meanings of complex words. Fodor argues that there is no sound justification for lexical decomposition (1998, 55): "I know of no reason, empirical or a priori, to suppose that the expressive power of English can be captured in a language whose stock of morphologically primitive expressions is interestingly smaller than the lexicon of English." The process of decomposing words – so the argument goes – merely defers the problem of meaning by passing it on to a metalanguage whose semantics generally remains unexplored. Nevertheless, Fodor believes in the *compositionality* of meaning – meanings are built up of smaller pieces.

Fodor is right to question the nature of primitives. But in doing so, he declares that we have no grounds for preferring one set of primitives to another, and that the default set of primitives is "the lexicon of English," that is, the set of words of which the lexicon is constituted. But surely we must consider carefully what constitutes the lexicon – what its parts are, what makes up words – before we decide that the *word* is the correct grain size for conceptual primitives. If words are themselves formally complex, can't they be semantically complex, and therefore might not the right grain size for semantic primitives be smaller than the concepts embodied in words? In other words, there may be nowhere to go but decomposition if one wants to talk about the meanings of complex words; I therefore take the leap into decompositional semantics in full knowledge of the philosophical problems it engenders.

There are, of course, many systems of semantic description in the literature which are decompositional in one way or another and which we might bend to our purposes. Nevertheless, I suggest that none of the currently available theories of semantic analysis has all the right properties for the job at hand.

First, Logical or Model Theoretic Semantics is not suitable for my purposes, as it does not yet allow for a sufficient focus on lexical aspects of meaning. Model Theoretic Semantics has concentrated primarily on aspects of propositional meaning including predication, quantification, negation, and the semantics of complementation. There has, of course, been work on lexical meaning, most notably the work of Dowty (1979) and Verkuyl (1972, 1989, 1993, 1999) on verbal aspect and verb classes generally. Dowty (1979) is especially notable in that he directly addresses issues of derivation as well as issues concerning the simplex verbal lexicon. Other researchers in this tradition have contributed enormously to our understanding of other lexical classes; see, for example, Carlson (1977), Kratzer (1995), on the individual/stage level distinction in adjectives and nouns; Landman (1989, 1996), Gillon (1992), Schwarzchild (1992), Schein (1993), among others on plurals; Bierwisch (1988) on prepositions; and Bierwisch (1989) on adjectives. Nevertheless, at this point Model Theoretic Semantics has not yet produced a system of decomposition that is sufficiently broad and cross-categorial, and at the same time fine-grained enough to address the questions I raise here.

Also available for our purposes are semantic systems such as those of Szymanek (1988), Jackendoff (1990), Pustejovsky (1995), and Wierzbicka (1996), all of which are decompositional in one way or another and more closely concentrated on the lexical domain. Although each of these systems has some attractive characteristics, none of them has all the characteristics that I believe are necessary to the task at hand.

Ray Jackendoff has, since the early seventies, developed a decompositional system of semantic representation or Lexical Conceptual Structure, as he calls it, which has many of the characteristics I mention above (Jackendoff 1972, 1983, 1987, 1990, 1991, 1996). Jackendoff's Lexical Conceptual Structures (LCSs) are hierarchical arrangements of functions and arguments. The primitives of the system are semantic functions such as BE, GO, STAY, ORIENT, CAUSE, TO, FROM, THING, and PATH, and in some later work (1990, 1991, 1996) increasingly smaller atoms of meaning represented as features (e.g., [bounded], [internal structure]) which allow for the discussion of aspectual characteristics of verbs and quantificational characteristics of nouns. I see my own work largely as an outgrowth and extension of the work of Jackendoff and related theorists (e.g., Levin and Rappaport Hovav 1988, 1995, Levin 1993), and I owe a great debt to their pioneering work. Nevertheless, Jackendoff's system as it stands is not entirely suitable to tackle the issues of morphological semantics I raised above. For one thing, his work has been heavily weighted towards the description of verbal meanings, and as yet is insufficiently cross-categorial to allow for a full discussion of the semantics of nouns and adjectives, which we would need in a full consideration of word-formation processes such as derivation, compounding, and conversion. Secondly, as I will argue in what follows, the "grain size" of many of Jackendoff's primitives is not quite right for our purposes. So although much of what follows will be couched in terms similar to those of Jackendoff, the system I will develop below will differ from his in significant ways.

Similarly, I cannot simply adopt the system of semantic description that has been developed in the work of Anna Wierzbicka (1972, 1980, 1985, 1988, 1996). Her framework is decompositional, and unlike Jackendoff's, it is very broadly cross-categorial. It is also admirably comprehensive. Wierzbicka, unlike most other semantic theorists, claims that the primitives of lexical semantics are a Natural Semantic Metalanguage comprised of word-sized chunks such as I, YOU, HERE, NOW, DO, HAPPEN, MANY, and the like (in Wierzbicka [1996, 28] the number of primitives is set tentatively at fifty-six):

> Semantic primitives are, by definition, indefinable: they are Leibniz's ultimate "simples", Aristotle's "prioria", in terms of which all the complex meanings can be articulated, but which cannot be decomposed themselves. They can, of course, be represented as bundles of some artificial features, such as "+Speaker, −Hearer" for "I", but this is not the kind of decomposition which leads from complex to simple and from obscure to clear. As pointed out earlier, the meaning of a sentence like "I know this" cannot be clarified by any further decomposition − not even by decomposition into some other meaningful sentences; and "features", which have no syntax and which are not part of natural language, have no meaning at all; they have to be assigned meaning by sentences in natural languages, rather than the other way around.

In other words, the only candidates for primitives in Wierzbicka's framework are chunks of meaning that cannot be explicated in simpler words; these chunks of meaning are themselves word-sized.

While I agree with Wierzbicka's judgment that putative primitives must be simple, I also believe, and hope to show in what follows, that the particular word-sized chunks that she deems to be primitives sometimes do not allow us to answer the questions about the semantics of complex words that I have raised above. The problem with Wierzbicka's system of lexical semantic description is therefore the one of "grain size."

Another attractive theory of lexical semantic representation is Pustejovsky's theory of the Generative Lexicon (1995). This theory, like Wierzbicka's, is broadly cross-categorial, and allows us to represent many aspects of the meanings of lexical items. A lexical semantic representation for Pustejovsky consists of four parts (1995, 58):

> These include the notion of *argument structure*, which specifies the number and type of arguments that a lexical item carries; an *event structure* of sufficient richness to characterize not only the basic event type of a lexical item, but also internal, subeventual structure; a *qualia structure*, representing the different modes of predication possible with a lexical item; and a *lexical inheritance structure*, which identifies how a lexical structure is related to other structures in the dictionary, however it is constructed.

The *qualia* part of the lexical semantic structure can in turn include several types of information about the meaning of a word (1995, 76): constitutive information ("the relation between an object and its constituent parts"); formal information ("that which distinguishes it within a larger domain"); telic information ("its purpose and function"); and agentive information ("factors involved in its origin or 'bringing it about'").

Pustejovsky's theory is decompositional, but he does not argue for a fixed number of primitives. Indeed, it is not clear that the descriptive elements in his lexical entries are primitives at all. What matters more for Pustejovsky is the process by which lexical items are combined – the ways in which their composition into larger units determines the meaning of each item in situ. His primary goal is to account for the polysemy of lexical items in the larger sentential context, for example, why we understand the word *window* to refer to an object in the sentence *She broke the window*, but an aperture in *She climbed through the window*.

With its emphasis on polysemy, the Generative Lexicon might seem to afford a possible framework in which to discuss the semantics of word formation. However, we will see that this system of description does not provide us with the means to discuss all the questions raised above – in particular the multiple-affix question – and that this latter question can in fact be answered only within a representational system that relies on a fixed (and presumably relatively small) number of primitives.

Finally, I must consider the descriptive system developed by Szymanek (1988) and adopted in large part by Beard (1993, 1995) for his *Lexeme Morpheme Base Morphology*. Unlike the descriptive systems provided by Jackendoff, Wierzbicka, and Pustejovsky, Szymanek's system is specifically intended to address questions of meaning in word formation. It therefore might seem the best place to start for the present endeavor. Further, Szymanek's system has several of the characteristics that we seek: it is broadly cross-categorial and decompositional, and relies on a (perhaps fixed) number of primitives. The problem, however, is with the primitives themselves.

These include semantic categories like the following: OBJECT, SUBSTANCE, PERSON, NUMBER, EXISTENCE, POSSESSION, NEGATION, PROPERTY, COLOR, SHAPE, DIMENSION, SIMILARITY, SEX, SPACE, POSITION, MOVEMENT, PATH, TIME, STATE, PROCESS, EVENT, ACTION, CAUSATION, AGENT, INSTRUMENT. Szymanek suggests a condition which he calls the Cognitive Grounding Condition (1988, 93): "The basic set of lexical derivational categories is rooted in the fundamental concepts of cognition." In other words, word formation is typically based on one or more of the semantic/conceptual categories above. I believe that Szymanek is right about the issue of cognitive grounding: derivation must be rooted in the basic concepts of cognition, as he puts it. But again it will become apparent that Szymanek's categories do not exhibit the right "grain size" needed to give interesting answers to the questions at the heart of this book. In fact, it appears that Szymanek adopts this list not so much for its intrinsic merit, but as a sort of first approximation, a useful heuristic: "Up to a point, then, the categorial framework to be developed will constitute a cumulative list of the fundamental categories of cognition as discussed by other authors. It should be noted, however, that we omit from the inventory a few concepts whose status seems rather dubious or simply non-essential from the point of view of the present study" (1988, 89). In other words, unlike Jackendoff and Wierzbicka, who are interested in establishing the nature and necessity of the primitives themselves, Szymanek is content with a list of provisional labels. These are, of course, labels that are useful in describing derivational processes, but I will try to show that answers to our basic questions begin to emerge only when we leave behind provisional labels such as AGENT and CAUSATION and try to establish the precise nature of the descriptive primitives in our system of lexical semantic representation.

Let me briefly outline the sort of framework of lexical semantic description which I think we need, and which I will develop in this book. As I mentioned above, I see my own work in some ways as an outgrowth and extension of that of theorists like Jackendoff, Wierzbicka, Pustejovsky, and Szymanek. But I distinguish my theory from theirs. First, I believe that noninflectional word formation – derivation, compounding, and conversion – serves to create lexemes and to extend the simplex lexicon; for that reason, I believe that the meanings it expresses ought to reflect the semantic distinctions that are salient in the simplex lexicon. That is, to the extent that we find semantic classes that are significant in distinguishing the behavior of underived lexemes, we might expect derivation, compounding, and conversion to extend those classes. And to the extent that we find polysemy in complex words, it ought to be like the polysemy we see in simplex lexical items.

Second, I conceive of lexical semantic representations as being composed of two parts, what I will call the Semantic/Grammatical Skeleton (or skeleton, for short) and the Semantic/Pragmatic Body (body, for short). The distinction I make here between skeleton and body is not particularly new, although some elements of both skeleton and body are designed in this theory to allow discussion of problems associated with the semantics of word formation. But the skeleton and body I develop in what follows do have elements in common with what Rappaport Hovav and Levin (1996, 1998) call respectively the "event structure template" and the "constant," or what Mohanan and Mohanan (1999) call "Grammatical Semantic Structure" and "Conceptual Structure."

The skeleton in my framework will be comparable in some but not all ways to Jackendoff's Lexical Conceptual Structures. It will be the decompositional part of the representation, hierarchically arranged, as Jackendoff's LCSs are. It will seek to isolate all and only those aspects of meaning which have consequences for the syntax. This part of the representation will be relatively rigid and formal. It is here that I will try to establish primitives, and specifically a small number of primitives of the right "grain size" to allow us to address issues of the semantics of derivation, compounding, and conversion. Instead of Jackendoff's semantic functions (BE, GO, CAUSE, etc.), Wierzbicka's simple concepts, or Szymanek's cognitive categories, I will propose a broadly cross-categorial featural system for decomposing meanings of morphemes.

The other part of the semantic representation, the body, will be encyclopedic, holistic, nondecompositional, not composed of primitives, and perhaps only partially formalizable. It will comprise those bits of perceptual and cultural knowledge that form the bulk of the lexical representation. The body will include many of the aspects of meaning that Pustejovsky encodes in his Qualia Structure – information concerning material composition, part structure, orientation, shape, color, dimensionality, origin, purpose, function, and so on (Pustejovsky 1995, 85–6).

My theory is consciously based on an anatomical metaphor. The skeleton forms the foundation of what we know about morphemes and words. It is what allows us to extend the lexicon through various word-formation processes. The body fleshes out this foundation. It may be fatter or thinner from item to item, and indeed from the lexical representation of a word in one person's mental lexicon to the representation of that "same" word in another individual's mental lexicon. But the body must be there in a living lexical item. Bodies can change with the life of a lexical item – gain or lose weight, as it were. Skeletons, however, are less amenable to change.

My main claim is that the semantics of word formation involves the creation of a single referential unit out of two distinct semantic skeletons that have been placed in a relationship of either juxtaposition or subordination to one another. The primary mechanism for creating a single referential unit will be the co-indexation of semantic arguments. Compound formation will involve juxtaposition of skeletons with concomitant co-indexing. Derivational affixation will involve the addition of skeletal material to a base whose own skeleton is subordinated; in other words, the semantic representation of a derivational affix will be a bit of semantic skeleton which subordinates a lexical base. The skeletons of which compounds are formed will typically have accompanying bodies, but derivational affixes will often have little or nothing in the way of semantic bodies. Both derived words and compounds may, however, over time, develop substantial and distinctive bodies as a function of their lexicalization. Lexicalization, we shall see, proceeds on an item-by-item basis, thus allowing a wide range of meanings to exist in items formed by the same process of derivation or compounding.

Semantic variation among items formed by the same process of derivation or compounding will not merely be a function of the lexicalization process, however. In fact, a concomitant of the claim that the semantics of derivation should reflect the semantics of the simplex lexicon is that the sorts of polysemy we find in the simplex lexicon should also be found in derived words. I will show in what follows that both of the main types of polysemy that are manifested in the simplex lexicon – what Pustejovsky and Boguraev (1996, 6) call "logical polysemy" and "sense extensions" – are to be found in derivational affixes as well. Logical polysemy will be seen to arise from the composition of skeletons, and specifically from the effects of underdetermination in skeletal meanings. It is here that the choice of primitives in our system will receive its justification: only a featural system such as the one to be proposed in this book will give rise to the right level of underdetermination of meaning to account for affixal polysemy. We will see that sense extensions sometimes arise in affixation, as well, although not as frequently as logical polysemy.

A word about the scope and limits of this book. I cannot hope to cover everything that needs to be said about the semantics of all sorts of word formation in all sorts of languages without promising to write a book I would never finish or could never hope to get published. I have chosen to narrow the scope of this work to three types of word formation that are well represented and fairly well understood – derivation, compounding, and conversion – and to limit my discussion in most cases to these processes in English.

This is not to say that inflection is unimportant, or to deny that there is an enormous amount that we could learn from scrutinizing word formation in languages other than English. In this work, I propose to confine myself to bona fide processes of lexeme formation in the hopes that the foundation of lexical semantics developed here will eventually allow us to proceed to a fruitful discussion of inflection. Other theorists such as Anderson (1992), Aronoff (1994), and Stump (2001) have tended to take the opposite route, building their theories primarily on the basis of a study of inflectional phenomena and giving shorter shrift to derivation, compounding, and conversion.[1]

Similarly, these theorists have tended to look at inflection in a wide variety of the world's languages, a methodological choice that has certainly borne fruit in the study of inflection. But specifically because of my concentration

---

1. Anderson (1992) devotes one chapter to derivation, and Stump (2001) part of a chapter.

on processes of lexeme formation in this work, I will tend to focus attention on a single language – English. My justification is the following: the sort of semantic work that I hope to do requires a detailed and intimate look at the meanings of lots of words formed with the same affix, or by the same type of compounding or conversion. Indeed, as will become apparent in the chapters that follow, I cannot even hope to provide an exhaustive description of the semantics of all of English word formation. Rather, I must narrow discussion to a series of case studies of particular realms of word formation: formation of personal/instrumental nouns; root and synthetic compounding; formation of verbs by affixation and conversion; negative affixation; and a few select others. These case studies are carefully chosen to reveal answers to the four central questions with which I began this introduction. So I beg the reader's indulgence on what might initially seem to be a rather narrow range of analysis. I cannot hope to do such detailed work with languages of which I am not a native speaker. I would hope that native speakers of other languages will eventually help to corroborate or criticize any of the theoretical apparatus that I build here.

In chapter 1, I begin to develop the theoretical apparatus needed to address questions of the semantics of word formation processes. I will concentrate on justifying a small set of lexical semantic features – [material], [dynamic], and [IEPS] – which allow us to distinguish broad semantic classes of nouns, verbs, and adjectives, the main classes of words that participate in derivation, compounding, and conversion. I will show that this simple featural system allows us not only to classify simplex items, but also to attribute semantic content of the right sort to affixes and in fact to predict a range of derivational affixes that ought to exist in English. I frame these issues in the context of a discussion of two English suffixes, *-er* and *-ee*, that present substantial descriptive problems in other frameworks of semantic analysis.

In chapter 2, I will turn to the second of the theoretical devices which I believe to be necessary in describing the semantics of complex words, namely co-indexation. I will first introduce this device and show how it allows us to explain a number of familiar observations about the interpretation of root and synthetic compounds. Then I will continue my discussion of the so-called agentive/instrumental affixes, and show how a simple extension of the device of co-indexation allows us to account for properties of these affixes.

Chapter 3 continues the discussion of derivational affixation focusing specifically on the polysemy and zero-derivation questions. Here, I will extend the feature system to permit an analysis of the so-called causative verb-forming suffixes *-ize* and *-ify*, and compare the semantic behavior of these affixes with that of noun to verb conversion. This comparison will lend support to formal analyses which treat conversion as relisting, rather than the addition of a phonologically null morpheme.

In chapter 4, I will speculate on how the simple feature system developed in earlier chapters might be extended. Specifically, I will explore the representation of concepts of time and space in our theory, concentrating on the semantic feature [Location]. I will show how this feature (in addition to the feature [IEPS]) allows us to characterize not only classes of simplex verbs, but also simplex prepositions. We will then look at the ways in which the feature [Location] allows us to explain the behavior of both negative affixes and prepositional affixes in English. What will emerge from this chapter is a clearer picture of the ways in which polysemy can arise in derivational word formation.

In chapter 5, I take a slightly different tack. Again, the focus is on extending the featural system that I began to develop in earlier chapters. Here, I expand the system to include quantificational features of meaning, building on work of Jackendoff (1991), Verkuyl (1993, 1999), Smith (1997), and others. What is important in this chapter is that the features that I justify are specifically lexical. Although quantificational aspects of meaning have been extensively discussed in the literature, the focus has always been on characteristics of meaning that manifest themselves at the phrasal and sentential levels, for example, telicity. I will argue in chapter 5 that telicity is not a lexical feature, but that there are nevertheless quantificational features that manifest themselves at the level of the lexical item. And not surprisingly these features (and not telicity) are exploited by the derivational system of English.

Chapter 6 will lead us to the issue of semantic mismatch: apparent cases of derivational redundancy, empty morphemes, and semantic subtraction in derived words. I will examine several cases of semantic mismatch in English derivation and argue that none of them constitutes a problem for my theory. Further, I will explore the general issue of semantic restrictions on affixation, and of redundancy and recursion in affixation and suggest that constraints on the complexity of meaning in derived words are largely a matter of pragmatics.

In chapter 7, I will look back and summarize what I think this book accomplishes, but more importantly look forward to the many questions it leaves unanswered, and the many paths of future research it suggests.

A last word on methodology. For the most part, the case studies that I develop in this book concern means of word formation in English which are uncontroversially productive, as measured by a variety of theorists in a variety of ways (e.g., Baayen 1989, Baayen and Lieber 1991, Plag 1999, Bauer 2001). I cull examples from a number of sources: the CELEX lexical database, Lehnert (1971), the OED, Marchand (1969), and the work of my colleagues. Generally, I try to arrive at the semantic representation of various affixes and word-formation processes by concentrating on the more transparently compositional data formed by those affixes and processes, acknowledging that each affix or process will also have given rise to forms that display semantic idiosyncrasies that can only be attributed to lexicalization and that ultimately defy any systematic explanation. If I have learned anything from years of delving in lists of English words, it is that words in general, and affixes in particular, are slippery little things. But I still believe it's worth trying to pin them down. Here then begins a first attempt to do so.

1   *Features*

In this chapter I begin to develop the descriptive system that I believe to be necessary for a discussion of the semantics of lexeme-forming word formation, that is, derivation, compounding, and conversion. As I argued in the Introduction, such a system must have a number of characteristics: it must allow us to treat lexical semantic properties (as opposed to properties of phrases, propositions, or discourses); it must be decompositional, and its atoms (or primitives)[1] must be of the right "grain size" to allow fruitful discussion of the semantics of word formation; finally, it must be broadly cross-categorial, allowing equally for the description of the lexical semantics at least of nouns, verbs, and adjectives. I begin with a discussion of the *skeleton*, as that is the part of the semantic representation that is formal, and will figure most prominently in the discussion of the semantics of derivation. As the discussion progresses, I will touch on the nature of the semantic body as well, and on its role in the ultimate determination of lexical meaning.

I start in section 1.1 with a problem which I think sets the agenda for anyone attempting to talk about the semantics of derivation. This problem – the meaning of the affixes *-er* and *-ee* in English – gives immediate insight into the issue of "grain size" of the primitives or atoms of meaning on which such a system might be based. I will touch briefly on the descriptive primitives made available in the work of other theorists (Jackendoff, Szymanek, Wierzbicka), and suggest that none of these systems gives insight into the problem raised

---

1. I am hesitant to call the descriptive categories that I propose here "primitives," preferring to call them instead "atoms" of meaning. As Jackendoff (1991) so eloquently argues, past research in all kinds of scientific fields has shown that levels of description which at one time were thought to be primitive come later on to be seen as composed of still smaller components. I expect that research in lexical semantics is likely to follow the same path. My claim in this chapter will merely be that atoms at least as small as the ones I propose are needed to discuss the semantics of word formation. Whether smaller atoms still may be needed for other purposes will emerge from future research.

by -*er* and -*ee*. In section 1.2 I propose the beginnings of a featural system which gives us atoms of a somewhat smaller grain size to work with, and try to justify them as plausible candidates for primitives, or at least provisional primitives. Section 1.3 will begin to apply this featural system to the analysis of derivational affixation, offering an initial solution to the problems posed in section 1 about the meaning of -*er*, -*ee*, and related affixes. Section 1.4 explores what the proposed system predicts about the scope and range of derivation that we should expect to find in a language like English.

Before I turn to the featural system which will be my first contribution to the formal representation of lexical semantics, let me briefly review those aspects of the formal system which I owe to previous work. Specifically, I will adopt the basic function and argument structure for semantic representations that has figured in both Model Theoretic Semantics and in the work of Jackendoff on Lexical Conceptual Structures, and perhaps less prominently in the work of Wierzbicka (1996).[2] Specifically, I will follow Jackendoff (1990) in assuming that the standard form of a lexical semantic representation – at least of the *skeleton*, which is what I will concentrate on first – contains two basic parts, a function and one or more arguments predicated of that function (1a). With Jackendoff, I will assume as well, that a skeleton may consist of a hierarchical arrangement of functions and arguments, as in (1b):

(1)   a. $[F_1 \text{ ([argument])}]$
        b. $[F_2 \text{ ([argument], } [F_1 \text{ ([argument])])}]$

I will also assume, following work of Williams (1981) and Higginbotham (1985), that all major lexical categories, that is, adjectives and nouns, as well as verbs, are argument-taking. Nouns, for example, take at least one argument, which has been called the "R" argument in previous literature. Williams (1981, 86) characterizes "R" as the external argument of a noun: "The label R is meant to suggest 'referential', since it is this argument position R that is involved in referential uses of NPs as well." The "R" argument of a noun may be discharged by linking it with an NP of which it is predicated (Williams 1981) or by linking with a determiner (Higginbotham 1985, Sproat 1985).

Where I part company with Jackendoff and others is in the nature of the functions that form the primitives of lexical semantic theory. In the next section I will try to justify this move on the basis of a problem in the semantics of derivational affixation.

2. Wierzbicka combines her primitives into sentence-like units that have a function and argument structure. So although she is not explicit about the structure of semantic representations, I believe it is safe to characterize her theory as being consistent with one in which semantic representations can consist of functions and arguments.

1.1 The problem: the meaning of -er and -ee

The problem I have in mind concerns a relatively familiar realm, the affixes *-er* and *-ee* in English, as well as related derivational affixes like *-ist* and *-ant/-ent*. At least the first two of these have been much discussed in the literature (e.g., Rappaport Hovav and Levin 1992, Barker 1998, Bauer 1987, 1993, Panther and Thornburg 1998, Booij 1986, Ryder 1999, Heyvaert 2001), but I think they bear looking at again, not only because aspects of their analyses remain problematic, but also because they provide great insight into what our semantic system needs to look like.

One of the things that has been noted in the literature is that words formed with these affixes have a wide range of interpretations:

(2)	-er	
	agent	writer, driver, thinker, walker
	instrument	opener, printer, pager
	experiencer	hearer
	stimulus	pleaser, thriller
	patient/theme	fryer, keeper, looker, sinker, loaner
	denominal noun	Londoner, villager, carpetbagger, freighter
	measure	fiver
	location	diner
(3)	-ee	
	patient/theme	employee, nominee, deportee
	agent/subject	escapee, attendee, standee, arrivee, resignee, recoveree
	indirect object	addressee, dedicatee, offeree
	governed preposition	experimentee, laughee, ejectee
	no argument	amputee
	denominal person noun	biographee, mastectomee, asylee, aggressee, inquisitee
(4)	-ant/-ent	
	agent	accountant, claimant, servant
	instrument	evacuant, adulterant, irritant
	experiencer	dependent, detestant, discernant
	patient/theme	confidant, insurant, descendant
(5)	-ist	
	denominal person noun	guitarist, Marxist
	deadjectival person noun	purist, fatalist

It has often been pointed out that for the affixes *-er* and *-ant/-ent* the most productive derivations are either agents or instruments. We want our theory to be able to explain why agent and instrument interpretations are frequently – not only in English, but also in other languages (cf. Booij 1986 for Dutch) – expressed by the same affixes, whereas combinations like agent and process or patient and place nouns never are.[3]

Another point which is significant for our purposes, one which is less frequently noted in the literature, is that there is a range of data in which the meanings of these affixes seem to overlap. Clearly, the suffix -*ee* most frequently and productively forms patient nouns, and the other affixes agent nouns or nouns with related "subject-oriented" interpretations (instrument, experiencer, stimulus). But still, there are a significant number of items formed with -*ee* which have agent or at least "subject-like" interpretations (*escapee*, *retiree*), and a number of -*er* and -*ant/-ent* nouns which are patients or themes, or at least "object-like" in their interpretation (e.g., *loaner*, *insurant*). We might be tempted to dismiss these last examples as lexicalized forms, odd survivals of unproductive processes, monsters of a sort. But there are enough examples to make one wonder how such monsters could come to be, or if indeed they are monsters at all. Why, for example, should *attendee* have a subject interpretation rather than a process or result interpretation (analogous to *attendance*)? Why should the territories of -*er* and -*ee* overlap with each other, rather than with other affixes that form nouns from verbs such as the action/process/result nominalizers -*ation*, -*ance*, -*ure*, -*al*, and the like?

Further, for both -*er* and -*ee* there are a substantial number of forms derived on nominal, rather than verbal, bases. Clearly these are related in some way to the deverbal derivatives: they are often person or instrument nouns, and they have roughly the same processual flavor that the deverbal forms do, but without the verbal base. This fact alone suggests that the affixes make some independent semantic contribution, beyond an effect on the argument structure of their base, in other words, that they actually mean something. The question then is what they mean.

My hypothesis is that it is not an accident that these affixes show the range of polysemy that they do and that their ranges of polysemy overlap. Rather, I suspect that these facts follow from the basic meanings of the affixes, that each of these affixes has a unitary meaning, and in fact that the meanings of -*er* and -*ee* are closely related. I will argue that a framework of lexical semantic representation which has atoms (or primitives) of the right "grain size" will allow us not only to describe the facts in an illuminating fashion, but to predict that they would have to be the way they are.

Before I do, I should point out that I am by no means the first in recent years to study these affixes and to seek a unitary characterization of their behavior.

---

3. Note that with nouns in -*er* even the denominal ones sometimes have a personal interpretation (e.g., *Londoner*) and sometimes have an instrument interpretation (e.g., *freighter*).

Booij (1986) provides such a characterization for Dutch, and Rappaport Hovav and Levin (1992) provide a solid and comprehensive analysis of *-er* for English. Barker (1998) is an excellent, detailed, and convincing study of *-ee*. But each of these articles confines itself to the analysis of only one of the relevant affixes and therefore does not treat the issue of their overlap in meaning, and each in turn fails to account for some of the observations I have made above concerning the range of derivatives in *-er* and *-ee*.

Rappaport Hovav and Levin (1992) (henceforth RHL) analyze *-er* at the level of argument structure, rather than at the level of semantic representation.[4] They argue that *-er* saturates or binds the external argument of the verb to which the affix attaches, noting that appeal to a syntactic argument position makes it unnecessary to list a variety of thematic roles (agent, experiencer, instrument, stimulus, and so on) in the analysis of the affix: *-er* can take on any of the roles that the external argument of a verb can, from agent and instrument to experiencer and stimulus.

Their analysis provides a neat account for the vast majority of forms in *-er*, namely the ones with the agent, instrument, experiencer, and stimulus readings. But it requires some special effort to account for some of the patient forms. For example, RHL treat the word *sinker* as formed from the inchoative alternant of the verb (*The ship sank*) and items like *looker* or *fryer* as formed from middle constructions (*She looks good*; *This chicken fries well*). But there are still a few items with the patient reading for which the external argument analysis cannot be made to work: neither the verb *keep* nor *loan* has an inchoative or a middle form, and yet *keeper* and *loaner* have patient interpretations.

Also problematic for RHL's analysis are the denominal forms. Although it has been argued that nouns have arguments, or at least the "R" argument (Higginbotham 1985), it is not clear that we would want to equate the "R" argument of a noun with the external argument of a verb; nominal arguments do not have thematic interpretations in the way that the arguments of a verb typically do. The "R" argument of a noun like *London* or *freight* is not interpreted as an agent, an instrument, or a theme, and yet nouns like *Londoner* or *freighter* receive respectively a personal interpretation and an instrumental interpretation. How do they get these interpretations if there is no verbal base whose external argument has the agent or instrument reading? How, indeed, do they get a processual meaning at all if they do not have a verbal base? In other words, there must be some semantic content to the affix that cannot be captured in a purely argument-structure theoretic framework, and therefore, good as RHL's analysis is, there seems still to be more work needed on *-er*.

---

4. RHL's analysis is quite similar to that presented in Booij (1986) for Dutch.

Interestingly, Barker (1998) argues that although an argument structure theoretic analysis of *-er* might be adequate (I suggest that it is not), an analogous treatment of *-ee* is completely unworkable. It is clearly too simplistic to say that *-ee* binds the patient/theme argument of a verb. Such an analysis does not account for cases where the referent of the *-ee* noun is the indirect object (*addressee*), the object of a governed preposition (*experimentee*), or the many cases where the *-ee* form receives an agentive, or at least a subject-oriented, interpretation (*escapee*, *attendee*).

Barker argues instead for a semantic analysis in which the affix *-ee* binds an argument of its base verb under three conditions: the argument bound by *-ee* must be episodically linked to the verb, by which he means roughly that the argument must be a participant in the event denoted by the verb; it must denote something sentient; and it must lack volitionality. For the canonical cases like *employee*, the affix binds the patient argument of the base verb rather than the agent argument, because that argument is both sentient and lacks volition. For indirect object cases like *addressee*, the theme may not be bound as it is not sentient, and the agent may not be bound because it is volitional. What is left to bind is the indirect object or goal argument. A similar analysis obtains for governed preposition cases like *experimentee*, where the first argument of the base verb that is both sentient and nonvolitional is the object of the governed preposition.

The cases where *-ee* binds a subject argument require a bit more work. For example, in the word *standee* Barker argues that the external argument is sentient and episodically linked, and is at least nonvolitional enough to suit – arguably standing doesn't require a high degree of agency. For *escapee*, a bit more special pleading is required: although the bound argument must be an agent in some sense (you have to do something on your own if you escape), Barker argues that the overall scenario lacks a complete sense of control (1998, 719):

> An escapee typically is volitionally, actively, and deliberately involved in bringing about the escaping event. Once the escape has been effected, however, the escapee undergoes a significant and relevant change of state: he or she is subject to consequences that are quite certainly not in their control and in fact are quite strongly negative, including pursuit, recapture and punishment for escaping.

He acknowledges, however, that the requirement that the argument bound by *-ee* lack volitional control is problematic in cases like these, and in other subject *-ee* forms such as *retiree* and *attendee*.

Barker's analysis also provides a plausible explanation for the word *amputee* where the affix appears to bind something which is not an argument of the base verb at all. The problem here is that none of the actual arguments of the verb *amputate* fulfill the full set of criteria, as the subject argument is volitional, and the object argument not sentient in the appropriate way. But the object argument (the limb) entails a possessor which is both sentient and nonvolitional. Hence, an *amputee* is understood as the possessor of the limb that has been removed.

Barker makes an excellent case that the analysis of *-ee* must take place at the level of lexical semantics. But his analysis still leaves some issues open. For one thing, it relies on semantic notions like sentience, volitionality, and episodic linking that are as yet loosely defined and not fully understood. Further, broad though Barker's analysis is, it does not cover all of the data, as he does not fully explore the semantics of *-ee* forms derived from nouns rather than verbs (*biographee, mastectomee*). Barker mentions these only in passing (1998, 717), and suggests that nouns can be eventive, just as verbs can, but he does not work out the details or implications of this idea. As in the denominal *-er* forms, these suggest a direct semantic contribution of the affix, and require us to look more carefully at Barker's notion of episodic linking: what does it mean to say that the affix episodically links an argument of a nominal base?

There is, then, still more that might be said about the analyses of *-er*, *-ee*, and related affixes, and especially about the relationship between the meanings of these affixes. One of the tasks still to be done is to identify the actual semantic contribution of each affix beyond the binding of a base argument by the affix. But how do we do this? Existing theories such as those of Jackendoff (1990), Wierzbicka (1996), or Szymanek (1988) do not provide us with the descriptive means to resolve the issues we have raised. We have seen that each of these theories provides some set of primitives or atoms of meanings that we might use to characterize this affixal semantic contribution, but for our purposes each offers chunks of meaning that are either too broad or too narrow.

Jackendoff's framework can form a starting point, but only that. Concentrating on verbal meanings, Jackendoff has tended to devote little attention to the description of nominal semantics.[5] His theory makes available only two candidates for characterizing noun-like arguments, THING and PLACE, the former

---

5. Jackendoff (1991) suggests some change in this respect. Concentrating on quantitative aspects of nominal semantics, Jackendoff's analysis of plurality, collectivity, and the mass/count distinction in this article suggests a framework more like the one I will develop below. Nevertheless, Jackendoff has not extended his descriptive system in a fully cross-categorial way, as I will try to do below.

clearly too broad to characterize either *-er* or *-ee*, and the latter semantically inappropriate.

Wierzbicka offers at least five primitives which she characterizes as "substantival": I, YOU, SOMEONE, SOMETHING, PEOPLE (1996, 35). Again, none seems like a likely candidate for the semantic content of *-er* and *-ee*. Clearly the pronominals I and YOU are not suitable, nor is PEOPLE. SOMEONE and SOMETHING are better candidates, especially when we understand that SOMEONE for Wierzbicka is a cover term which includes "person," and SOMETHING a cover term including "thing". But we would need to use both PERSON and THING to cover the agent and the instrument interpretations which *-er* forms allow, although in doing so, it is still not clear that we will have captured the processual nature of these nouns. The fit is not quite right, and we would need a disjunction of primitives. This in turn suggests that the primitives available in Wierzbicka's framework are not of exactly the right "grain size": why just this disjunction of primitives and not some other?

The disjunctive meaning problem is merely compounded if we try to make use of Szymanek's primitives. In this much richer system, we have more conceptual categories to choose from in characterizing the semantics of *-er* and *-ee*, among them "person," "agent," "instrument," and perhaps "object" for *-er* and "person," "object," and "agent" for *-ee*. But again, why just this combination of primitives? Merely listing them does not bring us any closer than before to saying what the affixes mean, or to explaining their behavior.

We need to characterize the meanings of these affixes in terms that are neither too broad nor too narrow. Too broad a semantic contribution is inadequate, as it predicts ranges of polysemy and overlap of meaning that do not in fact occur; too narrow a semantic contribution requires affixes to be characterized by disjunctions of separate chunks whose relationship to each other and co-occurrence with each other remains unexplained. We move on now to develop a system composed of atoms of meaning which are just the right size.

1.2   The features [material] and [dynamic]

1.2.1   Major ontological classes
I believe that, much maligned though they are in the literature, semantic features offer the best hope for capturing atoms of meaning of the right grain size for our purposes. At least one of the features that I will argue for here – [dynamic] – has already been proposed in various forms in previous literature (see, for example, Pinker 1989, Dowty 1979, Verkuyl 1972), and I will try to make a case for another feature – [material] – as well. Two things are new, I think,

about my use of semantic features. First, features will be used in a thoroughly cross-categorial way. And second, they will be used in both an equipolent and a privative way; that is, the features that I propose will be binary in value (i.e., positive or negative), but they may also be either present or absent in the semantic skeleton of a given item. Absence from a representation will indicate the irrelevance of the semantic feature for the item in question.

A note on this latter point. While it is generally frowned upon in syntactic or phonological theory to use features simultaneously in a binary and privative fashion – such use is said to impart extra and unwanted power to the grammar – I suggest that the lexicon should be treated differently. Specifically, the issue of power does not arise in the same way with respect to the lexicon. Although we should be concerned with the overall parsimony of the framework, we nevertheless need a way to say that a particular semantic dimension is or is not relevant to a particular set of lexical items. For instance, while animacy is a feature that we might use for partitioning nouns, it is irrelevant for the characterization of verbs; there are no animate or inanimate verbs. Instead of assigning verbs a value for the feature [animate], I would suggest that it is better to say that verbs are characterized by an absence of the feature [animate] in their skeletons.

For those that object strenuously to the use of features at the same time in a privative and a binary way, it would be possible to recouch the present theory in slightly different terms. In much the same way that Stump (2001) distinguishes for inflection categories like Gender or Number from features like [+/−feminine] or [+/−plural], using both categories and features in morphosyntactic representations, it would be possible here to distinguish semantic categories like SITUATION or SUBSTANCE/THING/ESSENCE from the features that may (but don't necessarily have to) instantiate those categories ([+/−dynamic], [+/−material]). Thus, a category such as SITUATION might be instantiated without one of its features being present. Categories, then, are privative, and features always binary. But as far as I know the distinction between this formulation and the one I opt for above is merely notational, and nothing substantive hinges on it.

Returning to the substance of my descriptive system, I propose the most basic of conceptual categories for our skeletons, a category comprising SUBSTANCES/THINGS/ESSENCES and a category comprising SITUATIONS. Each of these will be characterized by at least one binary-valued feature, the former by [+/−material] and the latter by [+/−dynamic]. These features may be defined as follows, keeping in mind that they are meant, at least for now, to be primitives, and primitives, by definition, are undefinable.

- [+/− **material**]: The presence of this feature defines the conceptual category of SUBSTANCES/THINGS/ESSENCES, the notional correspondent of the syntactic category Noun. The positive value denotes the presence of materiality, characterizing concrete nouns. Correspondingly, the negative value denotes the absence of materiality; it defines abstract nouns.
- [+/− **dynamic**]: The presence of this feature signals an eventive or situational meaning, and by itself signals the conceptual category of SITUATIONS. The positive value corresponds to an EVENT or Process,[6] the negative value to a STATE.

The terminology is bound to be awkward. Terms like SITUATION and SUBSTANCE/THING/ESSENCE are not meant to be primitives themselves, but mnemonic terms that we can use for referring to these large conceptual/ontological categories. While SITUATION seems to be a reasonably good shorthand for EVENTS and STATES[7] conceptualized together, I am at a loss for an appropriate single word to label the conceptual category defined by the feature [material]. For lack of anything better, I have therefore used a string of terms, SUBSTANCE/THING/ESSENCE. Any one of these terms alone is too narrow for the category I have in mind, the first making us think of an unbounded mass, the second of an entity, and the third of an abstraction. But I mean for the one conceptual category to cover all of these. The awkward concatenation SUBSTANCE/THING/ESSENCE is the best I can do for now, but as far as I can tell, nothing important hinges on the choice of this term.

How can these two features be used to define the major lexical syntactic categories: noun, verb, and adjective? Nouns are items which will bear at least the feature [material] as the outermost function of their skeleton;[8] I use the qualifier

---

6. Following Verkuyl (1989), I take Processes not to constitute a third category along with STATES and EVENTS. Rather, Process readings arise from the interaction of EVENTS with unbounded arguments.
7. I accept here Comrie's (1976, 9) definition of the distinction between an Event and a State: "With a state, unless something happens to change the state, then the state will continue: this applies equally to standing and knowing. With a dynamic situation, on the other hand, the situation will only continue if it is continually subject to a new input of energy: this applies equally to running and pure tone, since if John stops putting any effort into running, he will come to a stop, and if the oscilloscope is cut off from its source of power it will no longer emit a sound. To remain in a state requires no effort, whereas to remain in a dynamic situation does require effort, whether from inside . . . or from outside."
8. We will see that derivation involves the layering of skeletons, so we must specify that the outermost function determines the corresponding syntactic category of the lexical item.

"at least," because, as we will see shortly, some SUBSTANCES/THINGS/ESSENCES may also bear the feature [dynamic]. Verbs and adjectives will be characterized by the presence of the feature [dynamic] without the feature [material]. Verbs may denote either EVENTS or STATES, and therefore may be characterized by either the positive or the negative value of the feature. Adjectives are characterized by the feature [−dynamic]; that is, adjectives are conceptually identical to stative verbs in this system, although syntactically they differ from verbs in that (in English at least) they occur only in nonfinite form, that is, they do not bear tense.

The reader will certainly note that I have left the syntactic category of adpositions (prepositions in English) out of the discussion. My reason for this is simple: prepositions will be characterized by the absence of the major ontological features [material] and [dynamic], but by the presence of other features which I have not yet introduced. I will therefore defer a discussion of the semantics of prepositions until we begin to extend our system of features in chapter 4.

The semantic features [material] and [dynamic] are meant to be functions, in the same sense that Jackendoff's primitives (BE, GO, CAUSE, etc.) are, and as such they may take arguments. The basic form of a skeleton will contain one or more of these features, and one or more arguments. So, the simplest possible skeleton will be something like those in (6) for the concrete noun *chair*, the adjective *happy*, or the intransitive verb *snore*:

(6)   *chair*   [+material ([   ])]
        happy   [−dynamic ([   ])]
        snore   [+dynamic ([   ])]

Lexical items will always have at least one argument (the one argument of a noun being the one that is referred to in the literature as the "R" argument), but they may have more than one as well, as the lexical entries for the noun *leg*, the adjective *fond*, and the verb *kiss* show:

(7)   *leg*   [+material ([   ], [   ])]   (e.g., the leg of the table)
        fond   [−dynamic ([   ], [   ])]   (e.g., fond of pickles)
        kiss   [+dynamic ([   ], [   ])]   (e.g., kiss frogs)

These are only the most bare bones (pun intended) of skeletons. We will see that there are other features that may be useful in characterizing the semantics of lexical items. And further, each lexical item will of course have a body as well as a skeleton. We will leave the nature of the body for now and return to it later.

With the two features [material] and [dynamic] I can now begin to illustrate the important properties of my theory, first that features are active across syntactic categories, and second, that they may be used in both binary and privative fashion to allow us to characterize a useful range of lexical semantic subclasses.

Alone, each feature allows us to partition a lexical class into two subclasses, for SUBSTANCES/THINGS/ESSENCES a class of concrete items ([+material]) and a class of abstract items ([−material]). The SITUATIONS are divided into an EVENT class ([+dynamic]) and a STATE class ([−dynamic]).

(8)

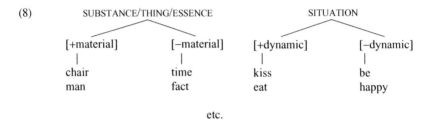

[+material]	[−material]	[+dynamic]	[−dynamic]
|	|	|	|
chair	time	kiss	be
man	fact	eat	happy

etc.

In a truly cross-categorial system, however, we should expect that the two features [material] and [dynamic] should not be mutually exclusive. But that leads us to ask what sort of lexical item might be defined by pairing the two features. The answer comes, I think, when we look more closely at the class of SUBSTANCES/THINGS/ESSENCES and observe that among the concrete and abstract classes, there are those which are processual in flavor, denoting states, events, actions, or even relations of some sort, and also those which lack a processual flavor. Among the former are nouns such as *parent, author, chef, boss, habit, war, effort*; the meanings of such nouns all intuitively involve doing something – having or caring for a child, writing a book, and so on. In Pustejovsky's (1995) terms, their TELIC senses are uppermost or most prominent.[9] Among the latter are the vast majority of simplex nouns, for example, *dog, chair, hand, fact, morning*, and so on. Such nouns may have purposes or functions, but these TELIC aspects of their meaning are not the most prominent. Let us assume that SUBSTANCES/THINGS/ESSENCES which are processual in nature bear some value of the feature [dynamic] as well as [material]:

---

9. Pustejovsky (1995, 86) cites "Built-in function or aim which specifies certain activities" as one of the main defining characteristics of the TELIC qualia.

(9)

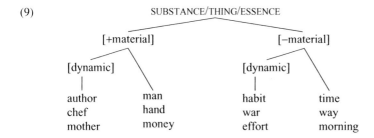

In other words, simplex nouns can be characterized semantically by the feature [material] and sometimes by the presence of the feature [dynamic] as well. Verbs and adjectives are characterized by the presence of the feature [dynamic] and the absence of the feature [material]. The feature [dynamic] is used in a binary way to define SITUATIONS, and in a privative way to distinguish processual from nonprocessual SUBSTANCES/THINGS/ESSENCES.

A word about the ontological implications of this claim. What I seem to be saying is that in some sense SUBSTANCES/THINGS/ESSENCES have ontological priority over SITUATIONS. Put informally, things can be processual, but processes, events, and states can't be "thingy" without, of course, ultimately being things. I think this is the right thing to say: SITUATIONS presuppose participants or arguments, which are usually SUBSTANCES/THINGS/ESSENCES, but SUBSTANCES/THINGS/ESSENCES do not presuppose situations. In some sense the semantic category SUBSTANCE/THING/ESSENCE is prior to, more fundamental than, and necessary for the semantic category SITUATION. In terms of formal representation, then, any skeleton with the feature [material] in its outermost layer is a SUBSTANCE/THING/ESSENCE but not everything with the feature [dynamic] is a SITUATION (although every skeleton with the feature [dynamic] in its outermost layer is in some way situational). Only a skeleton which lacks [material] in its outer layer is a pure SITUATION.

(10) illustrates skeletons for some of the situational or processual nouns:

(10)   *author*   [+substance, dynamic ([   ], [   ])]
        poet   [+substance, dynamic ([   ])]
        habit   [−substance, dynamic ([   ], [   ])]
        sunset   [−substance, dynamic ([   ])]

The question now obviously arises whether the binary nature of the feature [dynamic] has any use in characterizing processual THINGS/SITUATIONS/ESSENCES. I believe that the answer to this question is yes, at least sometimes. It has long been noted with respect to derived nouns that they may vary between what has been called a COMPLEX EVENT reading and a RESULT reading. According to Grimshaw (1990, 50–3), the COMPLEX EVENT reading appears prominently when derived nouns occur with temporal adverbs like *constant* and *frequent*, and especially when all of the arguments of the noun are present:

(11)   The frequent expression of one's feelings is desirable.

In contrast, the RESULT reading is compatible with determiners like *one* and *that*, and is obligatory when the noun is pluralized:

(12)   They studied that/one assignment.
(13)   The assignments took a long time.

Out of context, of course, derived nouns like *expression* or *assignment* are usually compatible with either the COMPLEX EVENT or the RESULT reading.

The same might be said for processual simplex nouns like *war*; with full expression of arguments, a COMPLEX EVENT reading is prominent, and with determiners like *that* or *one* and absence of a complement the RESULT reading is highlighted:

(14)   Barbara's constant war against the neighbors was distressing. (COMPLEX EVENT)
(15)   That/one war caused much destruction. (RESULT)

One way of encoding this distinction would be to say that the COMPLEX EVENT reading is characterized by the positive value of the feature [dynamic] in SUBSTANCES/THINGS/ESSENCES and the RESULT reading by the negative value of the feature [dynamic]. Nouns do not come with inherent positive or negative specifications for [dynamic], however; the positive and negative values are induced in a larger syntactic context by the presence or absence of determiners and the presence or absence of nominal arguments (see Lieber and Baayen [1999] for further discussion of this issue). For our purposes here, I will represent the skeletons of processual SUBSTANCES/THINGS/ESSENCES leaving the feature [dynamic] unspecified for value, and assume that further specification of this feature takes place at a higher level of semantic interpretation.

A final word about the features [material] and [dynamic]. It is important to point out that these features are not merely notational variants of the syntactic category features [+/−N] and [+/−V] that have figured in the literature of syntax since Chomsky (1970). [N] and [V] are features which have syntactic relevance but which lack semantic content; as such, they define four logically possible classes which are instantiated by the four categories Noun, Verb, Adjective, and Preposition. All logically possible permutations of these features are attested. The features [material] and [dynamic], on the other hand, represent pure semantic content and define only two major semantic categories, SUBSTANCES/THINGS/ESSENCES and SITUATIONS, the former corresponding largely to the syntactic class of Nouns, and the latter comprising two syntactic classes, Verb and Adjective.

1.2.2 Inferable Eventual Position or State

At this point, we have some of the apparatus we need to talk about the semantics of derivation, but not quite enough. That is, in order to talk in some detail about processes which form nouns from verbs (such as *-er* and *-ee*) or verbs from nouns (such as *-ize* and *-ify*) we will need to say something more about the semantic classes of verbal SITUATIONS. In order to do so, we will need to add one feature to our small inventory of primitives, specifically a feature which allows us to capture some of the major aspectual classes of verbs. This is the feature [IEPS] for "Inferable Eventual Position or State" which was developed and justified in earlier work with Harald Baayen (Lieber and Baayen 1999, 181–2):

- [+/− **IEPS**]: Let Φ be a variable that ranges over States and Places,[10] and x be the argument of Φ. Further, let i stand for the initial State or Place, f for the final State or Place, and $j, \ldots, k$ for intermediate States/Places. Then the addition of the feature [IEPS] to the skeleton signals the addition of the semantic component in (16):

(16) $[\Phi_i (x), \Phi_j (x), \ldots, \Phi_k (x), \Phi_f (x)]$

In other words, the addition of the feature [IEPS] signals the addition of a sequence of PLACES or STATES. Further, if the value of [IEPS] is positive, we will be able to make the inference in (17):

(17)   If [+IEPS], then $i \neq f \wedge \Phi_{j,k} \notin f$: $\Phi_i < \Phi_{j...} < \Phi_k < \Phi_f$

In plain English, if [+IEPS] is present, there will be a sequence of PLACES/STATES such that at any point between the initial and final PLACE/STATE, some progression will have taken place towards the final PLACE/STATE. If [−IEPS] is present, then we can make no inference about the progression of PLACES/STATES.

---

10. STATES and PLACES are themselves mnemonics for featural representations, the former for the feature [−dynamic], as we have seen, and the latter for the feature [+Loc], which will be introduced in chapter 4.

The addition of the feature [IEPS] to a skeleton in effect signals the addition of a PATH component of meaning. If [IEPS] is absent, the notion of PATH is irrelevant to the meaning of the lexical item; if it is present, a PATH is relevant. Further, [+IEPS] and [−IEPS] items are distinguished in terms of the kind of PATH they imply, the former signaling a direct PATH, the latter a random PATH.

As Lieber and Baayen (1997, 1999) argue, the feature [IEPS] permits us to distinguish a number of significant verb classes:

(18)

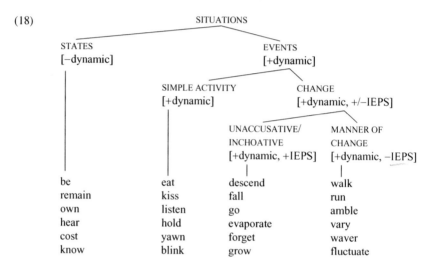

STATE verbs such as *know* and *possess* are characterized by the presence of the feature [−dynamic] in the outermost layer of their skeleton. I assume the usual tests for stativity, for example, that stative verbs do not occur in the progressive in English (**Daisy is knowing the answer*) or in the imperative (**Know the answer*), and so on (see Quirk et al. 1972, 94). Since the feature [IEPS] as I have defined it signals the addition of a PATH, and since a PATH involves a sequence of positions or STATES, it is by definition incompatible with the feature [−dynamic]. In other words, [−dynamic] verbs denote single STATES, not sequences of STATES, and thus do not bear the feature [IEPS]. A typical two-place STATE verb like *know* will therefore have the skeleton in (19):

(19)   know
         [−dynamic ([   ], [   ])]

All other verbs will have at least the feature [+dynamic]; these together will form the class of EVENT verbs, all of which can occur in the progressive in

English, can be used in the imperative, and so on. Referring again to Comrie's definition (1976, 49), they are actions which "will only continue if . . . continually subject to a new input of energy." Of these verbs, some will have only the feature [+dynamic]. This group, which I will refer to as SIMPLE ACTIVITY verbs, lacks the feature [IEPS]. Such verbs denote EVENTS for which the notion of a PATH is irrelevant. In other words, the notion of a PATH, as I have defined it, requires some change of position or state, which simply does not figure in the meaning of SIMPLE ACTIVITY verbs. The skeleton for a typical member of this class, *eat*, is given in (20):

(20)   eat
         [+dynamic ([   ], [   ])]

On the other hand, adding the feature [IEPS] to [dynamic] is possible, and adds two further subclasses to our typology. The presence of [IEPS], as I have said, implies the relevance of a PATH component of meaning; it defines those verbs in which some change of PLACE or STATE takes place. By way of example, consider the sentences presented in (21):

(21)   a. ?After having descended the ladder, Morgan found himself to be in
             exactly the same place he had started from.
         b. After having walked for five hours, Daisy found herself to be in exactly
             the same place she had started from.

(21a) is strange because the [+IEPS] change of place verb *descend* implies a PATH with non-equivalent initial and final points and a steady progression from one to the other.[11] In contrast, as illustrated in (21b), *walk* – a [−IEPS] verb – does not imply anything about the relationship between the initial and final place of its argument, or about the progression from one to the other, although the notion of a PATH is clearly relevant. In contrast, *eat* is a verb which lacks the feature [IEPS] entirely; nothing is implied in the meaning of the verb about the final position or STATE of its highest argument. Although many final positions or STATES can be envisioned, none is conventionalized as part of the meaning of the verb.

I have illustrated the interpretation of the feature [IEPS] by contrasting two CHANGE verbs with a SIMPLE ACTIVITY verb. I can elaborate a bit more on the former verbs, which bring together a number of lexical subclasses. The first subclass of the CHANGE group contains verbs which bear the features

---

11. Note that a verb like *descend* can be [+IEPS] even if an endpoint is never reached. That is, [+IEPS] does not imply either telicity or boundedness. See Lieber and Baayen (1997) for discussion of this point, and chapter 5 for a discussion of telicity and boundedness.

[+dynamic, +IEPS] in the outermost layer of their skeletons. These are the verbs which have traditionally been referred to as UNACCUSATIVES (for those involving change of PLACE) and INCHOATIVES (for those involving change of STATE). For all these verbs, the inference in (17) is possible, namely that there will be a sequence of PLACES or STATES implied by the action of the verb such that the initial and final PLACES/STATES are distinct, and at any point between the initial and final PLACE or STATE some progression will have taken place towards the final PLACE or STATE. The examples in (22) contain skeletons for the UNACCUSATIVE verb *descend* and the INCHOATIVE verb *grow*:

(22)   a. descend
           [+dynamic, +IEPS ([   ], [$_{Path}$])]

        b. grow (inchoative)
           [+dynamic, +IEPS ([   ], [$_{Path}$])]

I use the skeletons in (22) as an abbreviation for what might be more accurately but far less perspicuously represented as [+dynamic ([   ], [Φ_i ([$_x$]), Φ_j ([$_x$]), ..., Φ_k ([$_x$]), Φ_f ([$_x$])])], where Φ is again a variable ranging over PLACES (which will eventually be represented with the feature [+Loc]) and STATES (represented by the feature [−dynamic]), and the subscript x in the Φ arguments indicates that the same argument instantiates the sequence or PATH of PLACES or STATES. There is an empirical advantage to this abbreviatory device as well, as Lieber and Baayen 1997 have shown: as Φ has been defined to range over PLACES and STATES, we can express not only the similarities between UNACCUSATIVES and INCHOATIVES that have been noted in the literature (e.g., that they behave identically with respect to auxiliary selection in Dutch), but also the differences between them.

The second class of [IEPS] verbs will bear the features [+dynamic, −IEPS] in their outermost layer of skeleton. For such verbs, the inference in (17) does not hold. As I noted above, although a PATH is relevant to the meanings of these verbs, no inference is possible about the relationship between initial and final PLACES or STATES: the initial PLACE or STATE may be the same as the final one or not, and no steady progression between the two can be inferred. What is therefore highlighted in the meaning of these verbs is the MANNER OF CHANGE, either the manner of motion for verbs where a change of place is involved (e.g., *walk, run, amble*), or in the manner of change of state (e.g., *vary, waver, fluctuate*).[12] With verbs like *walk*, for example, one must change

---

12. Compare, for example, sentences like *The temperature fell* and *The temperature varied*. The former implies a change of state with a directed path, the latter a change of state with a random path.

position, but no inference is possible about the nature of the path involved. One may walk in place, walk in a circle, walk back and forth, etc.[13] Verbs in the MANNER OF CHANGE class will have skeletons like those in (23):

(23)   a. walk
           [+dynamic, −IEPS ([   ], [$_{Path}$])]
        b. vary
           [+dynamic, −IEPS ([   ], [$_{Path}$])]

Again, this skeleton is a somewhat simplified form of the skeleton we would have if we spelled out the feature [IEPS] as the sequence of PLACES or STATES that it really is meant to represent. The advantage again is not only a gain in perspicuity, but also an empirical claim that PLACES and STATES behave the same way for these classes of verbs.

I turn finally to one class of verbs which is not included in the typology in (20), namely CAUSATIVES. There is a good reason why this class does not appear in this initial typology. All of the verbs in (18) are ones which can be characterized in my system as simple SITUATIONS. It has been argued for some time in the literature that CAUSATIVES are not simple events or situations, but rather that they consist of two subevents, an ACTIVITY (x does something to y) and a RESULT (such that x causes y to become/go to z). This bipartite structure has been represented in various ways in the literature. Dowty (1979) and Levin and Rappaport Hovav (1995) make use of a structure something like [x DO y] CAUSE [y BECOME z]. Jackendoff captures a similar insight by adding an extra tier or layer to the LCS, with the upper tier representing thematic roles like agent and theme, and the lower one actor and patient. Here, I follow the general insights of this line of research, and suggest that CAUSATIVES should generally have a structure something like that in (24):

(24)   grow (causative)
        [+dynamic ([$_i$], [$_j$])]; [+dynamic ([$_i$], [+dynamic, +IEPS ([$_j$], [$_{Path}$])])]

In other words, a CAUSATIVE verb will typically consist of an activity event (x does something to y) and a causative event proper (such that the doing brings about some result). In the second subevent, the function [+dynamic] is layered on an INCHOATIVE or UNACCUSATIVE event. In the normal case, the first argument of the first subevent is co-indexed with the first argument of the second

---

13. Note that with verbs like *walk*, however, one may add an explicit path in the form of a prepositional phrase (e.g., *around the room, to Amsterdam*). Since prepositions like *to* themselves bear the feature [+IEPS], in composition with the verb they allow the inference in (15) to be made.

subevent, so that the "doer" of the activity is also the "causer" of the result. But the presence of a "doer" argument in both subevents allows for the possibility of indirect causation as well; in such cases, the first arguments of the two subevents would not be co-indexed. We will return to the representation of CAUSATIVE verbs in chapter 3, where we look at verb-forming derivation.

The sort of featural decomposition I develop here is not a notational variant of Jackendoff's (1990) system of representation. Jackendoff does not explicitly divide verbs into classes, but his primitives CAUSE, BE, INCH, and GO are used in a way that makes it possible to refer to some of the verb classes I have distinguished, but not to others. The primitive BE, for example, corresponds to my [−dynamic] class, that is, to STATE verbs. The primitive INCH together with BE corresponds to my INCHOATIVE verbs, and the primitive CAUSE (layered with INCH-BE or GO) to my CAUSATIVE verbs. The framework developed in Jackendoff 1990 gives no direct correlates in the area of SIMPLE ACTIVITY verbs, though, although in subsequent work, Jackendoff (1996) adds a primitive PERFORM which seems to have this function. PERFORM is left unanalyzed in that work, however, and its relation to other primitives remains unclear.

Further, Jackendoff does not class INCHOATIVES and UNACCUSATIVES together; the former are characterized by the primitive INCH and the latter by GO in his system. In light of the extensive evidence presented in Lieber and Baayen 1997 that these subclasses of verbs act uniformly with respect to auxiliary selection in Dutch – all and only [+IEPS] verbs in Dutch select the auxiliary *zijn* "be" in the perfect – I suggest that a system like mine is on the right track.[14]

---

14. In fact, in Jackendoff (1991, 1996), where some decomposition of these functions is attempted, they come out looking very different from each other. INCH appears as in (i), GO as in (ii), where [b] stands for "bounded," [i] for "internal structure," DIM 1d roughly for "conceived of as one dimensional," DIR for "directed," BDBY$^+$ for "bounded by a terminus or endpoint," and the parallel lines in (ii) for the device of structure preserving binding. I will not review all of these primitives and devices here. Suffice it to say that Jackendoff develops only a partial decomposition of his semantic functions, and that INCH and GO do not fall together in any obvious way.

    (i)   INCH (Jackendoff 1991, 37)

$$\begin{bmatrix} +b, -i \\ \text{DIM 1d DIR} \\ \text{BDBY}^+ ([_{\text{Situation}}\ x]) \end{bmatrix}$$

    (ii) GO (Jackendoff 1996, 322)

$$\begin{bmatrix} [1d] & & [1d] & [1d] \\ \| & & & \\ 0d & & \| & \| \\ \text{BE} & ([_{\text{Thing}}\ ],\ [_{\text{Space}}\ 0d]); & [_{\text{Time}}\ 0d] & \end{bmatrix}$$

Finally, Jackendoff does not have any way of referring to what I have called MANNER OF CHANGE verbs, or of classing together MANNER OF MOTION verbs with MANNER OF CHANGE OF STATE verbs. Verbs like *run, walk,* etc. are classed as GO verbs for Jackendoff, distinguished from UNACCUSATIVES only in having an added "Manner" component in their LCSs. Verbs like *waver, vary,* or *fluctuate,* the MANNER OF CHANGE OF STATE verbs, are not discussed at all. The two systems clearly differ in a number of respects.

1.2.3   A brief digression on the semantic body

Thus far, I have introduced three semantic features which serve as functional elements in semantic skeletons. We will see in the next section how these features will begin to offer an account of the polysemy of *-er* and *-ee.* But before I go on to the main point of this chapter, I should digress for a minute and give some idea of the composition of the semantic body. As I mentioned briefly in the Introduction, the semantic body puts meat on the bones of the skeleton; it consists of perceptual and cultural aspects of meaning, and of the sorts of things that Pustejovsky (1995) includes in his Qualia Structures: part/whole relationships, information about shape, color, dimension, orientation, origin, function, and so on.

I expect as well that the semantic body of a word may differ in individual speakers, with the representation being fatter or thinner from one speaker to the next. For example, in my own mental lexicon the word *flange* has quite an emaciated body: I know that a *flange* is something man-made – an artifact – and maybe that it has some mechanical function, although what that might be I don't really know. On the other hand, the word *dowitcher* has a more substantial body for me: I know that a *dowitcher* is something natural, a bird, in fact a wading bird favoring mudflats, and that it's a North American west coast bird. I expect that some speakers might know just the basics about this word, as I know only the basics about *flange.* Nevertheless, I would expect that all speakers would possess the same skeletal representation for these words, if they are familiar with them at all.

As for how we represent the body, in what follows I will be quite informal. For our purposes it will be enough to represent the semantic body as a list of bits and pieces of information in no particular order. We will return to the body in the next chapter.

1.3   Towards a solution

We have now developed barely enough of a framework to return to the problem raised at the outset of the chapter: what do affixes like *-er, -ee, -ant/-ent* and -*ist* mean, and why do they receive the range of overlapping interpretations that they do?

The most important claim of this section is that affixes, like simplex lexical items, can have skeletons, and that the semantic part of derivation involves adding the affixal skeleton as an outer layer to the skeleton of the base, thereby subordinating that skeleton. Affixal skeletons will consist of functions and arguments, just as simplex lexical skeletons do, and indeed of exactly the same atomic material that makes up simplex lexical skeletons. I assume, in other words, that affixes have actual semantic content. I will assume, as well, that affixation will require the coindexation or binding of an affixal argument with a base argument, a process that I will develop in detail in the next chapter. So for now, I will offer only one part of the analysis we need for this constellation of affixes, that is, the part concerning their semantic content.

The novel proposal I make here is that the vast majority of category-changing derivational affixes in English – and indeed in all languages – add a function that corresponds in featural content to one of the major semantic categories of simplex lexemes, namely the categories in (25):

(25)   **Basic categories for derivational affixes**:

[+dynamic]	creating SIMPLE ACTIVITIES
[−dynamic]	creating STATES
[+dynamic, +IEPS]	creating UNACCUSATIVES/INCHOATIVES
[+dynamic, −IEPS]	creating MANNER OF MOTION
bipartite	creating CAUSATIVES
[+material]	creating simple, concrete SUBSTANCES/THINGS/ESSENCES
[−material]	creating simple, abstract SUBSTANCES/THINGS/ESSENCES
[+material, dynamic]	creating concrete processual SUBSTANCES/THINGS/ESSENCES
[−material, dynamic]	creating abstract processual SUBSTANCES/THINGS/ESSENCES

In other words, the basic semantic categories – at least for category-changing derivation – are expected to be broad, general, and in fact quite abstract. We might expect affixes that derive statives or activity verbs by adding the features [−dynamic] or [+dynamic] respectively, or pure concrete or pure abstract nouns, or nouns that are concrete and processual or abstract and processual. The expectation that the system leads us to is one of rather extreme parsimony and underdetermination in affixal meaning. But I think that this expectation is exactly right.

Given the system I have outlined here, I propose that the affixes *-er, -ee, -ist,* and *-ant/-ent* actually make exactly the same fundamental semantic contribution to their bases. Specifically, all form concrete dynamic nouns: the skeletal contribution of these affixes will be nothing more than the features [+material, dynamic] and an associated "R" argument, that is, the highest argument of the semantic features:

(26)   *-er, -ee, -ant/-ent, -ist*
         [+material, dynamic ([   ], <base>)]

That is, this constellation of affixes fills one of the nine expected basic affixal types that the system predicts, a category of affixes that corresponds to simplex items like *author, chef, awl, victim,* and the like.

These four affixes are, of course, not completely identical. Obviously they take different sorts of bases: *-ist* takes nouns and adjectives, but predominantly nouns; the other three prefer verbs, although *-er* and *-ee* also sometimes take nouns. And, of course, their "argument-structural" properties are somewhat different: *-er* and *-ant/-ent* form predominantly subject-oriented nouns, *-ee* predominantly object-oriented nouns, although still with some overlap, as we have seen. We will have to account for these differences of course, and will do so once we add the device of co-indexation to our system in the next chapter. But with the featural system I have proposed, we can begin to see what the four affixes have in common. They are not specifically "agent" or "instrument" or "patient" or "subject" or "object" affixes, but they do add semantic content: specifically, they are affixes which create concrete and processual nouns, characteristics that agents, instruments, patients, experiencers all have in common. The two features [material] and [dynamic] in effect give us semantic means to characterize these affixes in a sufficiently abstract way to capture what they share. Thus, features like these appear to provide us with the right "grain size" for describing the semantics of this set of derivational affixes, unlike the primitives made available in other frameworks.

1.4   Wider implications: the paradigmatic nature of affixal semantics

The featural system that I have begun to develop in this chapter not only allows us to ascribe some sort of plausible unitary semantic content to the affixes *-er, -ee, -ant/-ent,* and *-ist,* but also possesses wider implications for morphology as well. Specifically, I believe that it makes it possible for us to say something about the semantic content of derivational affixes in general, including those that have been said in the past to be purely transpositional. According to Beard (1995), derivational morphology is transpositional when the only meaning change it induces on its base is that which is entailed by the change in syntactic category it effects. But what exactly is that meaning change? We can answer that question here: even transpositional affixes have semantic content in the form of features like [material], [dynamic], and [IEPS].

This featural system suggests something further as well. We have seen that there were nine main semantic classes into which we divided the simplex lexicon. If semantic features define a limited set of lexical semantic subclasses, and if derivation (and compounding and conversion as well) serve to extend the simplex lexicon, we predict that the range of lexical semantic subclasses appropriate for the simplex lexicon should be mirrored in the inventory of derivational affixes. In other words, we should expect to find affixes which create new lexemes falling into just those lexical semantic classes that we need for underived lexical items. In effect, the feature system I have begun to develop suggests that the semantics of affixation might be paradigmatic in nature. Just as features such as person (1st, 2nd, 3rd), number (singular, plural), and tense (present, past) serve to define the cells of an inflectional paradigm, we might look upon the semantic features [material], [dynamic], and [IEPS] as defining the cells of a semantic paradigm into which particular derivational affixes might be placed.

Let me be clear about what I mean here. I do not mean to say that all derivational affixes in English **must** fall into one of these nine categories. After all, these features are only the most basic of semantic features, and we must expect to add other semantic features, as we refine the system and extend its coverage to express other syntactically relevant semantic distinctions that figure in the simplex lexicon (in fact we will do so in chapters 4 and 5). We do not yet know the extent of the feature system that we will eventually need. But if we add other semantic features, we might expect to find these used by affixal semantics as well. Our prediction, then, is not that all derivational affixes in English will fall into one of the nine categories in (25), but rather a more modest claim that at least some will.

I believe this prediction to be correct; suggested members of each category are contained in Table 1.1. I have already suggested that English has a class of affixes including *-er*, *-ee*, *-ant/-ent*, and *-ist* that create concrete processual [+material, dynamic] nouns. What about the other classes?

English clearly has a large class of affixes which I believe should be characterized as abstract processual [−material, dynamic] nouns, namely nominalizing affixes like *-ation (examination)*, *-al (refusal)*, *-ure (closure)*, *-ment (amusement)*, and the like. These affixes are often characterized as being transpositional: they take verbs and make the corresponding nouns. What I take

Table 1.1 *Classes of English derivational affixes*

affixal skeleton	derivational affixes of English
[+material, dynamic ([ ],<base>)]	*-er, -ee, -ant/-ent, -ist*
[−material, dynamic ([ ], <base>)]	*-ation, -al, -ment, -ance, -ure*
[+material ([ ], <base>)]	*?-ware,* [compounding]
[−material ([ ], <base>)]	*-ness, -ity, -hood, -ship, -ism*
[+dynamic ([ ], <base>)]	[conversion]
[−dynamic ([ ], <base>)]	*-ic, -ive, -ary, -al, -ous, -y*
[+dynamic, +IEPS ([ ], <base>)]	[conversion]
[+dynamic, −IEPS ([ ], <base>)]	[conversion]
bipartite skeleton	*-ize, -ify*

this to mean is that they preserve the processual nature of their bases, while also making abstractions of them. Further, it has often been observed that these affixes form a constellation or cohort of rival affixes. This is to say that they have exactly the same effect on the meaning of their bases; all other things being equal, they are semantically interchangeable.[15]

We also have affixes like *-ness (happiness)* and *-ity (purity)* which create simple abstract [−material] nouns from adjectives, as well as a number of affixes which form abstract nouns from concrete nouns: among the latter are *-hood (knighthood)* and *-ship (stewardship)*. Although they take bases of different sorts, both affixes in effect mean the same thing, namely "abstraction having to do with X," where X is the denotation of the base.[16]

English also has a wide range of affixes which form statives, that is, [−dynamic] items, in the form of adjectives, including *-ic (dramatic), -ary (visionary), -ive (attractive), -al (architectural), -en (golden), -ous (poisonous), -y (fishy)*. Such adjectives are often termed Possessional or Relational adjectives (Beard 1995), and are glossed in a variety of ways including "in the nature of X," "pertaining to X," "characterized by X," "having X," "made of X," "belonging to X," and the like (cf. Marchand 1969). I claim that these multiple glosses are in fact symptomatic of the bare-bones nature of affixal semantics: the affixes do make a semantic contribution, but only insofar as they place their nominal and

15. They are not, of course, interchangeable in individual instances. For one thing, bases of particular sorts prefer one or another of these nominalizing affixes; verbs in *-ize* favor *-ation*, for example. Further, there exist doublets or even triplets of nominalizations (e.g., *committal, commitment, commission*) in which individual members have been lexicalized with distinct and idiosyncratic meanings. My claim here is more modest, simply that these affixes have the same range of effects when looked at over their whole range of bases.
16. See Aronoff and Cho (2001) for a discussion of the semantics of *-ship*.

verbal bases in the broad semantic category of STATES. Again, the semantic content of these transpositional affixes is a single semantic feature, in this case [−dynamic].

Finally, we have verb-forming affixes like *-ize (standardize), -ify (purify)*, and *en- (entomb)*. We will have much more to say about these affixes in chapter 3; specifically it will be necessary to consider whether it is correct to characterize them as "causative" affixes and if so, how we explain their characteristic polysemy (see Lieber 1998, Plag 1999). But for now, let's assume that "causative" is a close enough approximation to their semantic content, and recall that causatives are formed in the present lexical semantic system on the basis of a bipartite skeleton. Therefore, the verb-forming affixes *-ize, -ify*, and *en-* seem like good candidates for filling another of the expected affix types in this system.

There are plausible examples for at least five of the nine categories we would predict. Oddly, what we don't seem to find in abundance in English are affixes which create simple concrete [+material] nouns or simple verbs of any sort. In fact, I am hard-pressed to find any examples at all of a bona fide affix that creates concrete nouns. English does have a compounding stem – something which Marchand (1969, 356) might even call a "semi-suffix" – which fulfills this function, namely *-ware*: *glassware, tinware, hardware, software, flatware, Delftware*. But robust, productive suffixes seem not to be much in evidence.

Why might this be? One possibility is that it is simply an accident. Carstairs-McCarthy (1992, 185), discussing Beard (1981), cites an example from Serbo-Croatian which would seem to be the sort of concrete-noun-forming affix that we seek, a suffix *-ina* which means a number of things like "meat from," "skin from," "fat from," "tusks from," "wood from," and the like. What the suffix in fact seems to mean is something very general like "material stuff from," where its base is typically a natural SUBSTANCE/THING/ESSENCE like an animal species or a type of tree. I would say that the semantic content of *-ina* is nothing more than the feature [+material], with context and cultural expectations fixing the kind of "stuff" eventually lexicalized into the meaning of the word. So perhaps it is just an accident that English lacks an affix of this sort.

Another answer might simply be that languages tend to need fewer affixes forming concrete nouns, as the vast bulk of simplex nouns are concrete to begin with. Lyons (1977, 445–6) points out, for example, that the vast majority of concrete nouns are monomorphemic, whereas abstract nouns tend to be formed through a process of nominalization. It might be that English lacks derivational means for forming simple concrete nouns simply because such means are not particularly useful: we already have a large stock of monomorphemic concrete nouns.

The most plausible explanation, however, would seem to be that English has a highly productive alternate means of word formation for creating concrete nouns, namely root compounding. We can create a new name for a thing simply by putting together two already existing noun stems, and thereby extend the simplex noun lexicon infinitely.

English is also quite poverty-stricken in verb-forming derivational affixes. In fact, as we will see in chapter 3, the only productive suffixes we have are the causatives *-ize* and *-ify*. Again, there are a number of possible reasons for the dearth of verb-forming suffixes. For one, we have a large supply of simplex verbs of all sorts. And further, as was the case in the formation of concrete nouns, English has nonderivational means of word formation for the creation of new verbs, namely conversion.

The prediction that our theory makes seems largely, if not completely, to be borne out by the derivational morphology of English; we do find in abundance at least five of the nine major classes of affixes that we might expect to find, and the others are ones whose functions seem largely fulfilled in English by other morphological means, chiefly compounding and conversion.

Our theory can be made to yield another prediction as well, namely that there are certain things that affixes should **not** mean. With the featural system that we have created here, we should not, for example, expect to find an affix which creates at the same time both stative and activity verbs (that is, items some of which are [−dynamic] and others of which are [+dynamic]), or both processual and nonprocessual nouns, or an affix which creates nouns some of which are concrete and others of which are abstract (that is, some of which bear the feature [+material] and others [−material]). I believe that this prediction too is, in fact, correct, despite initial appearances to the contrary.

I know of no plausible candidate for an affix which creates both stative and eventive verbs in English, or both processual and nonprocessual nouns. But there is at least one affix in English which seems to run counter to our prediction about the nonexistence of affixes creating at the same time concrete nouns and abstract nouns, namely the suffix *-ery*. Consider the data in (27):

(27)   *-ery (-ry)*
      a. collectives: peasantry, tenantry, jewelry, machinery, crockery, cutlery, pottery
      b. place nouns: eatery, brewery, nunnery, piggery, fishery, bakery
      c. behavior characteristic of: snobbery, prudery, savagery, archery, midwifery

The suffix -*ery* forms, according to Marchand (1969, 282), both concrete and abstract nouns, and in fact seems to display an oddly heterogeneous range of meanings. *Piggeries* and *wineries* are places, *peasantry* and *jewelry* respectively collectives of people and things – all so far concrete – but *snobbery* and *midwifery* denote types of behavior characteristic respectively of *snobs* and *midwives*; they are surely abstract nouns. It appears that contrary to our prediction, then, English has at least one suffix which creates nouns that are sometimes concrete and sometimes abstract.

Further examination of this suffix suggests, however, that it is only an apparent counterexample to our prediction. I will argue in chapter 5 that -*ery* does not in fact mean "concrete" or "abstract" – that is, that its skeletal contribution is not the feature [material] at all – but rather that its semantic contribution is something else. Here, I will merely sketch the direction this argument will take.

Our first clue to the nature of this affix is that -*ery*, unlike the affixes we have looked at so far, does not change the syntactic category of the bases it attaches to. That is, it generally attaches to nouns and creates nouns. It is not a suffix of transposition. A second clue to solving our problem lies in the odd heterogeneity of meanings that -*ery* displays. We might at first be tempted to treat -*ery* as several homophonous suffixes – one a collective, one a place-naming affix, and so on. But there are two arguments against homophony. One is that historically, according to the OED, all forms seem to derive from a single French suffix -*erie*, which has a similar range of meanings. We cannot easily claim that several different affixes have fallen together as a single synchronic phonological form. A more compelling reason, however, is not historical. Rather, there is a second affix in English, the suffix -*age*, which seems to show quite a similar heterogeneity of meaning:

(28)   -*age*
      a. collectives: baggage, wreckage, poundage, plumage, spillage
      b. place nouns: orphanage, parsonage, hermitage

Although it does not show forms meaning "behavior characteristic of," the suffix -*age* does form both collectives and place nouns (the former more productively than the latter). It seems just as unlikely an accident that these two meanings should fall together in two different affixes, as it did that the meanings "agent," "instrument," and "patient" should fall together in the affixes -*er*, -*ee*, and the like. What this suggests is that -*ery* and -*age* again have some unitary meaning, that these meanings go together for a reason. If we can discover what this commonality is, it will no longer be an accident that just this constellation of meanings appears together, and it will also allow us to show why *-ery* does not constitute a counterexample to the prediction that we made earlier.

My solution here is provisional, as it requires us to go beyond the very simple system of three features that I have sketched and tried to justify in this chapter. I think the key to understanding derivational affixes like *-ery* and *-age* is that they form nouns with certain quantificational characteristics. We do not yet have the featural means to characterize their precise semantic content, but roughly, I propose that the central meaning of these affixes is one of collectivity and that the "place" sense is an extended sense of these two affixes that arises as a result of paradigmatic extension, a process that takes place when there is no particular affix in a language to supply a meaning (Booij and Lieber 2004). I will introduce the notion of paradigmatic extension in chapter 3. In chapter 5, I will extend our system to include several features which will allow us to capture quantificational characteristics of both simplex and complex words. At that point, I will return to the question of *-ery* and *-age*, and show why they do not constitute a real counterexample to the prediction made here. For now, however, I offer a promissory note.

1.5 *Conclusion*

What I have tried to show in this chapter is that it is possible to construct a system of lexical semantic representation which begins to have characteristics which will allow us to talk productively about the semantics of derivation. Features like [material] and [dynamic] allow us to partition the simplex lexicon into useful descriptive classes. This system is meant to be more than just a tool for characterizing the simplex lexicon, however. Indeed, it is meant to provide a framework in which we can not only describe affixal meaning, but actually predict what sorts of derivational affixes we might expect to find in English and indeed in any language. I have tried to show that the features [material] and [dynamic] are quite useful in characterizing the semantic contributions of various English derivational affixes.

Further, the framework I have been constructing begins to give a glimmer of an answer to two of the questions which were raised in the Introduction. A first pass at answering the so-called polysemy question is this. One reason that affixes tend to be highly polysemous is that their actual semantic content is vastly abstract and underdetermined. That is, given the kinds of skeletal representation I have proposed, we can begin to see how affixes manifest what Pustejovsky and Boguraev (1996) call "logical polysemy" – a kind of polysemy that results from an underdetermination of meaning. Given the "grain size" of our decompositional atoms, we have seen that it is possible, indeed necessary, to characterize affixal meanings very broadly and abstractly; when the underdetermined semantic contribution of the affix is combined with the more robust semantic contribution of the base (bases having both skeletons and bodies), and deployed in context, the semantic contribution of the affix can be lexicalized in a variety of related ways. We will see in detail in the chapters to come how this process of determination takes place.

We can also attempt a first pass at an answer to the multiple-affix question: there tend to be multiple affixes with the same meaning in any given language simply because there is a limited inventory of semantic contributions an affix can make, a limited number of slots in the semantic paradigm into which processes of lexeme formation can fit. If the features that constitute skeletal functions are severely limited in number, we predict a highly circumscribed realm of semantic functions which derivation can effect. Especially in languages like English, where there exist both a substantial native stock of derivational affixes and a large borrowed cohort of affixes, we would expect that the affixes would not differentiate in meaning, as simplex doublets often do, but would simply fall together into groups of rival affixes.

The key to making this idea work, of course, is to discover what that highly limited inventory should be. Here, I have done no more than to suggest the architecture of the system and a few plausible first guesses at features. What I think is important, however, is less the correctness of these particular features than of the general idea that some small set of semantic features should not only characterize broad semantic classes of simplex items, but also predict the scope and range of derivational categories. As I indicated at the outset, this is a work in progress. The next chapter will begin to refine the system and allow us to look in more detail at our tentative answers to the polysemy and multiple-affix questions. Following chapters will add depth and detail to the system.

2   *Co-indexation*

In the previous chapter we started to sketch a system of lexical semantic representation which is capable of answering some of the fundamental questions raised about the meaning of affixes. I argued that affixes have specific semantic content, and that affixal content can be quite abstract. Having suggested what some of that featural content might be, however, I offered only part of the system we need for exploring the semantics of derivation, compounding, and conversion. In this chapter, I will develop another part of the theoretical apparatus I think we need, namely a theory of co-indexation which allows us to integrate the referential properties of an affix with that of its base.

Why a theory of co-indexation? The creation of a new complex word, whether a derived word or a compound, always involves the integration of multiple parts into a single referential unit. It is this referential unit that determines how many arguments are eventually projected into the syntax. Co-indexation is a device we need in order to tie together the arguments that come with different parts of a complex word to yield only those arguments that are syntactically active. In this chapter I will first look at compounds in English to illustrate the process of co-indexation and its effect on the ultimate interpretation of complex words. Although this might seem to be a detour from our main goal – the four questions of the Introduction – I believe that compounding offers a good place to start in an investigation of co-indexation. I would argue that in fact co-indexation is responsible for much that is important in the semantic interpretation of compounds. We will look first at root compounds in English, both the normal *endocentric* compounds like *dog bed* and the slightly more exotic *copulative* compounds, sometimes called *dvandvas* (e.g., *producer-director*), and *exocentric* or *bahuvrihi* (e.g., *redhead*) compounds. We will then go on to look at the interpretation of synthetic compounds. I argue that a simple process of co-indexation in fact accounts for many of the observations about the interpretation of synthetic compounds that have previously been attributed in the literature to syntactic principles such as the First Sister Principle (Roeper and Siegel 1978), the First Order Projection Condition (Selkirk 1982), and the Argument Linking Principle (Lieber 1983), or to syntactic movement rules (Roeper 1988, Lieber 1992a).

In section 2.2, we go on to look at the process of co-indexation as it applies to derivational affixation, refining the process which we proposed for compounding, and finally returning to the problem we set in the last chapter, the analysis of the affixes *-er, -ee, -ant/-ent,* and *-ist.*

2.1   Co-indexation and compounding in English

Perhaps the most productive type of word formation in English is the process of compounding, which yields both root compounds such as those in (1) and synthetic compounds such as those in (2):

(1)   *root compounds*
        textile mill, towel rack, catfood, prince consort, etc.

(2)   *synthetic compounds*
        truck driver, meat-eating, home-grown, cost containment, waste disposal,
        word coinage, load tolerance, city employee, etc.

Root compounds are those compounds whose second stem is not derived from verbs. Synthetic compounds, in contrast, have a second stem which is deverbal. As has been observed many times (see Lieber 1983, 1992b for example), root compounding is most productive with noun and adjective bases in English.

A number of observations have been made about the semantic interpretation of compounds that any theory of word formation would have to account for:

- The first stem of any compound, either root or synthetic, is nonreferential in interpretation. That is, the first stem *cat* in the compound *catfood* cannot refer to any special cat.
- The compound as a whole takes the second stem as its semantic head. That is, the compound *catfood* denotes a kind of food rather than a kind of cat.
- The first stem in a synthetic compound receives an argument interpretation, often but not always the internal argument interpretation. For example, the stem *truck* in the synthetic compound *truck driver* is interpreted as the internal argument (i.e., the object) of the verb *drive*.
- Finally, synthetic compounds cannot be formed from obligatorily ditransitive verbs. For example, it is impossible to form synthetic compounds from verbs like *put* (**shelf book putter, *book putter on shelves,* etc.).

Such observations have been made frequently in the vast literature on compounding in the tradition of generative morphology (e.g., Allen 1978, Roeper and Siegel 1978, Selkirk 1982, Lieber 1983, 1992a, 1992b, DiSciullo and Williams 1987), but generally have been accounted for formally by appealing to the structure of the compound rather than to its semantic properties per se.

Let me first review briefly the different structural analyses attributed to different types of compounding and the reasons why they have been advocated. Perhaps least controversial over the years has been the structure proposed for root compounds, those compounds which consist of two stems where the right-hand stem is not deverbal. The agreed-upon structure is that in (3):

(3)

That is, there has been little disagreement that root compounds consist of two stems combined as one, with the compound as a whole bearing the category and morphosyntactic features of the right-hand stem.

Far more controversial has been the analysis of synthetic compounds, that is, those compounds whose right-hand stem is based on a verb. Two basic structures are conceivable for synthetic compounds:

(4)

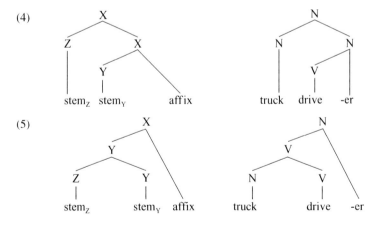

(5)

The structure in (4) is intuitively more plausible, and indeed the more frequently advocated in the literature – see, for example, Selkirk 1982 and Booij 1992, among others. In it, the deverbal noun is compounded with another stem, the derived word forming the head of the compound as a whole. The structure in

(5) was the one I advocated in Lieber 1983; in (5) a compound is first formed of the noun and verb stems, and then the derivational affix is added outside the compound. In retrospect, my choice of compound structure was driven by my statement of the Argument Linking Principle which required sisterhood in order for a noun stem to be interpreted as an argument of a verb.

But the structural analysis in (5) is less plausible for two reasons. First, it is unusual to attach derivational affixes on the outside of compounds. Second, as Booij 1988 pointed out, the structural analysis in (5) forces us to generate a sort of root compound – an NV compound – which in fact is highly unproductive; in other words, the basis of the productive category of synthetic compounds would have to be a sort of root compound which largely does not exist independently in English.

There are, of course, any number of other ways of capturing the argument relationship between the left-hand noun stem and the base verb in synthetic compounds that do not require the structure in (5), among them transformational or movement analyses (Roeper and Siegel 1978, Roeper 1988, Lieber 1992a). In such analyses, the argument interpretation of the left-hand stem follows from the fact that it starts out in the structural position of an internal argument (that is sister to V dominated by V′), and is moved into the compound by a process something like Baker's (1985) Incorporation.

However, it has become increasingly clear that the intuitively more plausible word structure for synthetic compounds is in fact the correct one based on the syntax of compounding, and that indeed no analysis involving movement or syntactic principles is needed to explain the interpretation of the first stem as an argument of the verb. Rather, what we need is a framework of lexical semantic representation that makes it possible to explain in a uniform way the interpretation of both root compounds and synthetic compounds and that does not appeal to the internal structure of those compounds. I argue in the next sections that the system of lexical semantic representations I have begun to develop – including both skeletons and bodies of lexical items – will allow us to account for all of the relevant observations about compound interpretation once we have added to our framework a simple principle of co-indexation. Indeed, I will show that the system we have been developing here will also make at least one prediction about compound interpretation that goes beyond those of previous analyses.

2.1.1 *Root compounds*

It has generally been noted that semantic interpretation in root compounds is quite free. That is, although both Lees (1963) and Levi (1978) attempted to fix a number of semantic patterns for root compounds (for example, "X made of Y" for compounds like *feather bed* or *iron lung*, "X used for Y" for compounds like *towel rack*, "X eaten by Y" for *catfood*, and so on), it is more generally acknowledged that the relationships between the first and second stems in root compounds are too numerous and too fluid to assign a fixed number of interpretive patterns. As Selkirk (1982, 22) puts it: "The semantic relation obtaining between the head constituent and its sister nonhead constituent can vary considerably, though, and a general characterization of the relation is probably impossible . . . it would seem that virtually any relation between head and nonhead is possible – within pragmatic limits, of course." I concur with Selkirk on this point, and believe that an adequate semantic analysis of root compounds must allow for the freedom of interpretation that we in fact find with root compounding in English.

There are nevertheless two specific observations about the semantics of root compounds that need to be captured, namely the first and second observations above. That is, any analysis of the semantics of root compounds must account for the fact that the first stem in root compounds (and indeed in any compounds) is nonreferential; the stem *cat* in *catfood* cannot refer to any special cat. It will also need to account for our second observation, namely that the relation between the first and second stems is one of hyponymy (Cruse 1986, 88–9): what is denoted by the compound is a subset of what is denoted by the right-hand stem; so *catfood* is a kind of *food*, and so on. This is the same observation that Allen (1978) formalized as the IS A Condition.

In order to account for these observations, let us look at the semantic operations involved in creating a root compound. When we form a new root compound we not only build a word structure like that in (3), which creates a single word from two stems, but also put together the semantic structures of those two stems. It is a reasonable assumption that the semantic structure – that is, the arrangement of skeletal parts – follows from the word structure. Let us say that the semantic operation associated with compounding minimally involves putting together the lexical skeletons of the two stems in a relationship of sisterhood, as shown schematically in (6):

(6) $[\alpha F_1 ([\ ])] [\beta F_2 ([\ ])]$

Further, I would argue that the semantic headedness of compounds follows from structural headedness. In other words, whatever principle determines that the second constituent is syntactically dominant will also determine the semantic dominance of that constituent; it is likely that the determination of headedness in compounds must be set individually for each language (see

Lieber 1980, 1992a for discussion of this issue). This will give us the effect of hyponymy (Allen's [1978] IS A Condition), as it will ensure that the denotation of the structural head will be the dominant denotation of the compound as a whole.

We must now account for the referential integration of the two skeletons. As the schematic representation in (6) stands, each stem has a separate "R" argument, and each therefore has a separate reference. But a compound has only a single referent. We must therefore look at how the reference of the two stems is tied together. The Principle of Co-indexation in (7) is a first attempt at formalizing the process of referential integration:

(7)   **Principle of Co-indexation** (preliminary): In a configuration in which
        semantic skeletons are composed, co-index the highest nonhead argument
        with the highest (preferably unindexed) head argument.

To interpret the Principle of Co-indexation, we must of course be able to identify what the "highest" argument of the skeleton is. This is straightforward: the highest argument is the argument of the outermost lexical function of the head. To anticipate later discussion, in a skeleton created by subordination of functions, such as would be the case in a derived word, schematically shown in (8a), the argument of F_1 is the highest. In a skeleton created by concatenation, such as would be the case in a compound, schematically (8b), the highest argument is the argument of F_2, which is the semantic representation of the syntactic head of the word:[1]

(8)   a. $[\alpha F_1 ([\quad], [\beta F_2 ([\quad])])]$
       b. $[\alpha F_1 ([\quad])] [\beta F_2 ([\quad])]$

We assume here that arguments with shared indexes share reference and interpretation, and are linked to a single constituent in the syntactic structure. That is, the Principle of Co-indexation is not only a principle which links

---

1. The reader might also raise the question of how lexical semantic representations such as the above schematic skeletons are ultimately linked to syntactic structures. Here, we enter a much vexed area of study. There is an enormous literature on this topic proposing solutions ranging from Baker's (1988) Uniformity of Theta Assignment Hypothesis (UTAH) to various thematic hierarchies (e.g., Jackendoff 1972, Bresnan and Kannerva 1989, Grimshaw 1990, Baker 1996, Van Valin and LaPolla 1997; see Newmeyer 2002 for discussion and criticism of the various proposals). For our purposes, it is not necessary to resolve this problem, as strictly speaking it is orthogonal to the issue of semantic interpretation of derived words. Co-indexation, in the sense used here, is a lexical semantic phenomenon that can be discussed without solving the linking problem in the larger sense.

arguments within a lexical semantic structure, but also a device which has logical consequences as well, namely the claim that the referential properties of the resulting word are set in a particular way. We must look closely at what exactly this means.

In the best of circumstances, co-indexation means that the reference of the first and second stems (nonhead and head, respectively) is completely identified. In order to see how this can happen, we now need to look not only at the skeletons of compounds, but also at their bodies. As I said in chapter 1, I imagine the semantic body to be much less formal in structure than the skeleton, to be nondecompositional, and to consist of all sorts of encyclopedic information, both cultural and perceptual, involving shape, dimension, color, trajectory, use, origin, purpose, and so on. For present purposes we can assume that the semantic body is merely structured as a list of bits and pieces of information, and that, unlike the skeleton, there is no fixed inventory of these bits and pieces. When I construct the body for any given lexical item in what follows, the inventory of body parts I list should be understood as merely a suggestion of what might be present in any given speaker's mental lexicon.

Returning now to the meaning of co-indexation, I repeat that in the best of circumstances co-indexation implies the complete identification of reference; the co-indexed items will be predicable of the same entity. I claim that complete identification can indeed happen, but only when both the skeletons and the bodies of the two stems are sufficiently similar or compatible to allow for complete identification. This in fact happens only in the so-called *copulative* compounds like *clergyman-poet*, *prince consort*, or *producer-director* whose first and second stems denote very similar sorts of entities.

Let me illustrate with an analysis of the compound *clergyman-poet*, paying attention now both to the skeleton, its concatenation and indexing, and to the bodies of the two stems.

(9)   skeleton   [+material, dynamic ([$_i$])]   [+material, dynamic ([$_i$])]
                          clergyman   *poet*
         body   <natural>   <natural>
                        <human>   <human>
                        <male>   <writes poetry>
                        <cleric>

Both nouns have similar skeletons – they're both dynamic nouns which allow a single argument. And both in fact are natural substances, as opposed to artifacts, and denote humans. In effect, the semantic representations, both skeleton and body, are so similar that they can in fact be identified, which is to say,

predicated of the same entity.[2] From this follows the coordinative interpretation characteristic of this sort of compound.

Most of the time, however, the skeletons and bodies of the nonhead and head stems in a compound will not be sufficiently similar to allow for complete identification. In the vast majority of cases – those typically referred to as *endocentric* compounds – co-indexing has a weaker effect: it forces a sort of merger of the two stems, that is, an effort to find some sort of common ground that allows them to be interpreted together. In effect, the result is that the nonhead stem is construed merely as having some plausible relationship to the head stem.

Consider, for example, a simple NN root compound like *dog bed*:

(10)   skeleton   [+material ([$_i$])]   [+material ([$_i$])]
                     dog   *bed*
       body   <natural>   <artifact>
                   <animate>   <furniture>
                   <canine>   <horizontal surface>
                                          <for sleeping>

Here, the skeletons are identical (both *dog* and *bed* are concrete nouns with a single argument), but their bodies are quite dissimilar. *Dogs* are natural, as opposed to artifacts, and are animate. I use the designation <canine> merely as shorthand here for the constellation of bits of information that allows a given speaker to distinguish the dogginess of dogs from, for example, the felinity of cats. *Beds*, on the other hand, are artifacts, items of furniture, which have a characteristic use, namely for sleeping. When the "R" argument of *dog* is co-indexed with the "R" argument of *bed*, what ensues is a process of co-interpretation. Since something cannot at the same time be natural and an artifact, the two representations cannot simply be identified or predicated of the same entity. Further, the "R" argument of *bed* is already committed to being an artifact, as *bed* is syntactically (and therefore semantically) the head of the compound. So the semantic characteristics of the nonhead can be placed only in relation to those of the head, which is to say, in some way to modify it. A *dog bed* is a bed somehow associated with a dog, context and knowledge of the world (and in

---

2. It is of course reasonable to ask how close two lexical semantic representations need to be for the copulative interpretation to be possible. Clearly, the two lexemes must have identical skeletons, and must share major bodily attributes; both must be natural substances or both artifacts, for example. Both must be human or not. But as far as smaller distinctions of meaning are concerned, it remains to be seen exactly how close corporeal attributes need to be to allow for complete referential identification. I leave this question open here.

this particular case lexicalization) determining what the ultimate relationship between the two stems will be.

Of course, there is surely a lot more to be said about the ultimate interpretation of individual root compounds – for example, why a *dog bed* is a bed that a dog sleeps in, whereas a *day bed* is a bed used during the day. I would argue that everything that goes on in arriving at a semantic interpretation of a root compound except for its referential properties and the semantic property of headedness involves context and encyclopedic knowledge: we do not want our theory to have anything to say about the ultimate lexicalized meanings of root compounds. The claim I make here is that lexical semantics fixes only so much of the interpretation of a newly coined compound, namely that the second stem determines the overall headedness of the compound, and that the compound as a whole has only a single referent. The rest is free.

The interpretation of root compounds can largely be said to follow then from the juxtaposition of semantic representations, skeletons and bodies, and from co-indexation. Before we look at synthetic compounds, whose interpretations are much more interesting, I should say something about the so-called *bahuvrihi* or *exocentric* root compounds. Although they do not represent a particularly productive type of compounding in synchronic English, compounds such as *dimwit*, *pickpocket*, *redhead*, and the like have nevertheless been much discussed in the literature. These are like root compounds in that their second stem is not derived from a verb. But they are unlike root compounds in that the second stem is not apparently the semantic head of the compound; the compound as a whole denotes something other than what the second stem denotes. So a *redhead* is not a kind of head per se, but a person who has red hair.

I accept here the analysis of *bahuvrihi* compounds proposed by Booij (1992) for Dutch. Booij (1992, 39) points out that compounds like *bleekneus* "pale person" (literally "pale nose") in Dutch may have an exocentric interpretation, but syntactically the second stem is clearly the head of the compound; the plural of the compound is straightforwardly determined by the second stem, for example. As for their semantic interpretation, Booij argues that these compounds are merely interpreted by whatever process of semantic inferencing allows us to interpret metonymic expressions in general: "A *bleekneus* . . . is not a *neus* 'nose', but this follows from the fact that referring expressions, either phrasal or lexical, can be used as pars-pro-toto." That is, even simplex items can be interpreted metonymically, as when we refer to a basketball player as the *shirt* (as opposed to the *skin*). Presumably whatever accounts for our ability to make this sort of inference can be put to use in the interpretation of the exocentric compounds as well. Following Booij's analysis, then, I assume that *bahuvrihi* compounds in English are interpreted precisely as endocentric root compounds are, with the skeletons of the first and second stems being concatenated, their arguments co-indexed, and the bodies of the two stems compared for compatibility, and related in some way. The resulting compound is then available for interpretation as a metonym, just as any lexical item would be.

2.1.2   *Synthetic compounds*

The process of co-indexation also plays a robust role in the interpretation of synthetic compounds. The thing that distinguishes synthetic from root compounds, and therefore that drives the interpretation of synthetic compounds, is the fact that the second stem of a synthetic compound is by definition a deverbal derivation, and in deverbal derivations we often have more than one argument available for co-indexing. Further, those arguments, by virtue of being verbal arguments, have distinctive thematic interpretations which contribute to the interpretation of any co-indexed stem. I will show now that most of the observations that have been made in the literature about the interpretation of synthetic compounds follow from the representations of derived words and compounds that we have already developed.

What observations about synthetic compounds do we need to account for? The most prominent of the observations are the third and fourth observations made above, namely that the first stem, the nonhead, of the synthetic compound is typically interpreted as the internal argument of the verbal base of the head, unless that argument has already been satisfied, and that verbs which take more than one obligatory internal argument (e.g., *put*) cannot form the base of synthetic compounds. These observations motivated principles like Roeper and Siegel's First Sister Principle (1978) and Selkirk's First Order Projection Condition (1982), as well as my own (1983) Argument Linking Principle.

The present framework accounts for these observations without appealing to syntactic structures or movement rules of any sort. Consider what the Principle of Co-indexation in (7) gives us for the compound *truck driver*. We must consider the skeletal representations both of the stem *truck* and also of the deverbal noun *driver*. The latter noun, of course, raises questions which we have only partially answered so far. We know that *driver* is formed by composing the skeleton of *-er* (shown in (11)) with that of the verb *drive* (12), but we have not yet fixed the means of integrating these two skeletal bits by co-indexation. Let us say, preliminarily, that the Principle of Co-indexation in (7) applies to derived words as well as compounds, that is, to skeletons that are composed hierarchically, as well as to skeletons that have been concatenated. We will therefore get the composed and co-indexed skeleton for *driver* in (13):

(11)   *-er*
       [+material, dynamic ([   ], <base>)]

(12)   *drive*
       [+dynamic ([   ], [   ])]

(13)   *driver*
       [+material, dynamic ([$_i$], [+dynamic ([$_i$], [   ])])]

In other words, the highest argument of the nonhead (the verb stem) will be co-indexed with the "R" argument of the affix *-er*. When the skeleton of the deverbal stem *driver* is concatenated with that of *truck*, we must co-index again. In this case, the "R" argument of the nonhead *truck* is co-indexed with the next available argument in the head constituent, namely the internal argument of *drive*:

(14)   [+material ([$_j$])]   [+material, dynamic ([$_i$], [+dynamic ([$_i$], [$_j$])])]
              truck   *-er*   *drive*

The nonhead stem of the synthetic compound is interpreted as an internal argument because the highest free argument of the base happens to be the internal argument of the verb *drive*. In other words, because the referent of the stem is co-indexed, and therefore identified with an argument that has a particular thematic interpretation, and since that thematic interpretation has not already been co-opted by the "R" argument of the affix, the first stem of the compound can simply and straightforwardly take on the thematic interpretation of the verbal argument.

Now compare the interpretation of the compound *truck driver* with that of *city employee*. The Principle of Co-indexation in (7) in fact makes a nice prediction with respect to compounds with a second stem in *-ee*, namely that the first stem should **not** receive the internal argument interpretation. The key here is the indexing that occurs with the suffix *-ee*. Let us say informally that the affix *-ee* preferentially binds the internal argument of its verbal base, as in (15) (section 2.2 will be devoted to working out exactly how this co-indexation works, as it obviously does not follow from the Principle of Co-indexation as it is now formulated, but for now an informal statement must suffice):

(15)   *employee*
       [+material, dynamic ([$_i$],   [+dynamic ([   ], [$_i$])])]
              -ee   *employ*

When this is compounded with another stem, according to (7) the "R" argument of the nonhead is co-indexed with the highest available argument of the head, which in this case is not the internal argument, but rather the external argument. This is represented in (16):

(16)   *city employee*
       [−material ([$_j$])] [+material, dynamic ([$_i$], [+dynamic ([$_j$], [$_i$])])]
           city   *-ee*   *employ*

This analysis in fact gives us what I think is the right interpretation of the compound *city employee* which is a person that the city employs. Note that principles such as the First Sister Principle (Roeper and Siegel 1978), the First Order Projection Condition (Selkirk 1982) and my own Argument Linking Principle (1983) would not have predicted the correct meaning for this compound.

Similar analyses follow for other synthetic compounds, once we have a lexical semantic analysis of the affix on which the second stem is formed. The indexing of the first stem of the compound will follow straightforwardly given the indexing associated with the derived second stem. Again, for now it is enough to say that the Principle of Co-indexation in (7) applies to affixes like *-ation*, *-ment*, and *-al*, co-indexing the "R" argument of the affix with the highest argument of the base verb.[3] Given this indexing, when the Principle of Co-indexation applies again in the indexing of the compound, it is the second argument of the verbal base which is free to be co-indexed with the argument of the first compound stem. Therefore, synthetic compounds whose second stems end in nominalizing affixes like *-ment*, *-al*, *-ance*, and *-ation* all receive interpretations analogous to that of *truck driver*. Representations for two representative compounds are given in (17):

(17)   a. *meat preparation*
       [+material ([$_j$]] [−material, dynamic ([$_i$], [+dynamic ([$_i$], [$_j$])])]
              meat   *-ation*   *prepare*
       b. *cost containment*
       [−material ([$_j$]] [−material, dynamic ([$_i$], [−dynamic ([$_i$], [$_j$])])]
              cost   *-ment*   *contain*

---

3. Indexing in nominalizations in *-ation*, *-ment*, *-al*, and the like is somewhat more complicated than this. The indexing assumed here is clearly the preferred indexing: although it is possible to get a reading in phrases like *the destruction of the city / the Huns* or *the city's / the Huns' destruction* in which the unindexed argument of the affix is identified with, or discharged by, the subject/agent argument, the predominant and preferred reading is the one in which the unindexed argument is the object/patient argument. It is possible, of course, to have both arguments discharged syntactically, as in a phrase like *the Huns' destruction of the city*. I leave a full treatment of indexing in these nominalizations to further research. Here, I only claim that the reading we get in synthetic compounds, and the predominant reading in phrases with syntactically manifested arguments, follows from the Principle of Co-indexation as it is now stated.

Slightly more complicated is the interpretation of synthetic compounds on passive participles, for example compounds like *handmade* or *home-grown*. These raise special issues, because they depend so heavily on our analysis of the effects of passivization. In other words, here we have something which has much more robust syntactic effects, and is not such a simple derivational process. To provide a complete analysis of passivization here goes well beyond the scope of this work. My analysis is therefore a bit more tentative.

It is generally observed that passivization eliminates the highest argument of the verb (e.g., Jaeggli 1986). I'm not exactly sure how to represent this in lexical semantic terms, especially the apparent continued availability of the subject argument as an implicit argument, but let us tentatively represent the unavailability of the subject argument by drawing a line through the first argument of the base verb. Let's say as well that the passive participle affix creates a semantically stative item, that is, adds the feature [−dynamic] and an argument. Again, assuming that something like the Principle of Co-indexation in (7) applies in the skeletal structures of derived words as well as compounds, the affixal argument will be co-indexed with the only available argument of the base verb, namely its internal argument:

(18)   [−dynamic ([$_i$], [+dynamic ([—], [$_i$])])]
            -en   *make*

When a passive participle is then used as the second stem in a compound, the only possible co-indexation is the one shown in (19) for the compound *hand made*:

(19)   [+material ([$_i$])] [−dynamic ([$_i$], [+dynamic ([—], [$_i$])])]
            hand   *-en*   *make*

In other words, there being no unindexed argument available, the "R" argument of the first stem, the nonhead, gets co-indexed with the argument of the affix, which in turn is co-indexed with the one remaining argument of the verb, its internal argument. What does this mean for interpretation? This indexing is rather like the one we saw in root compounds, in which the "R" argument of the first stem is co-indexed with the highest argument of the second stem. If indeed the indexing is alike, we would assume that the interpretation of this kind of synthetic compound would proceed in the same fashion as that of a typical endocentric root compound. The juxtaposed semantic representations – here even the skeletons, although of course we would expect that the bodies are quite dissimilar as well – are too unlike to be identified completely. We must then look at the skeletons and bodies of the first and second stem, and try to come up with some sort of common ground, finding some sort of plausible relationship between the concrete substance of the first stem and the stative situation of the second. Indeed, we find that the nonhead stem in compounds on passive participles is rather free in interpretation, sometimes being agentive, sometimes locative, sometimes manner, and so on. Again, this would seem to follow from the indexing that governs the interpretation of compounds in my account. The first stem in a synthetic compound based on a passive participle is free for exactly the same reason the first stem in a root compound is free: its indexing properties.

We have accounted for the observation that the first stem in synthetic compounds is often, although not always, interpreted as the internal argument of the verbal base of the second stem. We must still, however, account for the fourth of our observations, namely the fact pointed out by Selkirk (1982) that synthetic compounds cannot be built on obligatorily ditransitive verbs. Specifically, we do not find compounds like **shelf putter* or **book putter*. Nor, in fact do we find phrases like **shelf putter of books* or **book putter on shelves*, or compounds like **shelf book putter* or **book shelf putter*. What rules out synthetic compounds based on ditransitive verbs like *put*?

I believe that these facts follow at least in part from general principles of argument satisfaction. As Selkirk and many others have pointed out, verbs like *put* must obligatorily discharge all of their arguments. Thus, a compound like *book putter* or *shelf putter* would be ruled out on anyone's theory simply by the fact that the verb *put* fails to find one of its required arguments. Levin and Rappaport (1986, 631) also point out that for obligatory ditransitive verbs, neither of whose internal arguments can stand alone (e.g., *hand*), it is impossible to form an adjectival passive participle. They encode this restriction in a principle which they call the Sole Complement Generalization (SGC): "An argument that may stand alone as sole NP complement to a verb can be externalized by APF [Adjectival Passive Formation –R.L.]." The corollary of this, of course, is the generalization that arguments which cannot stand alone cannot be externalized by a word-formation process like APF. The data under consideration here suggest that this generalization is broader: perhaps it is safe to say that derivation generally eschews ditransitive bases whose internal arguments are both obligatory.

Why, however, can we not satisfy one argument of the verb *put* within the compound and one outside, as in a phrase like *a book putter on shelves*? This, I would suggest, follows from the referential properties of the first stem in compounds. Remember that the process of indexing the "R" argument of the first stem of the compound to some argument of the second stem results in depriving that first stem of any independent reference. The first stems of all compounds, we saw above, are always nonreferential. In phrases like *shelf putter of books* or *book putter on shelves*, the argument structure of the verb *put* is, strictly speaking, satisfied. But one of its arguments is nonreferential, and the other, being realized syntactically, has independent reference. Although I am not sure how to formalize this intuition, I'd like to suggest that the problem here stems from the mismatch in referentiality between the verb's arguments: both internal arguments must have the same referential status.

Why, finally, do we not get doubly compounded synthetic compounds like *shelf book putter* or *book shelf putter*? Here, the answer does not seem quite so clear to me. Note, for example, that doubly compounded synthetic compounds are often strange, even if the verbal base is simply transitive, and not ditransitive; that is, I find compounds like *garage car keeper*, *hand lace maker*, and even the compound *tree pasta eater*, which Selkirk finds grammatical, to be marginal at best. It's not clear within my theory, or anyone else's for that matter, why this should be the case. Further, we have seen that the Principle of Co-indexation does not forbid us to co-index a first (nonhead) stem with an unindexed verbal argument quite "far down" in the composed skeleton. But it seems clear that with compounds like *shelf book putter* we have gone too far:

(20)   [+material ([$_k$])] [[+material ([$_j$]] [+material, dynamic ([$_i$],
        shelf   *book*   *-er*

        [+dynamic ([$_i$],   [+dynamic, +IEPS ([$_j$], [+LOC ([$_k$])])])])]]
        put

Nothing so far within our theory prevents the "R" argument of *shelf* from being given the same index as the lowest argument of *put*. The typical indexing in synthetic compounds that we have seen is nonlocal in the sense that it dips down at least one level into the skeleton of the base of the second stem. Why, then, can't we dip down farther? I leave this question open, noting only that it is possible that whatever principle rules out compounds like *garage car keeper* will also solve this problem.

2.1.3   Root interpretation of synthetic compounds

There is one last point we must cover before we return to the analysis of *-er*, *-ee*, and related affixes. That is, it has been pointed out a number of times in the literature on compounding (e.g., Selkirk 1982, Lieber 1983) that compounds with deverbal second stems occasionally lend themselves to an interpretation other than the expected synthetic compound interpretation. For example, most native speakers can – with some difficulty – get a second reading for the compound *truck driver* in which *truck* is not the internal argument of *driver*, but is interpreted rather as a modifier of *driver*; in this reading, the compound *truck driver* might be used deictically to refer to the driver (maybe of a car) who is wearing a shirt with a picture of a truck on it.[4] In effect, in cases like these the interpretation is that of a root compound. How might the present theory account for this alternate interpretation?

I propose that such cases can be handled by assuming that the Principle of Co-indexation in (7) is a **violable principle**: the indexing procedure in (7) preferably co-indexes the highest argument of the nonhead with the highest unindexed argument of the head, thus normally giving rise to the argument interpretation. But the principle can be violated, in which case the highest argument of the first stem is simply co-indexed with the highest argument of the head, namely the "R" argument of *-er*:

(21)   [+material ([$_i$])] [+material, dynamic ([$_i$], [+dynamic ([$_i$], [   ])])]
            truck   *-er*   *drive*

How do we interpret this skeleton? The "R" argument of *truck* must in this case be identified referentially with the "R" argument of *driver*. In other words, they must be predicable of the same referent. Given that the semantic bodies of *truck* and *driver* are sufficiently dissimilar to preclude complete referential identification as in the case of *copulative* compounds, *truck* must be interpreted in relation to *driver* in the same way that the first stem must be interpreted as related in some way to the second stem in any endocentric root compound. The ultimate interpretation is then a result of context and encyclopedic knowledge combining to allow a plausible relationship to be inferred.

The alternative root interpretation of synthetic compounds can thus be made to follow if we assume that the Principle of Co-indexation is a violable principle. We will see in the next section that there is further reason to believe that the Principle of Co-indexation must be construed as violable.

2.2   *Co-indexation in derivation*

Having seen how the Principle of Co-indexation works in the interpretation of compounds, we now have enough apparatus developed to return to the problem with which we began the last chapter, namely the curious behavior of the cluster of affixes *-er*, *-ee*, *-ant/-ent*, and *-ist*. We have seen that what they have in

---

4. Note that occasionally compounds of this sort get lexicalized. A good example is the compound *Sunday driver* which is, of course, not interpreted (nonsensically) as a driver of Sundays but as someone who only drives on Sundays (and by inference, not very well).

common is a core of meaning represented by the features [+material, dynamic]. Of course, we would want to be able to characterize what differentiates these affixes as well. I suggest that it is not the semantic content of the affixes which does so, but rather the co-indexation properties of the affixal argument in each case. We therefore need to look briefly at how co-indexation of the affixal argument is effected, beyond the very informal treatment that we gave in the previous section.

Let us assume that when a derivational affix attaches to its base, the argument associated with the derivational affix – its "R" argument in these cases, as these are all noun-forming affixes – gets co-indexed with or bound to one of the arguments of its base. What co-indexing means in argument-structural terms is that the two arguments are identified referentially with each other, and must be discharged or satisfied by the same phrase in the syntax. In logical terms, they must be predicated of the same referent.

We have assumed so far that normally the affixal argument, in this case the head of the derived word, is co-indexed with the highest of the base or nonhead arguments. This clearly will not allow us to explain the behavior of affixes like *-er* and *-ee* fully – if the co-indexing principle treated them identically, we would expect these two affixes to behave alike. We must look further then into the process of co-indexation.

As Barker's (1998) analysis of *-ee* suggests, it appears that an affixal argument may sometimes impose specific semantic requirements on its co-indexed arguments. In effect, the affixal argument and the base argument it is co-indexed with must be semantically compatible, or at least semantically nondistinct in certain specified ways. For example, as Barker has pointed out, the argument of *-ee* must be sentient but nonvolitional. It cannot normally be co-indexed with a base argument which is nonsentient or volitional. The co-indexed arguments must match. We will obviously need to attend carefully to what we mean by terms like "sentient" and "nonvolitional," but for now let us use those ideas somewhat intuitively, as Barker does. If such semantic compatibility requirements are allowed for co-indexing, we might present a second approximation of a co-indexing principle, as in (22):

(22)　**Principle of Co-indexation**
　　　In a configuration in which semantic skeletons are composed, co-index the highest nonhead argument with the highest (preferably unindexed) head argument. Indexing must be consistent with semantic conditions on the head argument, if any.

As was the case with compounds, we assume that composition of lexical semantic skeletons follows from word structure. Assuming that an affix is hierarchically superior to its base (i.e., [af [base]] or [[base] af]), the lexical semantic structure will show the same hierarchical organization.[5]

Let us assume next that the affixes *-er*, *-ee*, *-ant/-ent*, and *-ist* have the specific lexical entries in (23)–(26), where each lexical entry now shows not only the features of the semantic skeleton, but also the particular semantic requirements (if any) of its argument, and also the syntactic subcategorizations of each affix (that is, the categories of base each affix attaches to):

(23)   *-ee*
        Syntactic subcategorization: attaches to V, N
        Skeleton: [+material, dynamic ([$_{sentient, \underline{nonvolitional}}$], <base>)]

(24)   *-er*
        Syntactic subcategorization: attaches to V, N
        Skeleton: [+material, dynamic ([   ], <base>)]

(25)   *-ant/-ent*
        Syntactic subcategorization: attaches to V
        Skeleton: [+material, dynamic ([   ], <base>)]

(26)   *-ist*
        Syntactic subcategorization: attaches to N, A
        Skeleton: [+material, dynamic ([$_{volitional}$], <base>)]

My claim is that the basic semantic contribution of all four affixes is exactly the same, but their syntactic subcategorizations and the co-indexation conditions of their arguments vary in small ways. The affixes *-er* and *-ant/-ent* place no semantic requirements on their co-indexed arguments. But *-ee* and *-ist* do have such requirements. I claim (following Booij and Lieber 2004) that *-ee* places a strict requirement of sentience and a somewhat weaker requirement of volitionality (weakness indicated here by underlining) on its co-indexed argument. Here, I agree with Barker that the characteristics of sentience and volitionality are relevant, but I differ from Barker in attributing differing strengths to these two requirements. The suffix *-ist*, I will argue, places a strict requirement of volitionality on its co-indexed argument. Let us now see how this analysis begins to account for a wide range of data.

I will start with the affix *-ee*, since it is the one which appears to place the most complex conditions on the co-indexation of its arguments. In many ways, my analysis recapitulates Barker's, but it differs in two respects. First, it makes far more explicit than Barker does why the noun-based derivatives are possible, and how they come to mean what they do. Second, as mentioned above, the

---

5. I will assume, however, that linear order is of no relevance in composed semantic skeletons.

present analysis claims that the semantic requirements on the "R" argument of *-ee* are not of equal strength.

Starting with the denominal cases then, consider the skeleton for an *-ee* form like *biographee*:

(27)
biographee
[+material, dynamic ([$_{\text{sentient, \underline{nonvolitional}}}$-i   ], [−material, dynamic ([   ], [$_i$])])]
                    -ee   *biography*

This complex noun is formed on the base *biography*, the nonhead, which is an abstract processual noun having two arguments of its own. The first of these is the "R" argument, and the second the argument which is syntactically realized as the object of an *of* prepositional phrase in English. The "R" argument in this case is the referent of *biography*, which is clearly nonsentient, not a good match with the conditions on the head argument. The only co-indexing in which conditions match is the one which takes the second argument of *biography*. The result is a concrete dynamic noun whose referent is sentient but nonvolitional, as required. There doesn't need to be a verbal base for *biographee* to be a "patient" noun of sorts; this reading follows from the semantic content of the affix combined with the semantic requirements on the co-indexation of the affixal argument.

The more prototypical deverbal derivatives follow straightforwardly in this analysis as well. Verbal bases, of course, have skeletons with arguments, and these arguments often have co-indexation conditions of their own with respect to sentience, volitionality, and the like. In co-indexing a nonhead (base) argument with the affixal argument, we must pay attention to matching as closely as possible the semantic conditions on the affix argument with those of the base. The noun *employee* receives the semantic structure in (28):

(28)   *employee*
         [+material, dynamic ([$_{\text{sentient, \underline{nonvolitional}}}$-i   ], [+dynamic ([   ], [$_i$])])]
                        -ee   *employ*

Assuming the verb *employ* is an activity verb, it has the skeletal feature [+dynamic] and two arguments, the first of which is volitional, and therefore incompatible with the "R" argument of the affix. The second argument is sentient but not necessarily volitional, and it therefore is more consistent with the semantic requirements of the affixal arguments. They are co-indexed, and the "R" argument then shares the "patient" reading of the co-indexed base argument.

A similar analysis can be given for the so-called "indirect object" and "object of governed preposition" cases *addressee* and *experimentee*. Consider the composed skeletons in (29) and (30), where both verbs are again activity verbs, and both the Goal argument of the verb *address* and the *on* argument of the verb *experiment* are introduced by a general Locational function [+Loc]:[6]

(29)
experimentee
[+material, dynamic ([_{sentient, nonvolitional}-i   ], [+dynamic ([   ], [   ], [+Loc ([_i   ])])])]
            -ee   *experiment*

(30)
addressee
[+material, dynamic ([_{sentient, nonvolitional}-i   ], [+dynamic ([   ], [   ], [+Loc ([_i   ])])])]
            -ee   *address*

We would need, of course, to justify the use of this new feature (we will do so in chapter 4), and distinguish the Locational functions of the two verbs more closely, but the skeletons in (29) and (30) at least give enough detail to allow us to see why the argument of -*ee* needs to be indexed as it is. That is, the first argument of both *experiment* and *address* is volitional, and the second argument sentient. It is only the argument of the Locational function in each case which is compatible with both the requirements of the affixal (head) argument.

Let us now turn to the -*ee* derivatives that are more challenging, namely the ones like *standee* or *escapee* which have "subject" interpretations. Why do these receive the interpretation that they do? Consider the verbal skeletons for *stand* and *escape*:

(31)   *stand*   [+dynamic ([   ])]
(32)   *escape*   [+dynamic ([   ], [+Loc ([   ])])]

Barker suggests that the sole argument of *stand* is not particularly volitional, even when it is sentient. But surely this is not quite right: *standing* can be involuntary, but it can also be as much under conscious control as any other activity. *Standees* can stand voluntarily and intentionally or not, this being part of the odd nuance of the derived word: it is often used of bus travelers whose standing is under their control, but who have no choice in a crowded bus but to stand (compare the word *stander* which has a much more clearly agentive

---

6. There is, of course, much more that needs to be said to justify this move. In chapter 4, I will begin to justify the feature [Loc].

meaning).[7] The reason that *standee* is possible is that there is in fact only one verbal argument for the affixal argument to be co-indexed with. Although that argument has the potential to be volitional, the requirement of nonvolitionality on the co-indexed argument of *-ee* is a weak one. Remember further that the Principle of Co-indexation in (22) is violable. If no consistent argument exists, it is sometimes apparently possible to co-index the head argument with the least incompatible nonhead argument. We therefore get a representation like that in (33) for *standee*:

(33)
standee
[+material, dynamic ([$_{sentient, \underline{nonvolitional}-i}$], [+dynamic, +IEPS ([$_{?volitional -i}$])])]
   -ee   *stand*

But I would argue that this is just the representation we want: the lexicon exploits the incompatibility of the co-indexed arguments in giving rise to the odd nuance of the word *standee* where the referent is not clearly volitional, but also not clearly nonvolitional. In other words, there is a semantic payoff for this weak violation of the Principle of Co-indexation. The referent of *standee* receives mixed and incompatible requirements, being construed at the same time as volitional and nonvolitional. Rather than this being impossible, it actually constitutes part of the nuanced interpretation of the derived noun.[8]

Let us turn to an even more vexed case, that of *escapee*. Remember that Barker (1998, 719) noted an odd nuance to this word as well. Although an *escapee* must initiate the activity of escaping, there is something about the gestalt of the situation that is not completely under the control of the *escapee*. Why is it interpreted as it is? Consider the composed skeleton in (34):

(34)
escapee
[+material, dynamic ([$_{sentient, \underline{nonvolitional}-i}$], [+dynamic ([$_i$], [+Loc ([   ])])])]
   -ee   *escape*

The affixal argument must normally be co-indexed with a nonhead argument that is compatible with its semantic requirements. The first argument of *escape* is

---

7. The word *stander* is in fact attested, and the OED gives citations like the following: "The crowd of sitters and standers gradually increases" (1815, *Sporting Magazine*); "The most obstinate stander on old ways" (1850, *Tait's Magazine*). Examples such as these suggest a fully agentive interpretation.

8. A quick search of the Internet yields an example that suggests that this hunch is on the right track: "And a stander may also be someone who helps another stand. So if the one who does the helping is a stander and the one [who] is helped is a standee, then he who helps himself is both a stander and a standee." (*Idiot's Delight Digest Archive*, issue 3056, http://www.cherk.com/idd)

volitional, and the second argument nonsentient (one generally escapes from an institution of some sort). In fact, none of the arguments is completely consistent with the conditions on the affixal argument. But again, the requirement of nonvolitionality is the weaker one, so the Principle of Co-indexation permits the less blatant violation, and the volitional argument of *escape* is co-indexed with the "R" argument of *-ee*. But again, I would argue that this mismatch in argumental interpretation is exploited by the lexicon: it apparently gives rise to the dubious two-sided meaning of the resulting derived lexical item. As Barker himself points out, although the *escapee* is in control of initiating the action, the consequences of the action and indeed the whole scenario are beyond his or her control.[9]

One would expect that this sort of mismatch of semantic conditions on arguments should not happen. That is, we might expect that words like *standee* and *escapee* should never be formed. They are, however, although this type of *-ee* form is intuitively far less productive than the usual "patient" forms. We might speculate that they are coined only when the argumental mismatch seems to allow for a nuance of interpretation that is useful or in some way contextually or pragmatically forced. That is, violation of the Principle of Co-indexation is possible, but it is not a preferred word-formation strategy and it happens only when it is dictated by pragmatic concerns.

There is one last *-ee* form that the present analysis accounts for nicely, namely the interpretation of the word *amputee*. Here, the referent of the affix is not an argument of the base verb itself, but an implied argument of one of the arguments of the verb. Suppose that the composed skeleton of *amputee* is the one in (35):

(35)   *amputee*
        [+material, dynamic ([$_{\text{sentient, nonvolitional}}$]   ], [+dynamic ([   ], [   ])])]
                         -ee   *amputate*

Assuming that *amputate* is an activity verb whose first argument is sentient but volitional and whose second argument is nonsentient, there is no good match for the semantic conditions on the affixal argument. But normally, the second argument position of the verb *amputate* is occupied by a noun like *leg* or *arm*,

---

9. Compare *escapee* with the word *escaper*, which is an attested word. Again, a quick search of the Internet yields an example which suggests that my hunch is correct: "[Squadron Leader Cross] was picked up by the Germans with three other survivors and all were made prisoners of war. Whilst in captivity Squadron Leader Cross became an experienced **escaper**. Both men had an active role in Operation 2000 . . . It was decided that the escape should go ahead later that month and the 200 **escapees** were then selected." (Squadron Leader IKP Cross DCF RAF, 103 Squadron, wysiwyg://49/http://www.elshamwolds.50g.com/escape.html) The word *escaper* is also used as a synonym for escape artist in some contexts.

which has its own two arguments, the second of which is its possessor, an argument which can be sentient and nonvolitional. Assuming that semantic interpretation above the lexical level involves the successive composition and integration of skeletons, the "R" argument of the affix will eventually come to an argument which is compatible with its semantic conditions, namely the possessor of the limb. And that is what ultimately gets co-indexed with the affixal argument. Again, this is not a preferred strategy, which is to say that this is not a productive way of forming new *-ee* nouns. But it is clearly not impossible.[10]

We can now extend the analysis to the suffix *-er*. In fact, the analysis that I propose here is very much like that of Booij (1986), Levin and Rappaport (1988), and Rappaport Hovav and Levin (1992) (RHL), described in chapter 1, except that I reformulate their argument-structure theoretic analysis in terms of lexical semantics. The move to a lexical semantic analysis has two advantages. First, it gives us a way of talking about denominal *-er* forms, which RHL could not explain in argument-structure theoretic terms, and second, it allows us finally to see how *-er* and *-ee* can come to have overlapping interpretations.

I begin with the denominals. As the lexical entry in (22) indicates, *-er* forms concrete processual nouns; its semantic content is exactly the same as that of *-ee*. But it differs from *-ee* in that it imposes no special semantic conditions on its "R" argument. In other words, the affixal argument is compatible with base arguments that are sentient or nonsentient, volitional or nonvolitional. Given the Principle of Co-indexation in (22), we would expect, then, that the argument of the head, the affix *-er*, will always be co-indexed with the highest nonhead argument, whatever that is. Composed skeletons for both agent nouns like *villager* and instrumental nouns like *freighter* will look like (36):

(36) *villager, freighter*
      [+material, dynamic ([$_i$], [+material ([$_i$])])]
          -er   *village, freight*

The affixal skeleton attaches to a concrete noun (*village, freight*) and makes it into a concrete dynamic noun. The "R" argument is co-indexed with the sole argument of the base noun. As there are no special conditions on the linked "R"

---

10. The case of *amputee* is the one that suggests most clearly that co-indexation of affixal arguments is not necessarily a local process. We saw that exactly how nonlocal referential identification could get was unclear. In the case of synthetic compounds like *shelf book putter* there appears to be some limit on how "far down" into a composed skeleton the Principle of Co-indexation can get. I leave this question unanswered here, and hope that further research will clarify the issue.

argument, it can receive either an agentive/personal reading if the derived noun is predicated of something sentient, or an instrumental reading if the derived noun is predicated of something nonsentient. The affix itself is compatible with either reading, as it does not specify the sentience of its argument. It is a matter of lexicalization, I would say, that *villager* is conventionalized with the personal reading and *freighter* with the instrumental one.

Deverbal forms in *-er* are analyzed in much the same way. Again, *-er* forms concrete dynamic nouns and imposes no semantic conditions on the linked base argument. The co-indexation principle (22) therefore always links the affixal "R" argument to the highest base argument, with the resulting *-er* derivative absorbing whatever thematic interpretation the verbal base argument has: agent in the case of *writer*, instrument in the case of *print*, and so on:

(37)   *writer*
        [+material, dynamic ([$_i$], [+dynamic ([$_i$], [   ])])]
                -er   write

(38)   *printer*
        [+material, dynamic ([$_i$], [+dynamic ([$_i$], [   ])])]
                -er   print

As RHL point out, if *-er* is attached to an inchoative verb like *sink*, whose highest argument is interpreted as a theme or patient, the *-er* form takes on that interpretation as well:

(39)   *sinker*
        [+material, dynamic ([$_i$], [+dynamic, +IEPS ([$_i$])])]
                -er   sink

Similarly, assuming that in the skeleton of a middle verb (e.g., *fry*) the highest argument is in fact the patient argument, the affixation of *-er* will involve linking the affixal argument to that argument.[11]

I have not yet given an explanation of forms like *loaner* and *keeper*, that is, those *-er* derivatives with an object (or patient) interpretation which cannot be derived from inchoative or middle forms of verbs. I promise such an explanation, but defer it briefly until I have completed the analysis of the affixes *-ant/-ent* and *-ist* in this section.

---

11. I assume here that the formation of a middle, like that of a passive, involves the elimination of an original external argument, with the result that the remaining patient argument becomes the "highest" argument. Further, the verb, although still in the finite form, becomes stative, that is [−dynamic]. Note also that although verbs like *fry* can have an *-er* form derived from their middle readings, there is nothing to prevent them also from having *-er* forms derived from their usual active verb readings. In this case, a *fryer* would simply be someone who does the frying.

The affix *-ant/-ent* in English has basically the same properties as the affix *-er*, although it attaches only to verbs. With respect to verbal derivatives, we see the same range of meanings – agent, instrument, experiencer, patient – and for the same reason. The affix *-ant/-ent* forms concrete processual nouns; its "R" argument carries no special semantic conditions. It therefore is co-indexed with the highest argument of its verbal base and carries whatever interpretation is consistent with that base:

(40)   *servant*
       [+material, dynamic ([$_i$], [+dynamic ([$_i$], [   ])])]
            -ant   *serve*

(41)   *evacuant*
       [+material, dynamic ([$_i$], [+dynamic ([$_i$], [   ])])]
            -ant   *evacuate*

(42)   *descendant*
       [+material, dynamic ([$_i$], [+dynamic, +IEPS ([$_i$])])]
            -ant   *descend*

We turn, finally, to the last of the affixes in this semantic cluster, the suffix *-ist*. This affix exclusively forms person nouns from adjectives and other nouns. I capture this fact, as the lexical entry in (26) indicates, by placing a semantic condition on the "R" argument of *-ist*, namely that this argument must be interpretable as volitional.

On an adjectival base like *pure*, *-ist* attaches and co-indexes as in (43):

(43)   *purist*
       [+material, dynamic ([$_{\text{volitional-}i}$], [−dynamic ([$_i$])])]
            -ist   *pure*

As the sole argument of *pure* has no particular semantic conditions of its own, it is compatible with the volitional requirement of *-ist*. A *purist* is someone who does something or appreciates something in a pure manner.

On nominal bases we see the effect of the volitionality requirement more clearly. Normally, the "R" argument of *-ist* would seek to co-index a semantically compatible base argument, that is, one whose referent shares its volitional characteristic. In the case of a proper noun like *Marx* which has a human referent, the co-indexation is unproblematic.

(44)   *Marxist*
       [+material, dynamic ([$_{\text{volitional-}i}$], [+material ([$_{\text{volitional-}i}$])])]
            -ist   *Marx*

But it is frequently the case that the referent of the nominal base superficially appears not to be semantically compatible; the "R" argument of *guitar* is nonsentient, as *guitar* itself denotes an inanimate object, and inanimate objects certainly cannot be volitional. Nevertheless, derivations such as *guitarist* have no special nuances, and are quite productive and indeed quite normal.

(45)   *guitarist*
        [+material, dynamic ([volitional-i   ], [+material ([i   ])])]
             -ist   *guitar*

I would suggest that there is a good reason that derivations like *guitarist* do not count as violations of the Principle of Co-indexation, and are not perceived as odd in any way: items which have the semantic characteristic of being non-sentient are actually unmarked for the characteristic of volitionality; that is, volitionality is irrelevant for them. Thus, when the "R" argument of *-ist* gets co-indexed with the "R" argument of *guitar* there is no violation of the Principle of Co-indexation, and the derivation gives rise to no special nuance of meaning. All forms derived with *-ist* are person nouns; the restriction on their "R" argument ensures that the derived word is interpreted as a doer of something associated with the base. This argument is not prevented from co-indexing with a base argument for which the semantic characteristic of volitionality is irrelevant.

There are obviously a number of points that need further attention. Just what, for example, do we mean by "sentient" and "volitional," and what do those intuitive characterizations correspond to in the featural system I am developing? Under what circumstances is it possible to mismatch the semantic characteristics of an affixal argument and a base argument in co-indexing?

I will return to these questions shortly. But here it is necessary first to give a clear answer to the question with which we began chapter 1, namely why it is that affixes like *-er* and *-ee*, although clearly distinct, nevertheless sometimes derive forms which overlap in meaning or function. The first part of the answer, we saw, was that the basic featural content of these two affixes is identical. Now we can add the second part of our answer: the Principle of Co-indexation allows the affixal argument to be linked to the same base argument – the highest one – under a number of specific conditions. The "R" argument of *-ee* is rather specific in its semantic conditions – far more so than that of *-er*. Since *-er* has no special conditions, its argument can sometimes come to be co-indexed with the patient argument of a base verb (e.g., *sinker, fryer*), specifically when that argument is the highest base argument. And since *-ee* can sometimes attach to verbs, none of whose arguments is perfectly compatible with its "R" argument, this argument can occasionally get co-indexed with an argument whose semantic conditions technically conflict, for example in a form like *standee*, with an argument which is more volitional in flavor. In other words, the overlap in the output of the two affixes follows from the precise operation of the Principle of Co-indexation.

2.3   *Sentience, volitionality, and the semantic body*

Before we tackle the final recalcitrant cases with *-er*, we must look in more detail at what we mean when we say that an argument of an affix may impose some sort of semantic condition on its co-indexed argument. We must explore not only what we mean by terms like "sentience" and "volitionality," but also how we determine whether a given argument is compatible with those conditions. What I would like to suggest here is that this information does not constitute part of the skeleton, but rather can be inferred indirectly from the semantic bodies of lexical items. Again, then, we will digress and think about the nature of the semantic body.

I have been assuming that an entity is sentient if it is both animate and conscious. Words denoting living humans are therefore clearly sentient.[12] Other animate entities can be sentient as well, but to some extent whether they are or not depends upon our culturally, and indeed sometimes individually, determined notions of animal consciousness. I, for example, have no trouble classing dogs (at least my own dogs) as sentient, but I am willing to acknowledge that non-dog people might question my sanity on this point. On the other hand, I think it more or less uncontroversial that amoebas, although clearly animate, are nonsentient in the relevant sense. With respect to other living beings, I expect that there might be some variation among speakers in their willingness to impute consciousness.

As for volition, I assume that action is volitional if it is deliberate and internally generated. Thus, there is a direct connection between sentience and volitionality: an entity cannot act deliberately without also being sentient, although clearly not all actions of a sentient entity are intentional and deliberate (e.g., involuntary actions like sneezing). There is a large literature which discusses in some detail the connection between volitionality and agency, and the relation of both notions to causation (see, for example, DeLancey 1984, 1985, Richardson 1985, Talmy 1985).

For our purposes, however, the relevant question is how we determine whether an argument in a skeleton is sentient or nonsentient, volitional or nonvolitional. Specifically, we must ask whether this information is encoded directly in lexical

---

12. I qualify the term human with "living" to rule out cases of words like *corpse* which are clearly human, but not animate.

semantic representations in the skeleton or the body. I think that the answer is no – information about sentience and volitionality can be inferred from the lexical semantic representation, but is nowhere encoded directly.

It seems fairly clear that (in English at least) the skeleton should not contain features like [sentient] or [volitional]. Semantic features are justified to the extent that they are relevant to the syntax, and as far as I know, there are no syntactic processes that depend on the sentience and volitionality of an argument; causatives, for example, are well known to allow both volitional subjects (*I broke the vase on purpose*) and nonvolitional subjects (*I broke the vase when I fell off the ladder*), and both sentient subjects (*I broke the vase*) and nonsentient ones (*The falling ladder broke the vase*).

Rather, I think that sentience and volitionality can be inferred from the composition of the semantic body, although they may not necessarily be represented directly in the semantic body. Sentience, as I suggested above, is arguably a matter of belief and cultural expectations. We can infer sentience from bodily elements like <animate> and <human>, but for merely <animate> entities, there is much leeway in the judgment that an entity is sentient. For volitionality, it seems that sentience is a prerequisite of volitional action. But sentient beings can also act involuntarily. Whether in a given case a verbal argument is ultimately construed as volitional or not follows from the selectional properties of the verb of which it is an argument, which in turn are probably represented either directly or indirectly in the semantic body of the verb. Exactly what the verbal body looks like we will leave open here.

2.4   *Rogue cases: -er and paradigmatic extension*

There are still, however, a few cases of *-er* forms in English which we have not yet accounted for. These specifically are the object-oriented *-er* forms that cannot plausibly be said to derive from verbs with inchoative or middle forms, that is, verbs in which the highest argument can be the Theme/Patient, Location, or Means. Example (46) shows some of these forms:[13]

(46)   *loaner, keeper, diner, sleeper, jotter, stroller, walker*

I would like to suggest that forms of this sort arise as violations of the Principle of Co-indexation under a particular sort of paradigmatic and pragmatic pressure. My argument here is based on Booij and Lieber (2004).[14]

---

13. See Ryder (1999) for an excellent compilation of data which suggests that there is some productivity to the formation of words of this type in English.
14. Booij and Lieber (2004) extend this argument to Dutch as well, which behaves much like English with respect to formations in *-er*.

In order to understand and explain these cases, we must return to and elaborate on the idea of the derivational paradigm that we mentioned briefly in chapter 1. Let us suppose that the featural system which defines the basic semantic classes into which items of the simplex lexicon fall also serves to define a set of possible derivational categories or semantic fields that might be available for extending the simplex lexicon by affixal means. Further, let us look briefly at six of the basic derivational categories that our system predicts (those based purely on the features [material] and [dynamic]), and at the extent to which the actual derivational affixes of English cover that paradigm.

(47) [+dynamic]   (conversion)
      [−dynamic]   *-ive, -ory, -al, -ic*, etc.
      [+material]   (compounding)
      [−material]   *-ship, -hood, -ism*, etc.
      [−material, dynamic]   *-ation, -ment, -al*, etc.
      [+material, dynamic]   *-er, -ee, -ant/-ent, -ist*

In fact, we need to look more closely at the last row, as that is the one that we are most concerned with here. Specifically, we need to break down this row according to the existence of what we might call subject-oriented vs object-oriented affixes:

(48) [+material, dynamic]
      subject   -er, -ant/-ent, -ist
      personal object   -ee
      non-personal object   **

What becomes obvious through this comparison is that English largely lacks the derivational means for extending the class of concrete, dynamic, non-personal object-terms. In English, at least, we have a productive affix *-ee* that creates personal object-oriented terms. Missing in English are specific affixes which serve to create concrete, non-personal object nouns, that is, nouns which would have the meaning "thing which has been Xed" or "thing which one Xes."

We must now explore what happens when a language has a pragmatic need for a term but lacks the specific derivational means for creating such a term. The basic idea that Booij and Lieber (2004) develop is one that they refer to as "paradigmatic pressure." By "paradigmatic pressure" they mean a situation in which there is a real-world need for a specific kind of word, but no available productive affix in a language with which to create such a word. In other words, context forces speakers to create a word – often on the fly – but the language does not have a specific derivational means for doing so. Booij and Lieber (2004) suggest that when such paradigmatic pressure exists, one of two things happens: either some sort of roundabout process (e.g., conversion or the substantivization of a participle) is employed, or – more interestingly – the semantically closest productive affix is put to use, even if it requires a violation of the Principle of Co-indexation in the process.

We have seen that the actual affixes available within a given language may in fact not cover the entire semantic space that can be expressed by items in the simplex lexicon. English occasionally uses the roundabout strategy of conversion to create terms for things affected by an action; consider conversion forms like *drink* "thing which one drinks" or *eats* "things which are eaten." But the strategy that speakers resort to in creating object-oriented forms seems more often to be the second one, in which the closest productive affix is employed, even if it requires a violation of the Principle of Co-indexation. For this purpose, English extends the use of the affix *-er* which is defined by the features [+material, dynamic], which does not place any particular semantic conditions on its argument, and which is the most productive of the affixes with these features.[15] But in order to make use of this affix, speakers must violate the Principle of Co-indexation in linking the "R" argument of the affix with an argument of the base other than the highest one. Thus the production of non-personal object-forms like *loaner* or *keeper* in *-er* is possible in English, but because they require a violation of the Principle of Co-indexation, they are much less productively formed than subject-oriented *-er* derivations, and are often heavily dependent on context for their interpretation.[16]

This leads us back finally to one of the central concerns of this book, **polysemy**, and specifically to the nature of polysemy in derivational affixes. One of the claims that I made at the outset is that the sorts of polysemy displayed by derivation should be like those found in the simplex lexicon. Copestake and Briscoe (1996, 18–19) distinguish two sorts of polysemy in the simplex lexicon, which they call "constructional polysemy" (also called "logical polysemy" in Pustejovsky and Boguraev 1996), and "sense extension":

> In what follows, we explore the hypothesis that systematic nominal polysemies of the kind outlined above can be divided into two types of process which we term constructional polysemy (sense modulation) and semi-productive

15. As mentioned above, very occasionally non-personal object forms are created with *-ee*, but only in highly restricted technical fields (cf. examples like *raisee* and *ascendee* from linguistic theory). I attribute the paucity of these forms to the lesser productivity of *-ee* with respect to *-er*, and to its more complex semantics.
16. Even less productive are *-ee* forms with non-personal object interpretations, for example *raisee* or *ascendee*. In fact, as Barker (1998) points out, these occur almost exclusively in restricted technical fields – notably in linguistic theory!

sense extension (sense change). In constructional polysemy, the polysemy is more apparent than real, because lexically there is only one sense and it is the process of syntagmatic co-composition (Pustejovsky 1991) which causes sense modulation. . . . Sense extension, on the other hand, requires lexical rules which create derived senses from basic senses, often correlating with morphological or syntactic change.

For the most part, the polysemy of *-er* is constructional polysemy, arising from the sparse nature of the featural composition of the affix and its interaction with the semantics of the base argument with which the affixal "R" argument gets co-indexed. But the extension of *-er* to object-oriented forms might be looked upon as the second kind of polysemy. In other words, paradigmatic pressure, the real-world need to form words of a certain sort combined with the lack of a specific derivational affix with the required sense, conspires to force a sense extension of *-er*. If this is the correct analysis, then we seem justified in saying that affixal polysemy is no different from the polysemy we find in the simplex lexicon. We will continue to explore the nature of affixal polysemy in the chapters to come, encountering further examples of both constructional polysemy and sense extension.

2.5   *Conclusion*

In this chapter I have proposed a Principle of Co-indexation which allows us to integrate the parts of a complex word into a single referential unit. The Principle of Co-indexation not only allows us to explain many of the often-observed facts of compound interpretation in English, but allows a more comprehensive and unified analysis of the polysemy of *-er*, *-ee*, and related affixes than has been available before. That analysis led us, finally, to the notion of paradigmatic extension. We will continue to explore affixal polysemy and the role of paradigmatic extension in the next chapter.

3 *The semantics of verb formation*

In this chapter I turn attention to the case of verb-forming word-formation processes in English. Here, I will offer an analysis of the affixes -*ize* and -*ify* which improves upon both my own previous research (Lieber 1998) and that of Ingo Plag (1999). In the course of this case study, I will continue to explore issues of affixal polysemy and the existence of multiple affixes with the same meaning. But I will also look in some depth at another productive source of new verbs in English, the process of conversion, and explore what the present theory has to say about the semantics of verbs derived without formal change from nouns. I will show in what follows that the range of polysemy exhibited by verbs formed by conversion in English cannot be explained as a result of the abstractness of skeletal material and variation in co-indexation, and indeed that conversion does not involve the addition of a single fixed skeleton, as derivation does. The semantic analysis of conversion that I will propose is consistent with, and lends support to, analyses of conversion that do not rely on so-called zero affixes, and therefore speaks to the third of the issues that I raised in the introduction to this work, namely the question of how we account for word formation in which there is semantic change with no concomitant formal change.

3.1   *Verbal derivation*

3.1.1   *Data*
English has three verb-forming suffixes and one verb-forming prefix:

(1)   -*ize*   legalize, unionize, criticize
       -*ify*   purify, acidify, speechify
       -*en*   darken, whiten, lengthen
       en-   enchain, enslave, entomb

Of these, however, only *-ize* and *-ify* have any degree of productivity in present-day English (see Plag [1999] for an excellent discussion of the productivity of this constellation of affixes), so I will confine discussion in this section to these two affixes.

Both *-ize* and *-ify* attach to nominal and adjectival bases, and it has been noted both in traditional literature on word formation (e.g., Marchand 1969) and in work in the generative tradition (Lieber 1998, Plag 1999) that the two affixes show a wide range of polysemy, and not surprisingly, very much the same range of polysemy. In (2) and (3) I give rough glosses for the different meanings exhibited by *-ize* and *-ify* forms, with Plag's labels for these categories in parentheses:

(2) *-ize*

"make x," "cause to become x"	(P: causative)	*standardize, velarize*
	(P: resultative)	*crystallize, unionize*
"make x go to/in/on something"	(P: ornative)	*apologize, texturize*
"make something go to/in/on x"	(P: locative)	*hospitalize, containerize*
"do/act/make/ in the manner of or like x"	(P: similative)	*Boswellize, despotize*
"do x"	(P: performative)	*philosophize, theorize, economize*
"become x"	(P: inchoative)	*oxidize, aerosolize*

(3) *-ify*

"make x," "cause to become x"	(P: causative)	*purify, diversify, acidify*
	(P: resultative)	*yuppify*
"make x go to/in/on something"	(P: ornative)	*glorify*
"make something go to/in/on x"	(P: locative)	*syllabify, bourgeoisify, codify*
"do x"	(P: performative)	*speechify, boozify*
"do/act/make/ in the manner of or like x"	(P: similative)	
"become x"	(P: inchoative)	*acidify, calcify*

Often, verbs formed with *-ize* and *-ify* mean "cause to become x" where x is a base denoting a state (*legalize, purify*). For these forms, there is sometimes an inchoative alternant meaning simply "become x" (e.g., *oxidize, calcify*). Sometimes, the base denotes a theme, so the derived verb can be glossed something like "cause x to go to/in/on something" (*anesthetize, glorify*). In other cases the base denotes a goal or a location, with the derived verb meaning something like "cause something to go to/in/on x" (*hospitalize, syllabify*). For the affix *-ize* at least, especially with bases that are names, the base can be interpreted as a manner argument, with the resulting verb meaning "act or do in the manner of x" (*Boswellize, despotize*); comparable examples meaning "act in the manner of x" seem not to exist for *-ify*, however. And finally, some forms simply mean "do x" (*philosophize, speechify*). Once again, the issue that these data raise is the one of polysemy: how do we account for the range of meaning that we find, and the fact that both affixes show the same range of polysemy?

Another issue that will figure in what follows is the relative robustness or productivity of each pattern. It appears, for example, that in Plag's list of twentieth-century neologisms in *-ize* from the OED, the most robust patterns are the causative, resultative, and locative patterns, with the ornative being somewhat less robust, and the performative and similative the least robust of all. It would be interesting to explain why this difference in productivity might exist, and I will attempt to do so below.

3.1.2   Past analyses

These questions were first raised within the generative tradition in Lieber (1998). There, using a modified version of Jackendoff's (1990) formalism, I suggested a range of LCSs for the suffix *-ize* (1998, 19–20):[1]

(4)   a. [$_{Event}$ **ACT** ([$_{Thing}$], [$_{Event}$ INCH [$_{State}$ BE ([$_{Thing}$],
            [$_{Place}$ AT ([$_{Thing, Property}$ base])])])])]
            (unionize, civilianize, epitomize, velarize)

        b. [$_{Event}$ **ACT** ([$_{Thing}$], [$_{Event}$ GO ([$_{Thing}$ base], [$_{Path}$ TO/ON/IN
            ([$_{Thing}$])])])]
            (carbonize, texturize, apologize)

        c. [$_{Event}$ ACT ([$_{Thing}$], [$_{Event}$ GO ([$_{Thing}$], [$_{Path}$ TO ([$_{Thing}$ base])])])]
            (summarize, hospitalize)

        d. [$_{Event}$ ACT ([$_{Thing}$], [$_{Manner}$ LIKE ([$_{Thing, Property}$ base])])]
            (criticize)

That is, in that article I encoded the range of meanings shown by forms in *-ize* in four separate LCSs, which, however, share their first semantic function, ACT. ACT, a semantic function borrowed from Pinker (1989), was meant to cover both causative meaning and a simple activity meaning for which Jackendoff provided no semantic function of his own. In this analysis, the suffix *-ize* is implicitly claimed to have four polysemous meanings, with the base playing the role of a Property, a Theme, a Goal, or a Manner argument. That the meanings are polysemous rather than homophonous was meant to follow from the presence of the function ACT in all four.

---

1. Boldface indicates the optionality of the ACT function. When this function is absent, the verb receives an inchoative interpretation.

As Plag (1999) points out, however, there are a number of problems with this analysis. First, given the four different LCSs, it is not clear how the polysemy of these affixes arises. Although all share the semantic function ACT, the four LCSs in (4) are also different in significant ways: (4a) uses the primitives INCH and BE, (4b,c) the primitive GO, and (4d) neither of these. The mere presence of the identical outermost function does not by itself constitute an explicit theory of polysemy. Second, as Plag notes, the LCS in (4d) is not sufficient to account for what he calls "performatives," those forms that I have glossed here as "do x" (*philosophize*, etc.); these arguably do not have a manner argument as Plag's similatives do. And finally, for what Plag calls the similatives, there is a problem with the LCS in (4d) in that it does not allow for the right number of arguments in the derived verbs, which are at least sometimes transitive rather than intransitive.

Plag (1999) offers his own analysis of *-ize* and *-ify* in terms of Jackendovian LCSs, claiming that the meanings of all *-ize* and *-ify* derivatives arise from a single LCS (1999, 137):

(5)   LCS of *-ize* verbs (generalized)
        CAUSE([$]_i$, [GO ([$_{Property, Thing}$ $]_{Theme/Base}$; [TO [$_{Property/Thing}$ $]_{Base/Theme}$])])

Underlining again represents optionality of this part of the LCS. For Plag, the difference between "locative" *-ize* forms like *hospitalize* and "ornative" forms like *patinize* is the position of the base in the LCS; for the former type, the base is the argument of the TO function, and for the latter, the base is the argument of GO. This much of the analysis is similar to the analysis proposed in Lieber 1998. For the "causatives" like *randomize*, Plag argues that the function GO can be used, rather than the functions BE/INCH which Lieber 1998 used (1999, 128):

> The crucial difference between these two categories [locative/ornative vs. causative – R.L.] is that the transfer denoted by the function GO is not of a physical nature with causatives. Whether we are dealing with a physical or a non-physical transfer depends on the semantic interpretation of the arguments of the GO function.

In other words, Plag proposes to generalize the GO function to cover not only physical change of position undergone by a thing, but also change of state undergone by a property. "Resultatives" like *peasantize* are subsumed under the same LCS as well. In fact, Plag argues that the base *peasant* could theoretically occupy the position of the argument of either GO or TO, giving rise to slightly different nuances of meaning: with the base as the argument of TO, *peasantize* would mean "cause to turn into a peasant," which is in fact its lexicalized meaning, whereas if the base is construed as the argument of GO the word might mean "cause peasants to go somewhere," as in *They peasantized the village*. Plag treats the inchoative class much as Lieber (1998) did, by making the outer CAUSE function optional.

This leaves the "similatives" and the "performatives." Plag argues that no special treatment is needed for these classes, but rather that the LCS in (5) works equally well for them. For similatives like *Marxize*, especially in their transitive forms, Plag suggests that an analysis that means "act like *Marx*" is not quite right. He points out that the base *Marx* can be understood metonymically as "the doctrines of Marx." If so, the base in *Marxize* could arguably be the argument of GO, yielding a meaning roughly like "x caused the doctrines of Marx to go somewhere." Plag also subsumes performatives like *anthropologize* under the LCS in (5). Again, the claim is that these forms do not mean "do X," but are more closely associated with the familiar locative, ornative, causative, and resultative cases. In (6) I show Plag's analysis for *anthropologize* (1999, 138):

(6)   LCS of *John anthropologized (in the field)*
        "ornative"
        CAUSE ([*John*]$_i$, [GO ([*anthropology*]$_{Base}$; [TO [   ]$_{Theme}$])])

The LCS in (6) can be paraphrased, according to Plag as "John applied anthropology to an unmentioned object."

Plag's analysis has the advantage of explaining more straightforwardly than my own earlier one how polysemy arises in *-ize* forms. All *-ize* derivatives share a core of meaning represented by a single LCS. The variations in meaning that they display are the result of the base occupying different argument positions in that LCS, of the base being interpreted metaphorically rather than literally, or of one of the arguments, GO, being interpreted as a change-of-state function, as well as a change-of-position function.

Plag's analysis is less than convincing, however, when it comes to the performative and similative classes. With respect to the performatives, while it is not entirely implausible at first glance to interpret *anthropologize* as "apply anthropology to some unmentioned object," we might first ask why the last argument – the TO argument, that is – is never projected in the syntax in these cases, and is not even implicit. Cases like *anthropologize* or *philosophize* are intransitives. Further, it would seem to require at least some justification to interpret the Jackendovian functions CAUSE and GO as "apply" in these cases; it sounds less plausible to say that *anthropologize* means "cause anthropology to go to some unspecified object." And finally, even the "apply" interpretation does not work for all performative *-ize* verbs. According to the OED, *despotize* and *hooliganize* are pure performatives meaning "act like a despot/hooligan"; given the LCS in (5), it's not clear why the performatives *despotize* and *hooliganize* don't mean "cause despots/hooligans to go to somewhere" or "cause someone to become a despot/hooligan" – just the interpretations that Plag himself gives for *peasantize*. Surely these are more plausible interpretations of the LCS in (5) than "apply despots/hooligans to some unmentioned object."[2]

Nor does Plag's interpretation work equally well for all similatives. While it is indeed plausible to interpret *Marxize* as "cause the doctrines of Marx to go somewhere," as in *They Marxized the proletarians*, a similar interpretation of *Boswellize* is not so plausible. As Boswell was not the proponent of a particular theory or doctrine, we have no choice but to interpret *Boswellize* literally, rather than metonymically, as "do something the way Boswell did it," that is, write in the style of Boswell. In other words, a metonymic interpretation of the similative cases works less well when the similatives mean "imitate x," arguably their core meaning.

A final problem we might note with both previous analyses is this: neither one accounts for a simple observation about *-ize* derivatives, that the goal-oriented forms (Plag's locative, causative, and resultative classes) are far more numerous than the theme-oriented forms (Plag's ornatives), and that the smallest classes of all are the performative and similative classes. I will argue in what follows that this pattern is not accidental, but rather that it can be made to follow from an analysis of *-ize* within the framework that I have been developing in this book.

3.1.3   "-ize," "-ify": *core cases*
The analysis I present here builds on both my own earlier analysis and that of Plag (1999). As in my treatment of the nominalizing affixes in chapters 1 and 2, I claim that the affixes *-ize* and *-ify* are associated with a unitary skeleton, and that the polysemy displayed by their derivatives arises from a combination of factors including the semantic category of the base and the positions in the affixal skeleton with which the base argument is co-indexed. In this section, I will discuss what I call the core cases derived with *-ize* and *-ify*, that is, those that fall into my own first three cases, which correspond to Plag's causative, resultative,

---

2. Horn (1989/2001, 107) gives a nice example of a pure performative when he cites Quine (1948, 7–12) as analyzing "*Pegasus is winged* into 'The thing which pegasizes is winged'."

ornative, and locative classes, as well as the related inchoative class. I will postpone for the moment discussion of the "act like x" or "do x" cases (Plag's similative and performative classes), returning to them in the next section, where I will argue that these cases are best treated a little differently from the other ones.

The skeleton that I propose for *-ize* and *-ify* is the skeleton I would attribute to causative verbs in general in English. Remember that in chapter 1 I suggested that causatives constitute complex SITUATIONS rather than simple ones; causatives consist of an activity which brings about the effecting of a result. As such, I adopted for them a form of the bipartite representation advocated by such researchers as Dowty (1979) and Levin and Rappaport Hovav (1995), Rappaport Hovav and Levin (1998), and Levin (1999). Couched in the formalism I have developed here, then, *-ize* and *-ify* would have the skeleton in (7):

(7)   *-ize, -ify*
       [+dynamic ([$_{volitional - i}$], [$_j$])]; [+dynamic ([$_i$], [+dynamic,
       +IEPS ([$_j$], [+Loc ([   ])])]), <base>]

Roughly, we might gloss this skeleton as adding to an adjectival or nominal base with the meaning "[x does something to y] such that [x causes y to become z/ go to z]."

Two notes on this skeleton. First, as I suggested in chapter 1, the directed change function [+dynamic, +IEPS] covers both change of location (Jackendoff's GO function) and change of state (Jackendoff's INCH/BE). As was shown in Lieber and Baayen (1997), there is good reason to believe that these are in fact the same function, as it is exactly this class of verbs that chooses the auxiliary *zijn* "be" in Dutch. The formalism adopted here allows us to express the identity of these functions without collapsing INCH/BE into GO as Plag (1999) does. Nor is it necessary any more to have separate skeletons for the causatives ("cause to become x") and the locatives ("cause to go to x"), as in my own earlier analysis.

Further, it appears that for the most part, the subject of *-ize* and *-ify* verbs needs to be a volitional agent (as opposed to an extrinsic agent or an instrument). Note that sentences like the following are somewhat odd:[3]

---

3. That is, they seem somewhat marginal, although occasionally such sentences in which the subject of the *-ize* verb is an inanimate actor are attested. My impression, after searching for such examples in the OED and on the Internet, is that they occur only infrequently.

(8)   *?The cold crystallized the water.*
       ?Charcoal purified the water.
       ?Circumstances unionized the faculty.

It therefore appears that these verb-forming affixes place a condition of volitionality on any argument with which they might be co-indexed. The significance
of this observation will become clear in the next section.

As we have seen before, in terms of lexical semantics, affixation requires the
integration of the skeleton of the base adjective or noun with the skeleton of
the affix. The cases we have looked at so far – compounding, and nominalizing
affixation like *-er* and *-ee* – suggested that a Principle of Co-indexation is
involved in this integration. I repeat the Principle of Co-indexation in (9):

(9)   **Principle of Co-indexation**
       In a configuration in which semantic skeletons are composed, co-index the
       highest nonhead argument with the highest (preferably unindexed) head
       argument. Indexing must be consistent with semantic conditions on the head
       argument, if any.

As before, I assume that this principle is a violable one.

Let us look now at the composed skeleton for *standardize* or *purify*.

(10)   *standardize, purify*
       [+dynamic ([$_{volitional-i}$], [$_j$])]; [+dynamic ([$_i$], [+dynamic,
       +IEPS ([$_j$], [+Loc ([$_k$])])]), [−dynamic ([$_k$])]]
                    -ize   *standard*
                    -ify   *pure*

The highest nonhead argument is the sole argument of *standard* or *pure*. This
argument must be co-indexed, according to (9) to the highest preferably unindexed argument of the head, that is of the affix. As the first two arguments of
both subevents are already indexed (and as the first argument of the activity
subevent of *-ize* or *-ify* must be volitional in any case), we pass over these
and co-index the argument of *standard* with the Goal argument of the second
subevent. The adjectives *standard* and *pure* are therefore interpreted as the end
states of the causative act. In other words, the skeleton in (10) receives an interpretation something like "x does something to y such that x causes y to become
standard/pure." Examples like *velarize, crystallize,* and *unionize* or *diversify*
and *yuppify* – that is, Plag's causative and resultative classes – can be treated in
the same way.

Examples like *hospitalize, containerize,* or *codify,* the class that Plag refers to as locatives, also receive this analysis, except that the Goal argument here represents a final position, rather than a final state of the causing act:

(11)   *hospitalize, codify*
        [+dynamic ([$_{volitional-i}$], [$_j$])]; [+dynamic ([$_i$], [+dynamic,
        +IEPS ([$_j$], [+Loc ([$_k$])])]), [+material ([$_k$])]]
              -ize   *hospital*
              -ify   *code*

Here, the sole argument of *hospital,* its "R" argument, is co-indexed with the highest available argument of the verbal head, again, the Goal argument. From this we get the rough gloss "x does something to y such that x causes y to go to/into *hospital/code.*"

Examples like *apologize, anesthetize, patinize, acidize,* and *glorify* – Plag's ornative group – can be analyzed using this basic skeleton as well, although we must assume that the ornative reading results from a somewhat less preferred indexing pattern. In these cases, the base nouns (*apology, patina, acid,* and the like) are not the end states or the final positions in the causative act, but rather themes: they are what gets transferred by the action.[4] How can we derive this indexing pattern?

We have seen that the Principle of Co-indexing may be violated under certain circumstances. Let us assume that violations may occur if the semantic properties of the base argument and the semantic properties of the highest available affixal argument are not compatible. In the case of the suffix *-ize,* the unindexed argument of [+Loc] is normally compatible with something that can denote a state (*standard, crystal*) or a location (*hospital, container*). Note that the bases in the ornative class are always nouns, and significantly nouns that do not normally denote states or locations (even metaphorical ones); rather they typically denote chemical substances (*anesthetic, acid*) or abstractions (*apology, glory*). Interestingly, these are nouns which denote moveable or transferrable entities, that is, entities which are more compatible with a theme interpretation.

---

4. In fact, as Plag rightly points out, some of the ornatives have alternate interpretations as resultatives; so *acidize* could mean "cause to become acid" or "cause acid to go to something." We would expect this sort of ambiguity to occur if the base noun is interpretable either as a state/location or as a transferable entity. One of Plag's examples is instructive here; he notes that *peasantize* can have either the resultative reading, if we construe *peasant* as a kind of end state (being like a peasant), or an ornative one, if we construe *peasant* as a concrete moveable entity (i.e., filling a village with peasants). Interestingly, the latter reading is the harder one to get.

The indexing they receive is the one in (12), where the semantic characteristics of the base are most compatible with those of the already indexed theme argument:

(12)   *anesthetize, glorify*
         [+dynamic ([$_{volitional-i}$], [$_j$])]; [+dynamic ([$_i$], [+dynamic,
         +IEPS ([$_j$], [+Loc ([   ])])]), [+material ([$_j$])]]
                  -ize   *anesthetic*

         [+dynamic ([$_{volitional-i}$], [$_j$])]; [+dynamic ([$_i$], [+dynamic,
         +IEPS ([$_j$], [+Loc ([   ])])]), [−material ([$_j$])]]
                  -ify   *glory*

This pattern, of course, represents a violation of the Principle of Co-indexation, but not a serious one. We would expect, however, that this indexing is somewhat dispreferred, and that we should find fewer items in the ornative class than in the causative, resultative, or locative classes. In fact, using Plag's list of twentieth-century neologisms in *-ize* from the OED, I would estimate roughly three times as many forms to be goal-oriented (Plag's locatives, causatives, and resultatives taken together) as theme-oriented (ornative), which accords with the slightly marked status of the latter category predicted by the present analysis.

We have accounted for most of the core cases with *-ize* and *-ify*: the causative and resultative group ("cause to become x"), the locative group ("cause to go to/in/on x"), and the ornative group ("cause x to go to/in/on something"). The only remaining central cases to be accounted for are the inchoatives ("become x"). Here, I will follow the analysis of Levin and Rappaport Hovav (1995) for all causative/inchoative alternations, that is, for simplex as well as derived verbs. LRH point out that the causative/inchoative alternation is typical of transitive verbs in which "the eventuality can come about spontaneously, without the volitional intervention of an agent" (1995, 102). They note that verbs in *-ize* and *-ify* often cannot detransitivize, as the end state or location denoted in the verb frequently cannot happen without an external agent (e.g., milk cannot *homogenize* by itself). But where an external agent is unnecessary, an inchoative form is possible, for example as in *The mixture solidified* (1995, 104). LRH analyze the general causative/inchoative alternation as a binding of the external cause argument (here the first argument of [+dynamic]) at the level of the lexical semantic representation (1995, 108). Binding, in their sense, ensures that the external cause argument is not projected to the syntax. Here, we will represent this "binding" as the deletion of the external cause argument from the composed verbal skeleton, although nothing crucial hinges on this particular means of formalization:

(13)
solidify (inchoative)
[+dynamic ([$_{volitional-i}$], [$_j$])]; [+dynamic ([$_i$], [+dynamic, +IEPS ([$_j$], [+Loc ([$_k$])])]), [−dynamic ([$_k$])]]
$$\Downarrow$$
$$\varnothing$$

As the eliminated argument is co-indexed with an argument in the second subevent, this argument will be eliminated as well. The result is a verb with the [+dynamic, +IEPS] function as outermost, in other words an inchoative verb.

3.1.4   *Non-core cases: performatives and similatives*
We turn now to the last two classes of *-ize* forms in English, the ones that Plag refers to as performatives ("do x") and similatives ("act like x"). Among the former are intransitive verbs like *anthropologize, philosophize, theorize,* and *speechify*. There are no *-ify* forms among the latter group, but for *-ize* there are intransitives like *Boswellize, hooliganize,* and *despotize*. Although Plag counts some transitives as part of this class as well, for example, *Marxize,* I will suggest that the transitive cases are not part of the similative class. Further, I argue here that the performatives and similatives stand outside the core of *-ize* formations, and that they in fact occur only as sense extensions of the normal *-ize* pattern under specific circumstances. Here I will appeal again to the notions of paradigmatic and pragmatic pressure introduced in Booij and Lieber (2004) and discussed in the previous chapter.

As I argued there, when a language lacks a systematic derivational means for creating a particular semantic class of lexemes, and under pragmatic pressure – the real-world need to coin a word belonging to that semantic class – the closest productive derivational process may be put to use to fill the semantic gap. I will first provide an analysis of the performative and similative classes based on the idea of sense extension, and then try to justify this move in terms of the larger picture of verb formation in English. This will lead naturally to a discussion of conversion in section 3.2.

My proposal is simple. I claim that the performatives and similatives arise as a sense extension of the more robust *-ize* patterns. With this sense extension, the *-ize* skeleton drops the second subevent, the one which denotes the end position or result of the activity. What remains is the skeleton of the first subevent, which is simply the standard skeleton for an activity verb:

(14)   *-ize* extension

[+dynamic ([$_{volitional-i}$], [$_j$])]: [+dynamic ([$_i$], [+dynamic, +IEPS ([$_j$], [+Loc ([   ])])])]

. . . .

↓

∅

Let us consider the performative class first. The composed skeleton for forms like *philosophize*, *anthropologize*, *theorize*, and the like would be that shown in (15):

(15)   [+dynamic ([$_{volitional}$], [   ]), [−material ([   ])]]
        -ize extension   *philosophy*

In other words, the base in these cases is composed with a simple activity verb skeleton. The base argument in (15) then needs to be co-indexed with the affixal skeleton. We have observed above that the first argument of the activity must be volitional. However, the class of performatives is formed on bases that typically denote abstract fields of inquiry; the "R" argument of nouns like *philosophy* is not compatible with volitionality. Therefore, the indexing that we arrive at is the one in (16), where the base argument is co-indexed with the second argument of the affixal skeleton:

(16)   [+dynamic ([$_{volitional}$], [$_i$]), [−material ([$_i$])]]
        -ize extension   *philosophy*

The interpretation that we get is roughly "do philosophy." Note that the fact that the performatives are intransitive follows from this indexing; such verbs have only one free argument to project to the syntax.

The similatives are based on the same extended skeleton, but they require, I would argue, a different pattern of indexing. Note that the similatives are formed on nominal bases denoting persons, either types of persons (*hooligan*, *despot*) or proper names (*Boswell*, *Marx*). As person-names are eminently compatible with the requirement of volitionality, there is nothing to prevent the indexing in the composed skeleton in (17):

(17)   [+dynamic ([$_{volitional-i}$], [   ]), [+material, dynamic ([$_i$])]]
        -ize extension   *hooligan*

In other words, in this pattern, there is nothing to prevent the "R" argument of the base from being identified with the highest argument of the affixal skeleton. This leads to what might seem at first glance like a rather odd interpretation:

theoretically, what a similative like *hooliganize* should mean is something like
"x hooligan-does." But perhaps this is just the right interpretation if we assume
that "to hooligan-do" means something like "to do as a hooligan does." In other
words, the manner interpretation of the base in these cases does not come from
a manner argument in the skeleton, but rather from the co-indexation of the
base argument with the volitional subject argument of the affix.

The performative and intransitive similative cases thus can both be treated
as sense extensions of the skeleton suggested for *-ize*, and, with this analysis, be given interpretations that are more natural than those suggested by
Plag (recall that he interprets *anthropologize* as "apply anthropology to an
unspecified object" and in fact provides no interpretation for the intransitive
similatives). However, as Plag (1999) points out, there seem to be transitive
cases based on person-names as well. For example, *Marxize* is attested in a
context like *The socialists Marxize the West* (Plag 1999, 139). The transitive
use of such forms obviously does not follow from the skeleton in (17), there
being no second unindexed argument to project to the syntax. But I would
argue that these transitive cases are in fact not members of the similative class;
as Plag himself analyzes them, they are resultatives or ornatives. That is, as
Plag points out, here the base *Marx* is not literally associated with the name,
but rather is interpreted metonymically as "the doctrines of Marx." Other transitive *-ize* forms derived from personal names denote specialized processes
invented by the person named (e.g., among the twentieth-century OED neologisms *Coslettize* and *Powellize*). As such, transitive cases based on person-
names will take the normal *-ize* skeleton, and will undergo indexing as the forms
discussed in section 3.1.3 do.

A final point we might make about the performatives and similatives is this:
as sense extensions of the suffix *-ize*, we would expect them to be the most
highly marked of *-ize* derivatives, and therefore the least productively formed.
As mentioned at the outset, these patterns are in fact the least robust of the *-ize*
patterns; a brief look at Plag's list of twentieth-century neologisms from the
OED shows that new intransitive forms in the performative and similative
classes exist, but they are far less frequent than causatives, locatives, resultatives, and even ornatives.

3.1.5   Summary

In this section, I have revisited the polysemy of the productive verb-forming
affixes *-ize* and *-ify* in English. My analysis is like that of Plag (1999) in that
I have suggested that for the most part the polysemy of these verbal affixes
follows from the existence of a single causative skeleton which may, given the

bases that the affix attaches to, undergo different patterns of indexing. In other words, the polysemy of *-ize* and *-ify* to a large extent qualifies as what we have called "constructional polysemy," that is, polysemy that follows from a single skeleton which is interpreted in a number of ways depending upon the bases with which it combines. The least productive senses of *-ize* formations were argued to qualify as sense extensions.

My analysis differs from Plag's in two respects. First, the nature of the skeleton I suggest is different. Plag's causative skeleton contains only a single event, whereas the skeleton that I suggest follows the bipartite analysis favored by Dowty (1979), Levin and Rappaport Hovav (1995), and others. Second, my analysis suggests a scale of productivity for *-ize* derivations, with goal-oriented forms being the most productive, theme-oriented forms less productive, and the performative and similative classes the least productive. I have suggested, in fact, that the performatives and similatives are not core cases, but rather arise from a process of sense extension which involves the dropping of the second subevent from the affixal skeleton, and therefore that their polysemy is of a somewhat different sort from that of the core cases.

While I believe I have provided a plausible analysis of the performative and similative classes of *-ize* verbs as an extension of the general pattern of *-ize* formation, I have not answered the most critical question that such an analysis raises: why should such a sense extension take place? What in the system of word formation in English motivates this extension? To answer this question we must now look more broadly at other means that the morphology of English makes available for the creation of new verbs.

3.2   *Conversion and the creation of new verbs*

Virtually the only other means of creating new verbs in English – besides affixation of *-ize* and *-ify* – is conversion. By conversion, I mean the creation of words of one lexical category from words of another lexical category with no overt formal change. In English, conversion can create nouns from verbs (*a throw* from *to throw*), verbs from nouns (*to boot* from *boot*), and sometimes verbs from adjectives (*to cool* from *cool*). In this chapter I will concentrate on verb-forming conversions.

We have seen in section 3.1 and in earlier chapters that it is typical for affixes to exhibit a range of polysemy, but that nevertheless they may generally be characterized by means of a unitary skeleton. We can now raise the subject of verbal conversion in English and explore whether or not conversion behaves like affixation in terms of lexical semantics. For decades a debate has raged over the proper analysis of conversion, specifically whether conversion is best analyzed as zero-affixation (Marchand 1969, Allen 1978, Kiparsky 1982), or the addition of some other phonologically null affixal element (Don 1993, Hale and Keyser 2002), as rebracketing (Dell and Selkirk 1978 for French, Williams 1981, Strauss 1982), or as something else such as relisting of items in the lexicon (Lieber 1980, 1981, 1992a) or innovative coinage (Clark and Clark 1979). In previous works I have argued in favor of a relisting analysis for English, showing specifically, on the basis of morphosyntactic patterns and patterns of verbal diathesis, that conversion does not behave like affixation. In Lieber (1992, 159) I stated the relisting analysis as follows:

(18)   Relisting
     i. The lexicon allows for the addition of new entries.
     ii. Conversion occurs when an item already listed in the lexicon is re-entered as an item of a different category.

In this section I will show that a careful analysis of verbal conversion in English – when compared to a semantic analysis of a true verb-forming affix like *-ize* – supports my earlier conclusion that conversion should be treated as relisting rather than as zero-affixation. In fact, as we shall see shortly, what I meant by relisting in my earlier analysis amounts to much the same position as that advocated in Clark and Clark (1979).

The argument goes as follows. If verbal conversion is zero-affixation, then it should be possible to analyze it with a single skeleton (or at most a single skeleton with a sense extension); we have seen that some degree of polysemy is to be expected in affixal semantics, and can be tolerated in a single-skeleton analysis. What I will try to show in what follows is that the semantic range exhibited by converted verbs is larger even than those of *-ize* verbs, and that the patterns into which converted verbs fall are quite different from those of *-ize* forms.[5]

Plag (1999) also argues for the greater semantic diversity of converted verbs than of *-ize* verbs, and we will take his analysis as a point of departure. Using the same semantic categories that he used in his analysis of *-ize*, Plag notes

---

5. In previous work (Lieber 1980, 1981, 1992a), I maintained that there was no reason to preclude a zero-affixation analysis when the facts of a language supported such an analysis. That is, if morphosyntactic patterns, patterns of verbal diathesis, and lexical semantic analysis all suggest that a conversion pattern in some language is like affixation, then there is no reason to rule out a zero-affixation analysis. My only claim here is that such an analysis cannot be justified for English verbal conversion.

that there are verbs converted from nouns or adjectives that fit into each of the relevant categories:[6]

(19)	locative	"put (in)to x"	jail
	ornative	"provide with x"	staff
	causative	"make (more) x"	yellow
	resultative	"make into x"	bundle
	inchoative	"become x"	cool
	performative	"perform x"	counterattack
	similative	"act like x"	chauffeur, pelican

But he notes that conversion verbs exhibit other meanings as well, citing the following three categories, with the instrument category being an especially productive one:

(20)	instrumental	"use x"	hammer
	privative	"remove x"	bark
	stative	"be x"	hostess[7]

Plag argues – rightly I think – that the semantic range of verbal conversion makes it unlike affixation with *-ize* (1999, 220): "What is important, however, is the growing consensus in the linguistic literature that the variety of meanings that can be expressed by zero-affixation is so large that there should be no specific meaning attached to the process of zero-affixation at all."

   In fact, I think an even stronger case can be made for the semantic diversity of verbal conversion in English. There are two ways in which the meanings of conversion verbs differ from the meanings of verbs formed by overt affixation in English.

   First, a look at Plag's appendix of twentieth-century conversion neologisms from the OED suggests that there are even more semantic categories exhibited by conversion than the ten that Plag himself lists. Specifically, there are many conversion verbs that have a motional meaning, with the base acting either as a manner component ("move in x manner") like *cartwheel* or *fishtail*, or as an instrumental component ("move using x") like *jet*, *lorry*, or *taxi*, or even a location ("move at x location") like *quarterdeck*. Interestingly, the first and last of these categories of motion verbs denote random motion, rather than directed motion.

---

6. For another, slightly different semantic categorization of conversion verbs, as well as extensive examples – both lexicalized and novel – see Clark and Clark (1979).
7. This is Plag's example. Better examples of stative conversion verbs might be *bay* and *landmark*, as – on my reading, at least – *hostess* is an activity verb.

Table 3.1 *Classes of English conversion verbs*

verb	gloss	Plag's category	proposed skeleton
archive, burlap	"put into x"	locative	analysis in (12)
coldcream, leaflet	"provide with x"	ornative	analysis in (13)
filthy, pretty	"make x"	causative	analysis in (11)
dolomite, puree	"make into x"	resultative	analysis in (11)
carbon, gel	"become x"	inchoative	analysis in (14)
boot, eyeball	"use x"	instrumental	[+dynamic ([ ], [ ], WITH [ ]), <base>]
bay, landmark	"be x"	stative	[−dynamic ([ ], [ ]), <base>]
audition, autopsy	"do x"	performative	analysis in (17)
buffalo, fink	"act like/as x"	similative	analysis in (18)
broadside, cartwheel	"move in x manner"		[+dynamic, −IEPS ([ ], [ ], LIKE [ ]), <base>]
jet, lorry	"move using x"		[+dynamic, +IEPS ([ ], [ ], WITH [ ]), <base>]
limehouse, quarterdeck	"move on/at x"		[+dynamic, −IEPS ([ ], [ ], [+LOC ([ ])]), <base>]
bark, peel	"remove x"	privative	see chapter 4

Second, the proportion of conversion verbs in the various categories appears to be very different from that exhibited among the *-ize* neologisms. As Plag points out, there are many instrumentals among the conversion verbs, and no *-ize* forms in this category. Nor are there any stative or motional *-ize* forms. But even where the categories overlap, there are marked differences. Among *-ize* verbs, the causatives, resultatives, and locatives predominate, and performatives and similatives are scarce. In comparison, among the conversion verbs, there are far more performative and similative verbs than any of the other categories. Verbal conversion simply does not behave semantically like derivation with *-ize*, *-ify* or any other verb-forming affix.

We can highlight the semantic diversity of verbal conversion even more clearly by suggesting rough analyses for various conversion verbs in English. Given the existence of both motion verbs and stative verbs formed by conversion, it would be difficult, using either Jackendoff's formalism or the one developed here, to find a single skeleton (even allowing sense extensions) that would cover all possible meanings. Remember that even with the polysemy of *-ize* derivatives, there was at least one thing that all *-ize* verbs had in common, namely the first [+dynamic] subevent. But some conversion verbs would need a [−dynamic] skeleton (*bay*, *landmark*) and some a motional skeleton, that is, one with [+dynamic] and some value of [IEPS]. Table 3.1 summarizes the categories of conversion verbs that appear in the OED neologisms, and the skeleton that I would propose for them. We have yet to develop the formalism within the present framework for either an instrumental or a manner component to meaning, so I have indicated these in Table 3.1 merely by using Jackendovian-style primitives WITH and LIKE. Clearly, we would need to clarify the nature of those components of meaning, to decompose them further into features, and to provide adequate justification for those features. Further, the formalism needed for privatives must wait until the next chapter; suffice it to say here that privatives require a semantic feature of negation added to a causative skeleton.

Nevertheless, even without a fully developed formalism, it is apparent that conversion verbs cover much the same semantic range as simplex verbs do. As we saw in chapter 1, there are four basic classes of simplex verbs (statives, activity verbs, unaccusatives/inchoatives, and manner of motion verbs) as well as the semantically more complex causatives; conversion verbs fall into all five basic classes. This range, of course, goes beyond even the broad polysemy exhibited by an affix like *-ize* and defies the assignment of a single unitary skeleton.

We can return now to the classic debate about the status of conversion in the grammar: if conversion were a form of affixation – specifically, affixation of a phonologically null element – then we would expect converted verbs to act semantically in the same way that verbs typically derived by affixation do. That is, we would expect a range of polysemy, the sort of polysemy that might be subsumed under a single skeleton, with perhaps a simple sense extension permitted. We have seen, however, that the broad range of meanings exhibited by conversion verbs in English goes beyond what we might reasonably pack into a single skeleton, and suggests once again that conversion should not be equated formally with affixation. The alternative is to argue that verbal conversion is just one form of coinage of novel lexical items, that it proceeds in the way that coinage of simplex items always proceeds, and that lexicalized conversion verbs are simply nouns that get relisted in the mental lexicon as verbs (essentially the relisting analysis set out in Lieber [1992a]).

How does such coinage work? As good an analysis as has ever been given is the one in Clark and Clark (1979). In effect, Clark and Clark argue that just about any noun can be used as a novel verb (and hence a new verb be coined), as long as it is interpretable in context. Interpretability requires adherence to a principle rather like Grice's cooperative principles (1975). Clark and Clark's principle of denominal verb interpretation is the following (1979, 787):

> THE INNOVATIVE DENOMINAL VERB CONVENTION. In using an inno-
> vative denominal sincerely, the speaker means to denote:
> a. the kind of situation
> b. that he has good reason to believe
> c. that on this occasion the listener can readily compute
> d. uniquely
> e. on the basis of their mutual knowledge
> f. in such a way that the parent noun denotes one role in the situation, and
>   the remaining surface arguments of the denominal verb denote other roles
>   in the situation.

I assume further that to the extent that novel verbs get reused and entrenched, they become fixed in the mental lexicon with some particular meaning; this is what I call relisting.

The relisting analysis in effect claims that conversion verbs are idiosyncratic coinages (albeit coinages taken from nominal or adjectival stock), and predicts that they should behave no differently from simplex coinages. We would expect that simplex verbs might be coined in any semantic class as need arises, and we should therefore expect a similar freedom with conversion verbs. The fact that we do find conversion verbs in all basic semantic classes therefore supports the relisting analysis.

We can now confront the fourth of the basic questions which we raised in the introduction to this work: how do we account for word formation in which there is semantic change without any concomitant formal change? The answer that emerges is a supremely simple one. In the case of conversion, the same semantic space is available for relisting of nouns and adjectives as verbs that would be available for the coinage of new simplex verbs. Conversion of verbs from nouns and adjectives in English simply **is** a form of coinage. Put slightly differently, a converted verb can have any of the skeletons that a simplex verb has, given the right context and pragmatic need. In a theory such as Szymanek's (1988) or Beard's (1995), in which the semantics of word formation is claimed to be different from the semantics of simplex lexemes, such a solution would be unavailable. But the present theory claims that word formation is intended to extend the simplex lexicon, and therefore that it can cover precisely the same semantic space as the simplex lexicon. The formalism developed here allows us to state this in a simple way.

3.3   *Paradigmatic extension and the case of* -ize

We must return now to the question raised at the end of section 3.1, namely, why -*ize* should be extended to allow the formation of intransitive performatives and similatives like *philosophize*, *Boswellize*, and *hooliganize*. The first thing we must point out is that these formations are quite rare as -*ize* derivations go. The performatives seem largely confined to bases that denote academic fields (botany, geography, astronomy, etc.), and new -*ize* forms based on names seem more often to denote specialized processes, to be transitives, and therefore to be analyzable as resultatives rather than as similatives. We are dealing with a very small class of items. The second thing to point out is that English is very poor in **systematic** ways of coining new verbs. Conversion is, to be sure, productive, but it is not **systematic**. Rather, it is a random and idiosyncratic process that can give rise to any kind of verb at all. The only systematic ways of forming new verbs that English has are the affixation of -*ize* and -*ify*, *en-* prefixation and -*en* suffixation being largely unproductive in present-day English.

The theory I have been developing in this book suggests that the simplex lexicon defines a semantic space represented paradigmatically as all the possibilities allowed by the featural system, any part of which can be occupied by an affix. Affixation functions to extend the simplex lexicon within some part of that semantic space. The affixes of a given language therefore form a kind of paradigm, or to put it a bit differently, occupy a space in a semantic paradigm. Given the features [dynamic], [IEPS], and [material], the semantic paradigm for verbs, for example, would define spaces for STATES, ACTIVITIES, UNACCUSATIVE/INCHOATIVES, MANNER OF MOTION and CAUSATIVES. The semantic paradigm for nouns would include space for SIMPLE CONCRETE, SIMPLE ABSTRACT, SITUATIONAL CONCRETE and SITUATIONAL ABSTRACT nouns (with some nuances of meaning, such as whether the derived forms are subject-oriented or object-oriented, following from particular patterns of co-indexing, as we saw in chapter 2).

As we have already seen, however, the semantic paradigm is not always fully covered by available affixes in a particular language. Even in the case of noun-forming derivation, where English has many available affixes, there is an affixal gap: no affix exists with the meaning "thing which is x-ed," where x denotes a verb. We saw that in the face of pragmatic pressure – the real-world need to coin a word with this meaning – the closest and most productive derivational affix available may be extended to create the needed word.

My analysis of the small class of performative and similative *-ize* forms claims that these items are oddities which, like the object-oriented *-er* forms discussed in chapter 2, are forced into existence, in effect, by the poverty of English verb-forming derivation. Strictly speaking, forms like *anthropologize* and *hooliganize* are not normal *-ize* derivatives, but there is no other systematic means in English for coining them. There is no special affix in English that can create verbs from nouns meaning "do x" or "act like x." The closest productive affix which could be extended in their creation is *-ize*. It is significant in this regard that the suffix *-ify*, which is less productive than *-ize*, has only three or four existing performatives (*speechify*, *versify*) and no similatives; further, there are no new coinages in either category. I would argue that the reason for this is that the more productive an existing affix is, the more it is available for paradigmatic extension.

3.4   *Conclusion*

In this chapter we have looked in some detail at the semantics of verbal derivation in English, comparing the meanings of verbs formed by affixation of *-ize* and *-ify* with verbal conversion. Two conclusions emerge from this case study.

First, even an affix with a rather broad range of polysemy can be characterized by means of a unitary semantic skeleton. The advantage in doing so for *-ize* is that the present theory yields some plausible predictions about the productivity or robustness of various sub-meanings, and therefore about the ease with which new forms displaying those sub-meanings should be coined.

Second, we can conclude that verbal conversion in English does not behave semantically like affixation, even like such a broadly polysemous affix as *-ize*. Rather, verbal conversion ranges over the entire semantic space available for new simplex verbs, and therefore is much more akin to coinage than to affixation. In other words, the semantics of verbal conversion in English lends support to structural analyses of conversion that do not rely on zero-affixation.

With respect to the third of the questions raised in the introduction to this work – how we account for semantic change unaccompanied by formal change – we now have an answer as well. We don't need to account specifically for semantic change unaccompanied by formal change any more than we need to account specially for the semantics of new coinages: the whole system I have developed so far in this book does that. Coinage of new lexemes can be expected to occur in any semantic area of the lexicon, and so it does with conversion.

4 *Extending the system – location*

My intention in this chapter is to extend our system of lexical semantic representation by focusing on the feature [Loc] for "Location," and by showing how an extended system can be used in the analysis of a number of affixes including privatives (*-less, de-*), negatives (*in-, -un-, non-, dis-*), and prepositional affixes (e.g., *over-*). My aim is to deepen our understanding of both the semantic skeleton and the body, and to explore further two of the questions with which I started this inquiry: why multiple affixes often occupy the same semantic space, and why at the same time these affixes exhibit polysemy. We will also begin to delve more deeply into the nature of affixal polysemy in this chapter.

The semantic features we have made most use of so far, [material] and [dynamic], define what we might refer to as major ontological classes of concepts/lexical items, perhaps the most basic of lexical classes: STATES, EVENTS, CONCRETE or ABSTRACT SIMPLE SUBSTANCES/THINGS/ESSENCES and CONCRETE or ABSTRACT SITUATIONAL SUBSTANCES/THINGS/ESSENCES. For a fuller description of the lexical semantics of a language like English we will clearly need to add features to these two, although how many and what sort is at this point an open question. To begin with, the semantic field of TIME/SPACE immediately suggests itself, as it has to do with concepts that are so basic to language, and indeed to human existence, that they must surely play some role in the meanings exhibited by lexical items.[1]

In section 4.1, I will define the feature [Loc], which has been mentioned only in passing in previous chapters, and discuss its relation to the feature [IEPS].

---

1. In grouping time and space together, I do not mean to claim that these concepts are the same thing, or that spatial concepts can be interpreted in terms of time or vice versa. Rather, I make an implicit claim that language often treats concepts of time and space in the same way, as has been claimed frequently in previous literature; see, for example, Lyons (1977), Jackendoff (1996b) and references cited therein, as well as Bierwisch (1996) and Talmy (2000).

Recall that we would hope that any new feature that we introduce would have a broad utility across lexical categories. We would also expect that a new feature would play an important role in the derivational morphology of a language as well as in its simplex lexicon. In this section, I will explore the use of the feature [Loc] in the simplex lexicon, considering its role in both verbs and prepositions. In section 4.2, I will look at how this feature might figure in the semantics of affixes. Specifically, I will try to make a case that both privative and negative affixes are best treated as having this feature at their semantic core; we will try to attribute their polysemy and overlap in function to the parsimony of the semantic skeleton. In other words, I will argue that negative affixes in English constitute a good example of constructional polysemy. Finally, I will consider the prepositional affix *over-*, which exhibits a broader type of affixal polysemy than we have encountered before. Here, I will argue that simplex prepositions are multiply polysemous, that their polysemy often involves sense extensions that can be represented in their semantic bodies, and that the semantic bodies of simplex prepositions carry over to their affixal use, allowing the prepositional prefix to exhibit a range of meanings wider than might otherwise be expected of a derivational affix.

4.1   *TIME/SPACE features*

Most theories of lexical semantics recognize a semantic primitive that denotes location in SPACE or TIME. Jackendoff (1983, 1990), for example, provides the function PLACE, Wierzbicka (1996) the primitive WHERE, and Bierwisch (1996) the primitive LOC. In addition, some theories – for example both Jackendoff's and Bierwisch's – distinguish pure location from path, that is, location with trajectory. I will continue to make a distinction between locations and paths by using two semantic features [Loc] for "Location" and [IEPS] for "Inferable Eventual Position or State," both of which I have already used at various points in this work. Here, I will go into more detail on how these features work.

Perhaps the most basic feature in the SPACE category is one which asserts the relevance of place or position in the conceptual make-up of a lexical item. [Loc] may be defined as follows:

(1)   [+/−**Loc**]: Lexical items which bear the feature [Loc] for "Location" are those for which position or place in time or space is relevant. For those items which lack the feature [Loc], the notion of position or place is irrelevant. Further, those which bear the feature [+Loc] will pertain to position or place. [−Loc] items will be those for which the explicit lack of position or place is asserted.

The presence of the feature [Loc] in a skeleton asserts the relevance of position in space to the lexical item. If the feature is absent, position or place is irrelevant to the meaning of the lexical item. If the feature is present, however, the plus value asserts position or place and the minus value denies position in space or time; in effect, it signals lack or privation. While the definition of [−Loc] as "privation" may seem to be rather far-fetched at this point, I will try to make the case that it might be of use in characterizing certain sorts of verbs and adpositions. This in turn will lead to a discussion of the notion of privation and its relation to negation in derivational affixes in the next section.

Let me suggest first a use for the feature [Loc] with stative verbs. Among the stative verbs, there are those that Levin (1993) characterizes as "verbs of existence," which might equally well be called verbs of location. As Levin (1993) points out, verbs of this class, among them *stay, remain, exist, dwell,* differ syntactically from other stative verbs (*know* or *hear,* for example) in being able to occur in "There Insertion" contexts:

(2)   a. There remained three survivors in the city.
        b. *There knew a man three solutions to the problem.

One way of capturing this difference would be to partition stative verbs – that is, verbs with the feature [−dynamic] – into a class which also bears the feature [+Loc] and a class without this feature. But given the featural nature of the system we are developing here, the existence of [+Loc] verbs suggests another simplex category, of course, that of [−Loc] verbs. While this may seem like an odd consequence of the featural representation, it is perhaps not a bad consequence. If [+Loc] verbs are stative verbs of existence or location, then [−Loc] verbs should be stative verbs (or adjectives) of nonexistence, or perhaps of privation of location. It seems that there are at least a few plausible candidates for verbs in English that might fall into this category:

(3)

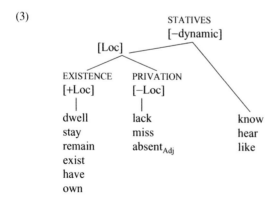

The privative meaning of the verb *lack* is fairly straightforward; "to lack" is "to not have." Similarly, the adjective *absent* has a transparently privative meaning: to be absent is not to be somewhere. (Remember that adjectives bear the feature [−dynamic], just as stative verbs do.) For the verb *miss*, the particular sense that I have in mind is the one that occurs in a sentence like *We missed you*, which in this case we might paraphrase as "we felt your absence." Perhaps an even better indication of the privative meaning of *miss* that I intend to focus on here occurs in the adjectival participle derived from this verb: *The screwdriver is missing again.*[2]

The second of our TIME/SPACE features is [IEPS] ("Inferable Eventual Position or State"). I have already defined this feature and discussed it in chapter 1, but I repeat the definition here for convenience, as it will be of use in the discussion of prepositions below:

(4)   [+/− **IEPS**]: Let Φ be a variable that ranges over States (i.e., [−dynamic] items) and Places (i.e., [+Loc] items), and x be the argument of Φ. Further, let *i* stand for the initial State or Place, *f* for the final State or Place, and *j*, . . . ,*k* for intermediate States/Places. Then the addition of the feature [IEPS] to the skeleton signals the addition of the semantic component in (i):

(i) $[\Phi_i(x), \Phi_j(x), \ldots, \Phi_k(x), \Phi_f(x)]$

In other words, the addition of the feature [IEPS] signals the addition of a sequence of PLACES or STATES. Further, if the value of [IEPS] is positive, we will be able to make the inference in (ii):

(ii) If [+IEPS], then $i \neq f \wedge \Phi_{j,k} \notin f$: $\Phi_i < \Phi_{j...} < \Phi_k < \Phi_f$

In plain English, if [+IEPS] is present, there will be a sequence of PLACES/STATES such that at any point between the initial and final PLACE/STATE, some progression will have taken place towards the final PLACE/STATE. If [−IEPS] is present, then we can make no inference about the progression of PLACES/STATES.

Recall that the feature [IEPS] adds a PATH component of meaning in a semantic skeleton. With respect to simplex verbs, it adds to the feature [+dynamic] to distinguish a subclass of verbs which denotes movement or change along directed paths from a subclass which denotes movement or change with a random path. The former subclass is composed of UNAC-CUSATIVE/INCHOATIVE verbs, and the latter of verbs that I dubbed in chapter 1 MANNER OF MOTION verbs. I repeat the taxonomy of simplex verbs from chapter 1:

---

2. The verb *want* used to have a privative sense as well, which survives in modern English only in negative contexts like *They don't want for anything.*

(5)

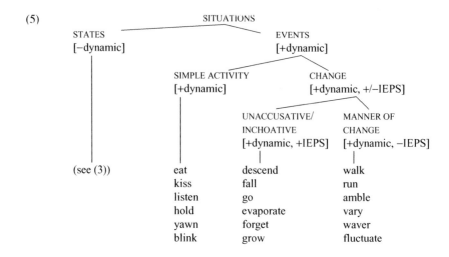

Verbs with the feature [IEPS] are those in which some change of PLACE or STATE takes place, either a directed change or a random change. Verbs without the feature [IEPS] are simple activity verbs for which the notion of PATH is irrelevant. Note that the feature [IEPS] treats SPACE and TIME in the same way. As Lieber and Baayen (1997) show, change of place verbs and change of state verbs behave identically in Dutch with respect to auxiliary selection. Arguably, change of state has to do with change over time and change of place, of course, with change of location. Yet the two notions behave alike in this linguistic context.

The TIME/SPACE features [Loc] and [IEPS] are clearly of use in distinguishing subclasses of simplex verbs. But they are also of use, I would argue, in characterizing the skeletons of simplex lexical items other than verbs. Up to this point, I have said virtually nothing about the category of prepositions (or more generally adpositions). Adpositions must be distinguished from the other lexical classes in one major way: as has been pointed out many times, adpositions form a closed class, unlike nouns, verbs, and adjectives. In semantic terms, adpositions are a category of lexical items for which neither the feature [material], which characterizes nouns, nor the feature [dynamic], which by itself characterizes verbs and adjectives, is relevant. The closed class of adpositions must then be characterized by features other than the major ontological ones in our system of lexical semantic representation.

The vast majority of prepositions in English denote spatial (and analogous temporal) relations, and those are the ones which will be of primary interest to us. Among the spatial prepositions, we can further distinguish those that are locational from those that imply trajectory. The former will be characterized by the presence of the feature [Loc] and the latter by the presence of the feature [IEPS]. The semantic distinction between [Loc] and [IEPS] prepositions is mirrored in a syntactic distinction as well. In English, for example, only [Loc] prepositions can occur with verbs of existence like *dwell*:

(6)   They dwelled on/above/behind the forest.
       *They dwelled to/into/through the forest.

In German, although the same prepositions can be either [Loc] or [IEPS], that is, either locational or directional, the former meaning is correlated with objects in the dative case and the latter with objects in the accusative case.

But the featural nature of the representation we have adopted here in fact goes beyond this relatively familiar distinction and suggests that there should in fact be two categories of [Loc] prepositions and two categories of [IEPS] prepositions. Again, although this seems somewhat unintuitive, it turns out to have interesting, and I think useful, consequences. Consider the taxonomy of a selection of English prepositions in (7):

(7)

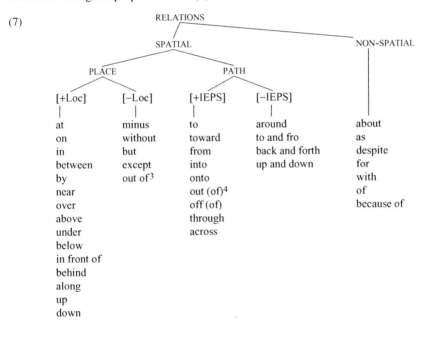

---

3. The sense I have in mind here is the one of deprivation: *We are out of milk.*
4. And here the sense is the purely directional one: *It flew out of the cage.*

As I suggested above, the minus value of [Loc] denotes privation. Indeed, there are a number of prepositions of privation in English, among them *minus* and *without* (*I'll have my burger minus/without the pickles*), and *but* and *except* (*We have everything but/except pickles*). The binary valued feature [Loc], odd though it may seem at first glance, gives us a convenient way of characterizing the core semantics of these prepositions.

It might seem equally strange to attribute a minus value to [IEPS] and use it to characterize prepositions. Nevertheless, in some cases I believe that this move makes sense. Remember that the negative value of [IEPS] signals a random path. Indeed there are at least two prepositions, *around* and (locational) *about*, and a few compound prepositions (*back and forth*, *to and fro*) which do seem to denote a random path: *We walked around/about/back and forth/to and fro all day, but never got anywhere.*

Prepositions will have skeletons as other categories do, only composed of features like [Loc] and [IEPS] rather than [material] or [dynamic]. And like other categories, these skeletons will represent not only the featural content of the prepositions, but also their arguments. Examples are given in (8):

(8)   in, on, at   [+Loc ([   ], [   ])]
       into, onto, to   [+IEPS ([   ], [   ])]

In (8), the first argument corresponds to what Bierwisch (1996, 65) calls the "theme" or the thing located, and the second to what he calls the "relatum," which is the syntactic complement of the preposition. Landau (1996) refers to these arguments respectively as the "Figure" and the "Reference Object." Intransitive prepositions like *back* or *away* will have one argument rather than two.

Of course, we might wonder how various [+Loc] prepositions like *in*, *on*, *at*, *near*, *over* or [+IEPS] prepositions like *into*, *onto*, *to*, *toward*, *from* are to be distinguished from one another. Here we must look to the contents of the semantic body. In fact, as has been pointed out in the literature, spatial prepositions in English show a rather rich paradigmatic structuring, systematically distinguishing a number of parameters including the dimensionality implied by their arguments, their axis of orientation, and whether they imply contact or mere proximity.

For example, it has frequently been noted (cf. Jackendoff 1996b, Bierwisch 1996, Talmy 2000, Landau 1996, and references cited therein) that prepositions differ in the dimensionality that is denoted by their second arguments (that is, their objects): *at* and *to* treat their objects as points, *on* and *onto* as surfaces, and *in* and *into* as volumes; consider, for example, the way we interpret the prepositional object in sentences like *The insect flew to/onto/into the milk*. The preposition *along* implies that its object is a line; a sentence like *The insect crawled along the milk* makes sense only if we can imagine milk enclosed in a container lying on its side, so that the length of the vessel represents a linear expanse.

Prepositions also differ in the implied focal point of their object (see Bierwisch 1988). To see what I mean by "implied focal point," consider prepositions like *to* and *from*. Both denote paths ending in points, but the former indicates progression towards the endpoint and the latter progression starting at the endpoint and ending back along some implied trajectory. To express this difference in focal point orientation, let us define two points, P_i for "initial point" and P_f for "final point," and a trajectory between them:

(9) $P_i. \dots\dots\dots\dots\dots\dots\dots\dots\dots\dots\dots\dots .P_f$

In most prepositions (e.g., *to*, *at*, *on*, *in*, *onto*, *into*), the focal point that is identified with the second (object) argument is P_f. But in some, like *from*, *off of*, and *out of* the focal point is set off from the final point; here we will designate this by identifying the second argument somewhat arbitrarily with P_i, although technically the focal point of these prepositions might be any point along the trajectory between P_i and P_f that is not P_f.

Prepositions also differ from one another with respect to the axis of orientation that they imply. Some prepositions like *at* or *to* imply nothing about axis of orientation, whereas others imply a vertical axis (*up*, *down*, *above*, *below*), a horizontal axis (*across*), or what might be called for lack of a better term an axis of depth in three-dimensional space (*in front of*, *behind*). To represent this, let us consider a three-dimensional space with three axes of orientation, each with an initial point and a final point, as follows:

(10)

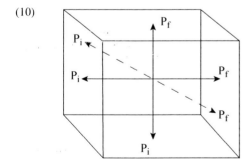

With this diagram I do not mean to make any formal or substantive claims about the mental representation of three-dimensional space, but only to provide a useful heuristic that will allow us to distinguish bodily characteristics of one preposition from another. In other words, I do not mean to imply that our mental representation of prepositions contains primitives like P_f and P_i, or a space like the one sketched in (10), but only that we have some way (perhaps even purely visual) to code such distinctions among prepositions.[5] Given this diagram, we can distinguish, for example, *up* and *down* from *behind* and *in front of*; the former prepositions imply a vertical axis, and the latter an axis of depth. Prepositions like *along* or *across* arguably refer to a horizontal axis.

One further parameter can be used to distinguish one preposition from another. As Jackendoff (1983) points out, some prepositions imply that the focal point is reached (*at, to*), while others imply only that the focal point is approached (*toward, behind*). Jackendoff refers to the former prepositions as bounded. I will represent the same notion with an element of meaning that I will call "limit." If the value of "limit" is positive, the preposition implies that the focal point is reached and that contact is effected; if negative, the preposition merely implies approach to the focal point. Again, my intention here is not to make a precise formal claim about the contents of mental representations, but simply to indicate how the relevant bodily distinctions between prepositions might be captured.

With these tools, we can arrive at a rough classification of both the skeletons and the bodies of some of the spatial prepositions in English, as illustrated in Table 4.1.

There are many things that remain unclear to me about the semantic representations of particular prepositions. I am not sure, for example, how to represent the fact that a preposition like *between* must have a split focal point, corresponding to the two individuals denoted by its plural or compound object (e.g., *between the posts* or *between the lamp and the table*). I am also not sure whether *across* is a [+IEPS] preposition or a [+Loc] preposition: perhaps the fact that one can say *She stood across the room* argues in favor of the latter, although *across* still seems to imply a path to me.[6] Nor is it clear to me whether prepositions like *up* and *down* imply the reaching of the limit or just approach to

---

5. Indeed both Lakoff (1987) and Tyler and Evans (2001) encode distinctions of this sort in the primary senses of the preposition *over* by using visual diagrams. Tyler and Evans (2001), for example, use symbols for what they call the Trajector (the object located), the Landmark (roughly, the location), and the vantage point from which the scene is viewed.

6. See Talmy (2000) for a discussion of the preposition *across*.

Table 4.1 *Semantics of English prepositions*

P	Skeleton	Dimension of object	Focus of object	Axis	Limit
at	[+Loc ([ ],[ ])]	0	P_f	any	yes
on	[+Loc ([ ],[ ])]	2	P_f	any	yes
in	[+Loc ([ ],[ ])]	3	P_f	any	yes
between	[+Loc ([ ],[ ])]	0	split P_f	any	no
by	[+Loc ([ ],[ ])]	0	P_f	any	no
near	[+Loc ([ ],[ ])]	0	P_f	any	no
over	[+Loc ([ ],[ ])]	0/2	P_f	vertical	no/yes
above	[+Loc ([ ],[ ])]	0	P_f	vertical	no
up	[+Loc ([ ],[ ])]	0	P_f	vertical	?
down	[+Loc ([ ],[ ])]	0	P_i	vertical	?
under	[+Loc ([ ],[ ])]	0/2	P_i	vertical	no/yes
below	[+Loc ([ ],[ ])]	0	P_i	vertical	no
in front of	[+Loc ([ ],[ ])]	0	P_f	depth	no
behind	[+Loc ([ ],[ ])]	0	P_i	depth	no
along	[+Loc ([ ],[ ])]	1	P_f	horizontal	no
to	[+IEPS([ ],[ ])]	0	P_f	any	yes
toward	[+IEPS([ ],[ ])]	0	P_f	any	no
from	[+IEPS([ ],[ ])]	0	P_i	any	yes
onto	[+IEPS([ ],[ ])]	2	P_f	any	yes
into	[+IEPS([ ],[ ])]	3	P_f	any	yes
off of	[+IEPS([ ],[ ])]	2	P_i	any	yes
out of (spatial)	[+IEPS([ ],[ ])]	3	P_i	any	yes
through	[+IEPS([ ],[ ])]	3	P_f	any	no
across	?[+IEPS([ ],[ ])]	2	P_f	horizontal?	yes
around	[−IEPS([ ],[ ])]		P_f	any	no
to & fro	[−IEPS ([ ])]			horizontal? or depth?	
back & forth	[−IEPS ([ ])]			horizontal? or depth?	
up & down	[−IEPS ([ ])]			vertical	

the focal point. Finally, I have said nothing about intransitive prepositions like *away*, *backwards*, and the like. Table 4.1 is, in other words, only a rough sketch of one way in which the semantics of prepositions might be represented. For now, however, it should be sufficient. The main point is that spatial prepositions have not only skeletons which are either locational or directional, but also bodies which express a number of different characteristics.

One point might be worth elaborating on, however. That is, prepositions often, indeed almost always, display a more complex polysemy than I have indicated here.[7] For example, prepositions like *over* and *under* seem to have several related senses. Central among the senses of *over* and *under* are a purely locational sense which implies mere approach to a limit, but not actual contact (e.g., *The helicopter hovered over the field; The chair is under the table*). Also prominent is another completive sense in which contact is implied (e.g., *They poured syrup over the pancakes; The bread is under the cloth*). The two senses seem to differ not only in whether the reaching of a limit is implied, but also in the dimensionality implied of the object: with the first sense, the object is conceived of as a point, but with the second (completive) sense, as more of a surface. I have therefore given the bodies of these prepositions two different values for the dimensionality and limit categories to reflect this lexical polysemy. Further senses of *over* include what might be called a "more" sense (*We saw over forty kinds of birds*) and an "excess" sense (*The milk flowed over the top of the glass*). These are perhaps best seen as sense extensions from the more central spatial meanings. We will return to this point and look at it more closely in section 4.2.3 below.

4.2   Location in derivation

If the feature [Loc] is of relevance in defining significant classes of simplex lexical items, we might expect it to figure in affixal meanings as well. In fact we should expect to find both [−Loc] affixes and [+Loc] affixes. Indeed, English has a wide range of prepositional affixes (*over-, after-, by-, down-, off-, through-*, etc.) which might be analyzed using the feature [+Loc]. We will explore one of these prefixes in section 4.2.3. More intriguing, however, would be the existence of [−Loc] affixes, and it is with this possibility that I will start. I will argue first in section 4.2.1 that English does indeed have two fairly straightforwardly [−Loc] affixes, the privative suffix *-less* and the verb-forming prefix *de-*. I will provide an analysis of these two morphemes, and then go on in section 4.2.2 to a larger question which suggests itself, namely the relationship between the notion of privativity and other sorts of negation. Specifically, I will explore the semantics of negative prefixes like *in-, un-, non-*, and *dis-* which have previously been discussed in work by Zimmer (1964) and Horn (1989/2001,

---

7. Indeed, in the framework of cognitive linguistics there is a wealth of literature on the preposition *over* disputing the number of primary senses. See Lakoff (1987), Brugman (1988), and Tyler and Evans (2001) for extensive discussion.

2002) and develop an argument that it makes sense to use the feature [−Loc] in characterizing these affixes as well. Further, I will argue that because negatives lack the richly paradigmatic body which we find in locative prepositions, this lack of a semantic body is played out in the nature of the polysemy – specifically constructional polysemy – exhibited by negative prefixes. In contrast, when we turn to prepositional affixes in section 4.2.3, we will see that the richness of the semantic body of simplex prepositions lends itself to a different kind of polysemy, namely sense extension, and that exactly this sort of polysemy is exhibited by prepositional affixes like *over-* as well. This section, then, has two goals, first to add to our description of the affixal semantics of English, and second, to look in more depth at the nature of polysemy that we might expect to find in derivational morphology.

4.2.1   Privative affixes

The simplest candidate for a privative affix in English is the suffix *-less* which productively forms adjectives from nouns (*loveless, hopeless, shoeless, heart-less, headless*).[8] As the semantics of *-less* are straightforwardly privative – *loveless* means "without love," *shoeless* "without shoes" – it makes sense to provide this suffix with a skeleton that adds not only the feature [−dynamic] but also the feature [−Loc]:

(11)   *-less*
          [−dynamic, −Loc ([   ], <base>)]

(12)   *shoeless*
          [−dynamic, −Loc ([ᵢ   ], [+material ([ᵢ   ])])]

In (12) I illustrate a composed skeleton for the word *shoeless* in which the Principle of Co-indexing has identified the argument of the affix with the "R" argument of the nominal base.[9]

Somewhat more intriguing is the prefix *de-* which most productively forms privative verbs from nouns:

(13)   *delouse, debug, deice, debark, dethrone*

---

8. Marchand (1969, 325) cites a number of deverbal forms like *tireless* and *exhaustless*, but this type of derivation seems never to have been particularly productive.

9. We find another privative element in the bound form *-free*, which is perhaps somewhere between a suffix and a compounding element, or what Marchand (1969) might call a "semi-suffix." *-free* is not quite identical to *-less*. Compare, for example, the words *shoe-free* and *shoe-less*: whereas the latter is purely privative and carries a rather negative emotive content, the former expresses privation, but along with privation a positive emotive content. Presumably the positive emotive content is part of the body of the independent morpheme *free*.

The prefix *de-* also attaches to verbs, most often to complex verbs formed with the suffixes *-ize*, *-ate*, and *-ify*, but also to some simplex verbs:

(14)   *demilitarize, denazify, decontaminate, deregister*

In these forms, the semantics of the affix might plausibly be called privative as well, although as we shall see below, it becomes more difficult with deverbal *de-* forms to distinguish purely privative meaning from more general negative semantics. We will therefore start our analysis with the denominal forms, in which the privative meaning is clearest.

In some sense, the verb-forming prefix *de-* is the privative correlate of the causative suffixes *-ize*, and *-ify*, and the unproductive prefix *en-*. In fact, there are pairs like *decolor* and *colorize*, and *dethrone* and *enthrone* that might serve as near-antonyms. Roughly paraphrased, to *delouse* is to cause something to come to be without lice, and to *dethrone* someone is to cause him or her not to be on the throne. In other words, the action denoted by *de-* verbs is one in which the first argument – the agent – does something such that the second argument is deprived of the base noun. The skeleton that suggests itself is precisely the same bipartite one I adopted for the causative suffixes *-ize* and *-ify* (repeated here in (15)), with the exception that the [+Loc] function of the causatives is replaced by the [−Loc] privative function:

(15)
-ize, -ify
[+dynamic ([$_{volitional -i}$], [$_j$])]; [+dynamic ([$_i$], [+dynamic, +IEPS ([$_j$], [+Loc ([   ])])]), <base>]

(16)
de-
[+dynamic ([$_{volitional -i}$], [$_j$])]; [+dynamic ([$_i$], [+dynamic, +IEPS ([$_j$], [−Loc ([   ])])]), <base>]

The indexing that obtains in *de-* derivatives is precisely the one that the Principle of Co-indexation would predict, with the base argument being identified with the lowest (unindexed) argument of the affix:

(17)
deice
[+dynamic ([$_{volitional -i}$], [$_j$])]; [+dynamic ([$_i$], [+dynamic, +IEPS ([$_j$], [−Loc ([$_k$])])]), [+material ([$_k$])]
de-   *ice*

The assumption that privation is a manifestation of the feature [Loc] therefore allows us to adopt an analysis of the prefix *de-* which makes clear its relationship with other verb-forming suffixes in English.

But the analysis does raise one question. That is, as pointed out in (14), *de-* attaches to verbs as well as to nouns, and primarily to verbs which themselves are complex, formed with the causative affixes *-ize* and *-ify* (e.g., *degasify, demilitarize*). One might wonder in cases like *degasify* or *demilitarize* whether *de-* still adds the whole causative skeleton in (16) to a complex word which already has the causative skeleton in (15). The most obvious answer would be that it does not (the resulting skeleton would seem unnecessarily complicated), and that instead on a verbal base *de-* merely changes the positive value of the [Loc] function to a negative one. But we should note as well that the feature-changing analysis carries with it an implication that privative *de-* has two representations, one when it attaches to nouns and another when it attaches to verbs. I will adopt the feature-changing analysis provisionally here, and defer until chapter 6 an initially less intuitive analysis which involves adding the skeleton in (16) to an already causative skeleton. In that chapter, I will look at other cases in which the same semantic material seems to be repeated in affixed forms with little or no semantic effect, and the double causative analysis of deverbal *de-* will cease to look so unintuitive.

The analysis I have provided for *-less* and *de-* here suggests that the feature [−Loc] is not an implausible addition to our arsenal of semantic features; it allows a simple analysis for the purely privative affixes. But perhaps there is more to be said about privation and privative affixes than this. For one thing, there are seemingly privative forms derived from affixes such as *un-* or *dis-* that we might otherwise characterize as negative or reversative; consider, for example, the verbs *unnerve*, which is plausibly paraphrased as "deprive of nerves," or *disarm*, which might be paraphrased as "cause to be without arms (i.e., weapons)." Further, there are at least a few denominal *de-* verbs like *deplane, detrain* which might plausibly be said to carry a reversative meaning ("get off a plane/train") rather than a purely privative one (where presumably they would have to mean something like "remove planes/trains from"). The question concerning the nature of the relationship between privation and other sorts of negation thus naturally arises. It is to this question that I will turn in the next section.

4.2.2   Negative affixes

Negation is an extremely complex semantic process that has been of interest to philosophers, logicians, and linguists alike for centuries, if not millennia. According to Horn (1989/2001), at least as far back in the western philosophical tradition as Plato, a major issue has been to determine whether all types of negation can be reduced to a single characterization. For Plato, negation is defined simply as "otherness"; not-P is "that which is distinct from P" (Horn 1989/2001,1). Aristotle admits two sorts of negation (Horn 1989/2001, 14–21): term negation, also called internal or strong negation by later logicians, involves (in structural terms) negation of a constituent ("Socrates is not intelligent") or negative affixation ("Socrates is unintelligent") and expresses either contrary or privative meaning, whereas predicate denial involves negation of an entire proposition ("It is not the case that Socrates is intelligent"), and expresses contradictory meaning. The main thread of modern logic has tended to reduce all negation to something more or less akin to predicate denial or external negation; Horn identifies the standard modern logical treatment (Frege's) with the Stoic's notion of *apophatikon*, essentially an external negative particle which may be iterated (Horn 1989/2001, 21–3). Again, the main reading of negation is reduced to the contradictory one.

We have already discussed the notion of privation, but it might be useful to digress at this point and unpack the notions of "contradictory" and "contrary" negation as they have figured in the philosophical and logical literature. Horn defines the former reading as in (18) and the latter as in (19):

(18)   Horn (1989/2001, 270)
        "Contradictory terms . . . exclude any middle term, an entity satisfying the
        range of the two opposed terms but falling under neither of them . . ."
(19)   Horn (1989/2001, 268)
        "As we have seen, any two mutually inconsistent terms are contraries in the
        broad sense; two sentences are in contrary opposition if they can be
        simultaneously false but not simultaneously true."

Contradictory negation results in two terms (P and not-P) which cannot both be true at the same time; additionally, one must be true and the other false (either P or not-P). In the standard terminology of logic, contradictory negation follows the Law of the Excluded Middle. Contrary negation also implies that two terms (P and not-P) cannot be true at the same time, but it allows for both terms to be false at the same time; it does not adhere to the Law of the Excluded Middle.

It is not my purpose here to survey the logical and philosophical literature which attempts to reduce all negation to a single operator, much less to settle this thorny issue. Rather, as an entree into the semantic behavior of affixal negation, I point out that there has been a long-standing debate over this issue. We have seen that the system of lexical semantic representation I have proposed makes available a function [−Loc] which nicely characterizes the notion of privation or lack. But what is the relationship between the notion of privation, and notions like contrary and contradictory negation? Is it possible that the same semantic function should be used to characterize all three notions? This is an especially interesting question for us, as it appears that the main negative affixes of English – *in-*, *un-*, *non-*, and *dis-* – can often express a whole range of privative, negative (both contrary and contradictory), and for that matter reversative meanings. We might therefore wonder whether it is in fact the right move to have only a single semantic function to represent them all.

In (20) I illustrate the range of lexical categories that each of the negative affixes *un-*, *in-*, *non-*, and *dis-* attaches to, and the range of polysemy that each affix exhibits.[10]

(20)   a. *un-*   on A: *unbreakable, unhappy*
                on N: *unease, untruth, uncola*
                on V: *undress, uncork, unlearn*
        b. *in-*   on A: *inaccurate, infinite, inarticulate*
                on N: *incapacity, inaction*
        c. *non-*   on A: *nonmoral, nonviolent, nonflammable*
                on N: *nonsmoker, nonviolence, nonpayment*
        d. *dis-*   on A: *discourteous, disloyal, disengaged*
                on N: *discomfort, disrespect*
                on V: *dislike, disobey, disrobe*

I note first that these affixes vary in productivity, and further, in their productivity with respect to particular syntactic categories; negative *in-* and *un-* favor adjectives, with *un-* being the more productive of the two. *In-* only infrequently attaches to nouns, and *un-* perhaps a bit more often; as Horn (2002) shows, it is possible to find a surprising number of nonce forms with *un-* on nouns. Reversative *un-* and *dis-* are both relatively productive on verbs. *Dis-* sometimes attaches to adjectives and nouns as well, but not with a high degree of productivity. *Non-* is the only one of the four with any productivity with respect to nouns; it is quite productive with adjectives as well. Productivity aside, however, I intend to look at the full range of forms with negative prefixes, as this gives us a better picture in the end of their lexical semantic behavior.

10. In this and what follows, I use examples culled from the CELEX database and the OED. I do not attempt to categorize all items listed with these affixes in these sources exhaustively, but rely on a large and (I hope) representative sample. In some cases, as with *un-* on nouns and the other unproductive categories, I have been relatively exhaustive in listing attested items in the lists in sections 4.2.2.1–4.2.2.3.

In terms of semantics, the most restrictive of the negative affixes is *non-*. *Non-* does not attach to verbs, and therefore does not display either a reversative or a privative meaning. It is strictly negative, and in fact, as has been pointed out by both Zimmer (1964) and Horn (1989/2001), more often than not gives a contradictory reading. This generalization seems quite solid when *non-* is attached to nouns (someone is either a smoker or a nonsmoker, for example – there is nothing in between). And it seems generally, although not always, true when *non-* is attached to adjectives; for example, I can find a movie neither violent nor nonviolent but there is nothing in between flammable and nonflammable for me; a substance is either one or the other. For me, then, *violent* and *nonviolent* are contraries, *flammable* and *nonflammable* contradictories. Examples with the contrary reading are, however, relatively hard to find.

The other affixes in (20) – *un-*, *in-*, and *dis-* – show a much wider range of interpretation. The majority of forms with these prefixes have contrary or contradictory negative readings. For example, *unhappy*, *inarticulate*, and *discourteous* have contrary readings; one can be neither *happy* nor *unhappy*, neither *articulate* nor *inarticulate*, neither *courteous* nor *discourteous*. On the other hand, *unbreakable*, *infinite*, and *disengaged* have contradictory readings for me; things are either *breakable* or *unbreakable*, *finite* or *infinite*, and people either *engaged* or *disengaged* with something – there is no middle ground to be occupied.

Verbal forms in *un-* are usually not negative (either contrary or contradictory), though, but rather reversative; *undress* means to reverse the action of dressing. In fact, at least the negative and reversative *un-* prefixes seem historically to be distinct in English (Marchand 1969, Horn 1989/2001), and at least one scholar has in recent years claimed that the negative *un-*, which attaches to adjectives, and the reversative *un-*, which attaches to verbs, are still synchronically distinct and homophonous (Dowty 1979; Horn 1989/2001, 287 cites Covington 1981 as maintaining this position). But Horn himself casts some doubt on this continued distinctness: "Given that what so-called reversative *un-* actually reverses is not the action denoted by the verbal base but rather the result of that action, the semantic relation between the two sets of derived forms [reversatives and negatives – R. L.] may be closer than first appears" (2001, 287), and Horn (2002) takes an even stronger stand on this issue.[11] It is not all that implausible, in other words, to link the reversative meaning with the negative meanings. *Dis-* shows both negative meanings on verbs (e.g., *dislike*) and reversative

11. Marchand (1969) seems to share this opinion.

meaning (e.g., *disrobe*). Further, as mentioned at the end of the previous section, some verbs in *un-* and *dis-* even display a privative meaning.

The picture that emerges is one in which there are multiple affixes which display multiple related meanings. Why should this be? It has been the main hypothesis of this book that the existence of multiple affixes overlapping in meaning is a result of the parsimony of the featural system on which the semantic skeleton is based, and that polysemy – at least constructional polysemy – arises from the interaction of the rather abstract meanings attributed to affixes with the meanings of different kinds of bases. I will next try to argue that it makes sense to say that the feature [−Loc] is the only feature needed for affixal negation, and that this single representation gives rise to four slightly different nuances of meaning – privation, contrary negation, contradictory negation, and reversativity – depending on the type of base to which it attaches.

I argue in what follows that a single semantic feature characterizes the skeletons of the negative affixes *in-*, *un-*, and *dis-*, namely the feature [−Loc]. Given this semantic representation, these prefixes impose an interpretation of nonlocation/nonexistence over some part of the base skeleton. In fact, I assert that they provide the same skeleton, namely that in (21):

(21)   *in-, un-, dis-*
         [−Loc ([   ], <base.>]

These affixes therefore differ from the privative affixes discussed in the previous section only in that they carry nothing but the feature [−Loc] in their skeletons. I must now argue that the various interpretations of negation – from reversative on verbs through contradictory and contrary readings on other categories – follow from the interaction of this feature with various semantic features of the base to which the feature attaches. In order to show this, we will need to look more carefully at the data.

4.2.2.1   [−Loc] on verbal bases

I start here with the negative prefixes *un-* and *dis-* which attach to verbal bases. It has been noted in previous literature that *un-* attaches selectively to particular types of verbs. Both Dowty (1979) and Horn (2002) consider the distribution of *un-* on verbs. Dowty (1979) suggests that *un-* prefers accomplishments in the Vendlerian classification – that is, verbs that are telic but involve change of state. Horn (2002) points out that *un-* occasionally attaches to verbs of other sorts as well. Let us first look at the distribution of *un-* and *dis-* on verbs in terms of the featural classes that we developed in chapter 1:

(22)

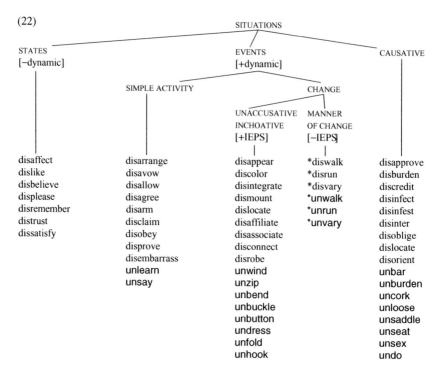

STATES [−dynamic]	SIMPLE ACTIVITY	UNACCUSATIVE INCHOATIVE [+IEPS]	MANNER OF CHANGE [−IEPS]	CAUSATIVE
disaffect	disarrange	disappear	*diswalk	disapprove
dislike	disavow	discolor	*disrun	disburden
disbelieve	disallow	disintegrate	*disvary	discredit
displease	disagree	dismount	*unwalk	disinfect
disremember	disarm	dislocate	*unrun	disinfest
distrust	disclaim	disaffiliate	*unvary	disinter
dissatisfy	disobey	disassociate		disoblige
	disprove	disconnect		dislocate
	disembarrass	disrobe		disorient
	unlearn	unwind		unbar
	unsay	unzip		unburden
		unbend		uncork
		unbuckle		unloose
		unbutton		unsaddle
		undress		unseat
		unfold		unsex
		unhook		undo

Certain generalizations emerge when we look at the data in this way. First, only *dis-* attaches to stative verbs, and for the most part it is the only negative affix compatible with SIMPLE ACTIVITY verbs (*unlearn* and *unsay* are the only examples from the CELEX lexical database that fit into this category, and they strike me as slightly strange).[12] Second, neither *dis-* nor *un-* attaches to verbs which bear the feature [−IEPS], that is, those verbs which imply some change, but not a directed change. *Dis-* and *un-* both attach relatively freely to verbs which are causative or causative/inchoative alternants, although clearly there are differences in the lexical semantics of the particular sets of verbs they favor. Specifically, *un-* selects for causative and/or inchoative bases which imply a result that is not fixed and permanent; in these verbs, the feature [−Loc] takes scope over the result, asserting that it no longer has existence. So if *button*

---

12. Note, for example, that they are most comfortably used in negative or subjunctive contexts: *You can't unsay what you said* vs. *?You can unsay what you said* or *I wish I could unlearn that bad habit* vs. *?I unlearned that bad habit.* Horn (2002, 14–15) gives an insightful analysis of such cases, arguing that the *un-* on activity verbs actually changes the lexical class of its base, turning them into change of state verbs. So *unsay* means something like "cause to come into a state in which one takes back the saying of something."

means something informally like "cause to go into a state of being buttoned," and "being buttoned" is a state which is mutable, then the *un-* verb results in the interpretation "cause to go into a state of being not buttoned" – which is interpreted as a reversal of the action. The fact that *un-* cannot attach to a causative/inchoative verb like *explode* (**unexplode*), whose resulting state (being in bits) is quite permanent, suggests that I am on the right track.

On the other hand, *dis-* allows a broader selection of bases. In fact, it takes causatives and inchoatives of various types. Where its bases are those which imply a result which is not fixed or permanent, that is, where its bases overlap semantically with those of *un-*, it too delivers the reversative meaning. Note, for example, that we have verbs like *disrobe* alongside *undress*, and *disinter* alongside *uncover*. Where its bases are causatives and inchoatives of other types, or indeed statives or simple activity verbs, it delivers a more standard negative reading.

This look at the data suggests that there is no need so far to postulate a reversative meaning distinct from the general negative [−Loc] meaning.[13] The reversative reading is not distinct to a single prefix, but arises whenever the semantic structure (skeleton and body) of the base is such that the feature can take scope over a result which is interpretable as not fixed or permanent.

4.2.2.2   [−Loc] on adjectival bases

In this section I argue that, just as it is unnecessary to postulate a distinct reversative skeleton within my framework, it is unnecessary to proliferate affixal skeletons to derive the distinction in reading between contradictory and contrary negation. To show this, we must now take a closer look at negative prefixes on adjectival bases. In considering the data in Table 4.2, several points emerge. First, all three negative prefixes attach to adjectives – both gradable and nongradable ones. In fact, the attachment of any of these three prefixes has no effect on the gradability of the resulting derived forms; gradable bases yield gradable derived forms and nongradable bases nongradable derived forms.

A further pattern emerges from the data in Table 4.2. Prefixed forms derived from gradable adjectives yield contrary readings, whereas nongradable forms allow only the contradictory reading. I interpret this pattern as follows. In order for a contrary reading to be possible, the base must denote a scalar quality where it is in some sense easy to conceive of an intermediate state; the easier it is to conceive of such an intermediate state (e.g., between *happy* and *unhappy*), the easier it is to get a contrary reading. Where an intermediate state is less plausible

---

13. In this, then, I concur with the earlier analyses of Maynor 1979, Andrews 1986, and Horn 2002.

Table 4.2 *English negative prefixes* dis-, in-, un-

	Base is gradable?	Derived word is gradable?	Derived form has Contradictory (CD) or Contrary (CR)?
discontented	yes	yes	CR
discourteous	yes	yes	CR
dishonest	yes	yes	CR
disingenuous	yes	yes	CR
disinterested	yes	yes	CR
disloyal	yes	yes	CR
dispassionate	yes	yes	CR
dissimilar	yes	yes	CR
disengaged	no	no	CD
inaccurate	yes	yes	CR
inadequate	yes	yes	CR
inappropriate	yes	yes	CR
inarticulate	yes	yes	CR
incompetent	yes	yes	CR
inconvenient	yes	yes	CR
incurious	yes	yes	CR
indecisive	yes	yes	CR
indefinite	yes	yes	CR
indirect	yes	yes	CR
ineffectual	yes	yes	CR
inelastic	yes	yes	CR
inflexible	yes	yes	CR
inhuman	yes	yes	CR
inalienable	no	no	CD
incongruous	no	no	CD
incurable	no	no	CD
inanimate	no	no	CD
incalculable	no	no	CD
incomparable	no	no	CD
indivisible	no	no	CD
inedible	no	no	CD
ineligible	no	no	CD
inexact	no	no	CD
infinite	no	no	CD
innumerable	no	no	CD
unbeatable	no	no	CD
unable	yes	yes	CR
unaccustomed	yes	yes	CR
unaware	no	no	CD

Table 4.2 (*cont.*)

	Base is gradable?	Derived word is gradable?	Derived form has Contradictory (CD) or Contrary (CR)?
unbalanced (in psychological sense)	yes	yes	CR
uncertain	yes	yes	CR
uncivil	yes	yes	CR
undecided	yes	yes	CR
undeniable	no	no	CD
uneven	yes	yes	CR
uneventful	yes	yes	CR
unfamiliar	yes	yes	CR
unfit	yes	yes	CR
unfriendly	yes	yes	CR
ungenerous	yes	yes	CR
ungrateful	yes	yes	CR
unhealthy	yes	yes	CR
unjust	yes	yes	CR
unkind	yes	yes	CR
unlikely	yes	yes	CR
unnatural	yes	yes	CR
unpleasant	yes	yes	CR
unmatchable	no	no	CD
unAmerican (not acting like an American)	yes	yes	CR
unalienable	no	no	CD
unbeaten	no	no	CD
unborn	no	no	CD
unbroken	no	no	CD
undone	no	no	CD
undue	no	no	CD
undying	no	no	CD
unfeeling	yes	yes	CR
unimpeachable	no	no	CD
unknown	no	no	CD
unlawful	no	no	CD
unlettered	no	no	CD
unmarried	no	no	CD
unparliamentary	no	no	CD
untrue	no	no	CD
unequal	no	no	CD

(for example, I find it harder to think of an intermediate state between *curable* and *incurable*, than between *happy* and *unhappy*), the contradictory reading is favored.

Note that the judgments on gradability are my own. I fully expect that others might find some adjectives which I find gradable to be ungradable for them, and vice versa. What I would also expect, however, is that these judgments would still correlate with the particular negative reading, as I have suggested here: gradability correlates with the contrary reading, nongradability with the contradictory one.

What this means for my analysis of the negative prefixes is that once again, it is possible to attribute the polysemy exhibited by affixed forms to interactions between the semantics of the affix and that of the base. *In-*, *un-*, and *dis-* all allow either the contradictory or the contrary reading, but the contrary or contradictory reading is generally correlated with the gradability of the base adjective.

It is worth pointing out that my examination of the data gives a somewhat different picture of the behavior of *un-*, *in-*, and *non-* on adjectives from Horn (1989/2001).[14] Horn makes the following generalizations concerning these prefixes (Horn 1989/2001, 282–3):

> *iN-* tends to combine only with scalar predicates on their evaluative readings; the resultant derived forms are lexicalized, semantically and phonologically opaque, and tend to be assigned a contrary and generally depreciatory . . . sense or connotation, often involving an opposition to some expected or established norm.
>
> *non-* is much freer in its connotations . . . ; the resultant derived forms are in general unlexicalized, semantically and phonologically transparent, and involve the formal and/or descriptive (rather than emotive or evaluative) dimensions of meaning.
>
> *un-* forms are situated between the *iN-* and *non-* forms with respect to these criteria, depending on how productively or freely the prefix combines with a given base; the less productive, the more like *iN-*; the more productive, the more like *non-*.

We will return to a discussion of *non-* shortly. The data in Table 4.2 suggest that *in-* does attach to nongradable bases, contrary to Horn's claim, and that when it does, the resulting forms tend to have the contradictory reading. Further, again contrary to Horn's claim, many forms in *in-* are semantically transparent (e.g., *indirect, ineffectual, incurious, incurable,* among others).[15]

---

14. Horn (1989/2001) does not discuss adjectives in *dis-* in detail.

15. Horn himself is equivocal on this point. Later in his discussion of affixal negation, he offers much the same observation that I have made (1989/2001, 281), citing Sapir (1944) and Ducrot (1973) as previous proponents of this view: "In each case, the contrary reading is possible to the extent that an adjectival stem can be regarded as a GRADABLE or SCALAR value."

Table 4.3 *English negative prefixes:* non-

	Base is gradable?	Derived word is gradable?	Derived form has Contradictory (CD) or Contrary (CR) reading?
noncontentious	yes	no	CD
nonmoral	yes	no	CD
nonassertive	yes	no	CD
noncontributory	no	no	CD
nonflammable	yes	no	CD
nonresident	no	no	CD
nonrestrictive	yes	no	CD
nonstandard	yes	no	CD
nonverbal	yes	no	CD
nonwhite	yes	no	CD
nonrational	yes	no	CD
nonprofessional	yes	no	CD
nonAmerican	no	no	CD
nonbreakable	no	no	CD
nonviolent	yes	yes	CR
nonsane	yes	yes	CR
nonsubstantial	yes	yes	CR

Oddly, Horn himself indicates later in his chapter on affixal negation that some forms with the prefix *in-* (*inconceivable, impossible*) have the contradictory reading (1989/2001, 298). In fact, the data in Table 4.2 suggest a far stronger correlation between gradability and negative reading (i.e., either contrary or contradictory) than Horn's analysis would suggest.[16]

We turn now to the prefix *non-* where Horn is perhaps closer to correct in his characterization. Consider the data in Table 4.3, where again the judgments are mine. Table 4.3 suggests that *non-* attaches to all kinds of adjectival bases, both gradable and ungradable, and quite consistently forms negatives that are both nongradable and contradictory in meaning. But not always. For me, as noted above, the form *nonviolent* is gradable and carries a contrary reading; to this pair might be added forms like *nonsane* and *nonsubstantial* which for me are identical in meaning to their more frequent cousins *insane* and *insubstantial*; further, all carry the contrary reading. What then is the semantic contribution of *non-*?

16. Horn (2002, 10), however, does acknowledge a strong correlation between gradability and the contrary reading.

A clue might be found when we look at other bases which occur with more than one of the negative affixes. Horn has observed that *non-* often has a slightly more neutral evaluative flavor than *un-* and *in-* (Horn 1989/2001, 280): "As noted by Jespersen, Marchand, and other descriptive morphologists, *un-* and (especially) *iN-* derivatives tend to negate the emotive senses of the stems to which they attach, while *non-* and (to a lesser degree) *un-* prefixes negate objective or descriptive content." Horn cites such examples as *immoral* versus *nonmoral*, *unprofessional* versus *nonprofessional*, and *unscientific* versus *nonscientific*. That is, although there are pairs of negatives like *insubstantial* and *nonsubstantial* and *insane* and *nonsane* for which (at least for me and the OED) there seems to be no difference in meaning, the vast majority of couplets of this sort tend to pick up specialized meanings.[17] When they do, the *in-* or *un-* forms tend to express evaluative negation and the corresponding *non-* forms a more evaluatively neutral negation. This is certainly the case with pairs like *nonmoral* versus *immoral*, *nonAmerican* versus *unAmerican*, and *nonprofessional* versus *unprofessional*. Further, I observe that the more evaluatively neutral the interpretation of the base, the less gradable its interpretation. For example, someone either holds American citizenship or not, or practices some profession or does not; these are the senses of *American* and *professional* that we find in the *non-* derivatives. In contrast, *American* in *unAmerican* means something more like "displaying the qualities of an American" and *professional* in *unprofessional* something like "acting like a professional." These are qualities that are more scalar in nature.

A possible analysis then suggests itself. The prefix *non-* carries precisely the same skeleton that the other negative affixes do:

(23)   *non-*
         [−Loc ([   ], <base>)]

That is, it makes no special semantic contribution. This accounts for the ability of the prefix to give rise to both the contradictory and the contrary meanings, as happens with the other negative affixes. The preference for the contradictory reading arises not from the meaning of the affix itself, but rather from the tendency of the affix to select for the evaluatively neutral meaning in bases which admit of polysemy; the evaluatively neutral sense of the base in turn disfavors a gradable interpretation. Where a base has no evaluatively neutral sense (as I think is the case with *sane*) or no evaluatively charged sense (as is the case with *substantial*), the *non-* form behaves exactly as the other negative prefixes do.

17. We might attribute this to the often cited tendency to avoid synonymy in the lexicon.

4.2.2.3 [−Loc] on nominal bases

The only set of negative-prefixed forms that we must still consider are the ones with nominal bases. In (24) I give examples of nouns derived with *in-*, *un-*, *non-*, and *dis-*:

(24)

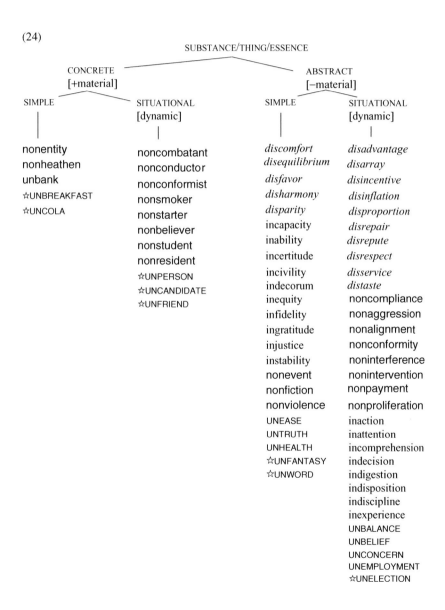

SUBSTANCE/THING/ESSENCE

CONCRETE [+material] ABSTRACT [−material]

SIMPLE | SITUATIONAL [dynamic] | SIMPLE | SITUATIONAL [dynamic]

SIMPLE	SITUATIONAL [dynamic]	SIMPLE	SITUATIONAL [dynamic]
nonentity	noncombatant	*discomfort*	*disadvantage*
nonheathen	nonconductor	*disequilibrium*	*disarray*
unbank	nonconformist	*disfavor*	*disincentive*
☆UNBREAKFAST	nonsmoker	*disharmony*	*disinflation*
☆UNCOLA	nonstarter	*disparity*	*disproportion*
	nonbeliever	incapacity	*disrepair*
	nonstudent	inability	*disrepute*
	nonresident	incertitude	*disrespect*
	☆UNPERSON	incivility	*disservice*
	☆UNCANDIDATE	indecorum	*distaste*
	☆UNFRIEND	inequity	noncompliance
		infidelity	nonaggression
		ingratitude	nonalignment
		injustice	nonconformity
		instability	noninterference
		nonevent	nonintervention
		nonfiction	nonpayment
		nonviolence	nonproliferation
		UNEASE	inaction
		UNTRUTH	inattention
		UNHEALTH	incomprehension
		☆UNFANTASY	indecision
		☆UNWORD	indigestion
			indisposition
			indiscipline
			inexperience
			UNBALANCE
			UNBELIEF
			UNCONCERN
			UNEMPLOYMENT
			☆UNELECTION

Examples with stars are taken from Horn (2002). I note first that negative prefixes seem generally less productive on nouns, and in some cases quite unproductive. On the whole, *non-*, *dis-*, and *in-* favor abstract bases, and of the abstract bases, situational (often deverbal) ones. In other words, the more "verby" the noun base is, the more productive negative affixation is with nouns. While there is not a huge number of nouns in *un-*, Horn (2002) shows that these forms are indeed more frequent than one might expect. There are in fact quite a few examples of *un-* on concrete nouns and on proper names in the corpus that Horn has collected. Of the four negative prefixes, *non-* seems most comfortable on nouns; it is the one which attaches most often to concrete nouns, in particular people or instrument nouns.

Second, all four prefixes yield a negative or privative reading when attached to nouns, and generally, the prefixes behave just as with adjectives with respect to alternation between the contradictory and contrary readings. *Non-* favors the contradictory reading, although again, to the extent that a noun can be descriptive of a scalar property, the contrary reading is permitted. The other prefixes allow either the contradictory or the contrary reading, depending on our ability to conceive of the base as having scalar properties or allowing some sort of intermediate state:

(25)   a. *non-*

        *He was neither a smoker nor a nonsmoker.   (CD)

        He was neither a player nor a nonplayer (meaning some   (CR)
           one who matters or is a significant participant in some affair)

    b. *un-*

        *His state was one of neither employment nor unemployment.   (CD)

        Her attitude was one of neither ease nor unease.   (CR)

    c. *dis-*

        *His state was one of neither equilibrium nor disequilibrium.   (CD)

        Her feeling was one of neither comfort nor discomfort.   (CR)

    d. *in-*

        *He displayed neither fidelity nor infidelity.   (CD)

        She showed neither experience nor inexperience.   (CR)

Horn (2002) argues that nonce nouns in *un-* also often have a privative reading, rather than a contrary or contradictory one. For example, an *unperson* is someone who lacks significant human characteristics, and an *uncola* a soft drink which is missing some of the salient characteristics of a cola.

Again, I think that the data support the present analysis. There is no need to distinguish privativity from other types of negativity, or to build the contradictory/contrary distinction into our theory of lexical semantics. The interpretation of various negative-prefixed nouns follows from the properties of the prefix together with the semantic nature of the noun and whether or not it can be construed as scalar.

There is one final point that I should address before I finish my discussion of negative prefixes. That is, it has long been observed that negative prefixes tend not to attach to simplex bases which themselves have substantial negative content; indeed Zimmer (1964) is solely devoted to an exploration of this generalization, and Horn (1989/2001) looks carefully at this claim as well. The generalization is as follows: we tend to find *unhappy* but not *unsad*, *unhealthy* but not *unsick*, and so on. Although this issue has been a central one in discussions of negative affixation in previous literature, I will defer discussion of it to chapter 6, where I will look more generally at the issue of semantic restrictions on affixation.

4.2.2.4   Summary

The negative prefixes *in-*, *un-*, *dis-*, and *non-* are all polysemous, and they overlap in meaning. But they also differ in the kinds of bases they attach to and in the readings that emerge with different classes of bases. The reversative meaning arises only when a negative affix is attached to a verbal base which implies a result which is mutable. The contrary meaning appears only when the base (either adjectival or nominal) has a scalar or gradable interpretation. The contradictory meaning arises from bases that have strictly nonscalar interpretations. The particular kind of negative reading therefore does not need to be attributed to multiple representations of the affix, but as we have seen before, arises from the parsimony of the single affixal skeleton and its interaction with the syntactic and semantic properties of different bases. The negative affixes of English are therefore a prime example of constructional polysemy.

Further, we can now see again why English has multiple affixes that cover the same ground. If the semantic system that characterizes core lexical meanings – that is, the feature system of which skeletal functions are composed – makes available only one function [−Loc] with which to characterize negation, then any prefix with a negative meaning would have to fall into this single semantic slot. English historically had its own native negative prefix (*un-*), but when it borrowed non-native negative affixes (*in-*, *dis-*, *non-*), there was nowhere for them to go but into the same semantic space.

4.2.3   *Prepositional affixes*

English has many prepositions which double as prefixes, among them *after* (*aftershock*, *afterthought*), *out* (*outhouse*, *outsell*), *under* (*underarm*, *undervalue*), and *down* (*downspout*, *downplay*). Perhaps the most interesting of the prepositional prefixes is, for our purposes, the prefix *over-* which attaches to

nouns, adjectives, and verbs, and displays extensive polysemy. When it attaches
to verbs, it shows interesting and systematic effects on the argument structures
which are correlated with different senses. In this section, I will explore the
polysemy of *over-* and try to determine to what extent it is constructional (that
is, to be attributed to the parsimony of the semantic skeleton) and to what extent
it is the result of sense extension. We will see that the polysemy of *over-* largely
follows and is derived from the polysemy of the independent preposition *over*,
and therefore is much richer and more complex than the polysemy of affixes
that have no derivational source in the simplex lexicon.

In (26) I illustrate the three central uses of the prefix *over-* on bases of various
categories:

(26)   a. pure locational sense
           on N: *overlord, overarm*
           on V: *overfly, overarch, overhang*
        b. locational and completive
           on N: *overcoat, overshoe*
           on V: *overrun, overpower*
        c. to excess
           on N: *overconfidence, overdose*
           on V: *overdevelop, overcharge*
           on A: *overfond, overgenerous*

In its purely locational sense, the prefix *over-* denotes position higher than,
above, or outermost. Slightly different is the sense displayed by the examples in
(26b), which add to the locational meaning a sense of completion. An *overcoat*
or *overshoe* is a coat or shoe that is completely covering other garments; to
overrun is to spread over something to the extent that it is completely covered.
Perhaps most frequent and productive with the prefix *over-* is the sense which I
have labeled "excess"; this sense occurs on bases of all lexical categories, and
adds the meaning "too much." So an *overdose* is too large a dose, to *overvalue*
is to value too highly, and so on.

The prefix *over-* not only displays polysemy, but also has systematic effects
on the argument structure of its bases. With the purely locational or locational
and completive senses, it often, but not always, adds an argument:

(27)   a. locational: *overfly, overarch*
           *The airplane flew the field.   The airplane overflew the field.
           *The tree arched the driveway.   The tree overarched the driveway.
        b. locational and completive: *overrun, overshadow*
           *The enemy ran the battlefield.   The enemy overran the battlefield.
           The trees shadowed the driveway. The trees overshadowed the driveway.

With the "excess" sense it most frequently has no effect at all on the argument structure of the base verb; notably, even with an intransitive base, this *over-* does not add an argument:[18]

(28)   *overdevelop*:   They developed the area.   They overdeveloped the area.
        overexpose: They exposed the film.   They overexposed the film.
        oversleep: The children slept.   The children overslept.

We will want our analysis of the prefix *over-* to account not only for the polysemy which the affix displays, but also for the argument structure effects of the affix.

The key to understanding the semantic and syntactic behavior of the prefix *over-* is to realize that this prefix (and other prepositional prefixes) have something that the other derivational affixes we have looked at so far do not have, namely a body. That is, whereas *-er* or *-ize* or *un-* consist semantically of pure skeleton without body, if an affix like *over-* is simply a bound form of its lexical counterpart, we would expect it to have a much more complex semantic representation. Whereas the polysemy of affixes like *-er*, *-ize*, and *un-* must largely come from the interaction of skeletal features with bases of various kinds, the more complex semantic representations of prepositional affixes can give rise to a much richer and more complex polysemy. Let us look, then, in a bit more detail at the prepositional meanings of *over*.

Prepositional *over* occurs both in transitive and in intransitive (for the OED "adverbial") contexts. Transitive *over* can be purely locational (*The bird flew over the tree*) or locational and completive (*He threw a blanket over her*; *There were cottages spread over the moor*). Intransitive (adverbial) *over* shows both of these senses as well (locational: *He bent over*; locational and completive: *The dress was studded over with sequins*). Both transitive and intransitive *over* can display the "excess" reading as well: *Your article is over the page limit* (example from Tyler and Evans 2001, 749); *The milk spilled over*.

Both transitive and intransitive *over* can have metaphorical senses as well. In a sentence like *The king presides over his subjects* the location is extended metaphorically to the realm of power or authority. In *The payment was spread over five years* the preposition is extended to the temporal realm. Both transitive and intransitive *over* also display a sense which is locational but seems not to imply a vertical axis, for example in sentences like *The ship sailed over the seas* or *He climbed over*; here *over* means something close to "across." Intransitive

18. Oddly, however, there is one verb in *over-* with the "excess" sense that seems to lose an argument: *overeat* (She ate (pickles) / *She overate pickles). While the base verb *eat* may have an internal argument or not, the prefixed verb *overeat* does not occur with an internal argument. We will return to this case below

over has a number of other uses as well, including senses like "past" (*The movie is over*) and "repetition" (*I had to do it over*). See Tyler and Evans (2001) for an analysis of the complex polysemy of *over* in the framework of cognitive linguistics.

In section 4.1, I suggested briefly that *over* has a single skeleton, but also displays some variation in its bodily characteristics. The lexical entry for *over* was suggested there to be something like (29):

(29)   *over*
        skeleton: [+Loc ([   ], [   ])]
        body: dimension-0/2; focus-P_f; axis-vertical; limit-no/yes

That is, *over* is a locational preposition which takes two arguments. It is distinguished from other locational prepositions in its bodily characteristics, treating its object argument sometimes as a point, and sometimes as a surface. Its focal point is P_f, meaning implied progression towards the endpoint. It implies (at least in the senses we will be concerned with here) a vertical axis of orientation. And, as we saw above, *over* sometimes implies mere approach to the endpoint and sometimes the reaching of the limit.

The representation in (29) is not quite detailed enough for our purposes, however. First, as *over* may be either transitive or intransitive, we must indicate the optionality of the second argument; I will do so here somewhat arbitrarily by underlining the second argument. Second, it should be made clear that the dimensionality and limit characteristics often correlate with one another. Generally, with the purely locational meaning (e.g., *The bird flew over the tree*) the object argument is interpreted as point-like and the prepositional relation is one of approach but not contact with the object; a bird can only be over a tree if it is not actually touching the tree. With the completive sense, however, the object is more often conceived of as a surface, and contact with that surface is implied. So in a sentence like *They poured syrup over the pancakes*, the pancakes are two-dimensional objects every bit of which is touched by syrup. I propose, then, that the semantic representation of prepositional *over* should have a single skeleton, but at least two variant bodies:

(30)   *over*
        skeleton: [+Loc ([   ], [___])]
        body-1 (locational):   dimension-0; focus-P_f; axis-vertical; limit-no
        body-2 (locational/completive):   dimension-2; focus-P_f; axis-vertical; limit-yes

This would account for two of the main senses of *over*. Perhaps other combinations of body characteristics will be needed for some of the other senses of *over* (e.g., "across"), but I will leave this issue open, as it does not figure in what follows.

The third, "excess," meaning of *over* is generally seen as a sense extension from the more central locational senses. Tyler and Evans (2001, 756–7), for example, suggest that it proceeds naturally from an inference that greater elevation implies greater quantity, and that greater quantity in turn leads to going beyond the capacity of a real or metaphorical container. That is, in this sense, *over* is still locational, but in our terms its body adds the notion of going beyond the limit of the focal point P_f:

(31)   *over* (excess)
        [+Loc ([   ], [   ])]
        body-3 (excess): dimension-0; focus:-P_f; axis-vertical; limit- >P_f

In effect, then, the polysemy of the preposition *over* is manifested by a variety of different bodies that arise as sense extensions.

The simplest hypothesis that we could make is that prefixal *over-* is nothing more than a bound version of prepositional *over*, taking on much of the polysemy of its independent counterpart. Not surprisingly, the prefix *over-* displays a large part of the semantic range of its prepositional counterpart. In its prefixal form, *over-* takes three of the possible meanings of the preposition and adds them to lexical bases, adding not only the meaning conveyed by the affixal skeleton, but also the bodily characteristics borrowed from the free form:

(32)   *over-*
        a. locational   skeleton: [+Loc ([   ], [   ], <base>)]
                          body: dimension-0; focus-P_f; axis-vertical; limit-no
        b. locational/   skeleton: [+Loc ([   ], [   ], <base>)]
           completive
                          body: dimension-2; focus-P_f; axis-vertical; limit-yes
        c. excess   skeleton: [+Loc ([   ]), <base>)]
                          body: dimension-0; focus-P_f; axis-vertical; limit- > P_f

The lexical semantic representations of the prefix *over-* are identical to those of the simplex preposition *over* in all respects but one; that is, in (32c), the "excess" sense of the prefix *over-* is associated with an intransitive skeleton. We will return to this point shortly.

The skeletons (and bodies) in the lexical representations in (32) add to lexical bases, and the Principle of Co-indexation integrates affixal arguments with base arguments, linking the highest nonhead argument with the highest (preferably unlinked) head argument, consistent with semantic conditions on the head argument, if there are any. In this case, following many current treatments of prefixation in English (Lieber 1992a, DiSciullo and Williams 1987), it is the base which is the head, and the affix which is the nonhead, in the sense that the base, rather than the prefix, determines the syntactic category of the derived word.

Our next step is to look at what happens when the skeleton of *over-* is composed with bases of various sorts. Let us consider first what results when the three forms of *over-* attach to verbs, as this brings us directly to the second complex and interesting issue raised by this prefix, namely its effect on argument structure. A look at data from the CELEX database and examples from Marchand (1969) suggests that locational *over-* shows a marked preference for intransitive or inchoative verbs, those which we have characterized with the features [+dynamic] and [+/−IEPS], and completive *over-* perhaps a slight preference for this class. Both locational and completive *over-* do, however, attach to verbs of other classes. Excess *over-* is much more eclectic in the range of verbs to which it attaches.

(33)   a. **locational**   *intransitive bases*: overarch, overflow, overfly, overhang, overlap, overleap, overlook, overreach, overspill, overtop, overcanopy, oversoar, overrise, overtower, overlay, overlie
transitive bases: overprint, overturn, overeye

b. **completive**   *intransitive bases*: overcloud, overgrow, override, overshadow, overrun,
transitive bases: overcrowd, overcover, overcurtain, oversweep

c. **excess**   *intransitive bases*: overact, overdress, oversleep, overstay, overeat?
transitive bases: overbid, overburden, overcapitalize, overcharge, overcompensate, overcook, overdevelop, overdo, overdose, overemphasize, overestimate, overexert, overexpose, overheat, overindulge, overpraise, overproduce, overrate, oversell, oversimplify, overstate, overstock, overstrain, overtax, overvalue, overwork, overpay, overeducate, overbook

Locational or completive *over-* add their skeleton to an intransitive verb base, giving representations like those in (34):

(34)   *overfly, overrun*
[+Loc ([ᵢ   ], [   ], [+dynamic, −IEPS ([ᵢ   ])])]
       over-   *fly, run*

According to the Principle of Co-indexation, the single argument of the base verb is co-indexed with the highest argument of the (nonhead) affix, identifying the two and ensuring that they are discharged by the same phrase in the syntax.

The second argument of locational and completive *over-* is free, however, and we would expect it to be discharged syntactically. That is, if *over-* is a transitive affix when it attaches to verbs, we would expect it to add an argument to an intransitive base. And so it does, as the data in (35) show:

(35)   *The airplane flew the field.   The airplane overflew the field.
        *The enemy ran the battlefield.   The enemy overran the battlefield.

As locational *over-* tends to favor intransitive bases, we neatly account for much of the data in (33a), and many of the completive cases in (33b).

What happens when the skeleton of *over-* attaches to a transitive base such as *print* or *crowd*? Assuming that these verbs are activity verbs, we would get the composed representation in (36):

(36)   *overprint, overcrowd*
       [+Loc ([$_i$], [   ], [+dynamic ([$_i$], [   ])])]
           over-   *print, crowd*

The Principle of Co-indexation identifies the first argument of the base with the first argument of the prefix, again ensuring that they are discharged by the same phrase in the syntax. The representation in (36) suggests that the composed skeleton of the derived word leaves three arguments to be filled syntactically (the shared argument, the second argument of the prefix, and the second argument of the verbal base), but this is not correct. The verbs *overprint* and *overcrowd* are transitive, not ditransitive, so we need to look beyond the most straightforward analysis.

Prefixation of *over-* seems in fact to behave in terms of argument structure like verbal compounding in English. Although clearly not productive in English, verb-verb compounds occasionally do get coined; among the more recent ones are examples like *stir-fry*, *blow-dry*, and *slam-dunk*. The behavior of arguments in this sort of compounding seems to go beyond the Principle of Co-indexation that has seen us through to this point: verbal compounding requires not just the identification of the first argument of the head with that of the nonhead, but complete identification of all arguments of the head verb with those of the nonhead. In other words, when they are compounded, the first and second verbs come to share precisely the same arguments. Typically both verbs must be transitive, and the resulting compound is transitive.[19]

19. We might make the same observation about copulative compounds which have more than one argument, for example, *prince consort* or *producer-director*. In these cases, too, all arguments of the compounded stems are identified.

I am not sure at this point how to formalize this observation, but it seems to be relevant to cases like *overprint* and *overcrowd*. As is the case in verb-verb compounds, prepositional affixes never result in an argument structure with more than two arguments. When prefixed to an intransitive verb, they can add an argument. But with transitive bases they may not add an argument. Rather than adding a third argument in the derived form, the prefixal arguments are completely identified with the base arguments. The result is that if the base verb is transitive to begin with, there will be no overall change in its argument structure.

We have suggested that excess *over-* has a somewhat different skeleton from locational and completive *over-*, as it is obligatorily intransitive. We therefore might expect that excess *over-* should have no overt effect on verbal diathesis, and this is largely what we find. When excess *over-* attaches to intransitive verbs it yields intransitive verbs, and on transitive verbs it yields transitive verbs:

(37)   *oversleep*
       [+Loc ([$_i$], [+dynamic ([$_i$])])]
              over-   *sleep*

(38)   *overdo*
       [+Loc ([$_i$], [+dynamic ([$_i$], [   ])])]
              over-   *do*

Verbs derived with excess *over-* maintain the syntactic argument structure of their base verbs.

It is odd, then, that there is one verb whose argument structure does seem to be changed by prefixation of *over-*. The verb *eat* usually allows an internal argument (*we ate / we ate pickles*), but *overeat* is usually used intransitively (**we overate pickles*). It is interesting that the internal argument is disallowed only when the "excess" part of the semantic body of *over-* would implicitly have to take scope over that argument. If *she overate pickles* were to be acceptable, it would have to have the meaning "she ate too many pickles." On the other hand, in the more typical cases where *over-* has no effect on argument structure, the "excess" meaning added by the prefix is typically interpreted as having scope over the verb phrase. That is, *they overworked the peasants* can be paraphrased as "they worked the peasants too hard" and not as "they worked too many peasants." (Note that an adjunct of quantity is precluded with *over-* verbs: **they overworked the peasants too hard*.) Again, although I am not sure how to formalize this observation, it seems plausible to say that *over-* does not actually delete an argument when it attaches to the verb base *eat*, but rather chooses as its base the intransitive form of the verb, avoiding if it possibly can taking scope over an overt object.

Most of the intricate effects of *over-* prefixation on the argument structure of verbal bases follow then from its skeletal representation. This is true with nominal and adjectival bases as well. Nouns and adjectives with a single argument do not gain arguments when *over-* is prefixed, nor do nouns and adjectives which have more than one argument undergo any change in their argument structures as a result of prefixation (e.g., *anxiety about her future ∼ overanxiety about her future*; *fond of pickles ∼ overfond of pickles*). This makes sense: note that the vast majority of nouns, and all of the adjectives, with the prefix *over-* carry the excess meaning. As the second argument of excess *over-* is filled with a semantic constant, we would not expect prefixation to add an argument on nominal or adjectival bases.

There are, of course, a handful of nouns in which *over-* has the locational or completive senses (*overbridge*, *overbrow*, *overcheek*, *overworld*, *overking*, *overlord*; *overcoat*, *overshirt*, *overshoe*). We might assume for these either that the process of *over-* prefixation is no longer productive (or was never productive) with nouns, and therefore that these forms are lexicalized, or that only the intransitive form of the prepositional affix attaches to nouns. As the overall number of examples is rather small, I will not decide between these alternatives here.

4.3   *Conclusion*

In this chapter, we have added a feature [Location] to our arsenal of semantic atoms, and explored its consequences both for the simplex lexicon (prepositions) and for derivational morphology (privative, negative, and prepositional affixes). My focus has again been on two of our central questions: why are there often multiple affixes fulfilling the same function in a language, and why do affixes display so much polysemy? Again, the discussion of privative and negative affixes in sections 4.2.1 and 4.2.2 suggests that the existence of multiple affixes with the same meaning follows from a parsimonious system of lexical semantic representation. If negation is to be characterized by a single semantic atom – in our system the feature [−Loc] – then we would expect to find the sort of complex overlap in negative affixes that we indeed do find in English. Further, I argued in section 4.2.2 that the rich polysemy of negative prefixes in English can be attributed to the interaction of the feature [−Loc] with bases of different semantic types; we do not need to postulate separate skeletal representations for privative, contrary, or contradictory negation, or indeed for the reversative sense of verbs like *undress* and *disrobe*.

In section 4.2.3, I tried to expand our view of affixal polysemy; specifically, I proposed that not all polysemy in affixes must be attributed to the interaction of a highly abstract skeleton with bases of different kinds. What prepositional affixes like *over-* show us is that affixes derived from simplex lexical items can show the same sort of polysemy that the corresponding simplex items display. For prepositions, a category which displays a richly paradigmatic semantic body, polysemy may arise from small variations in body characteristics. Those same variations are taken on when the preposition is used as a bound form. Thus, the polysemy of *over-* does not arise so much from the interaction of skeleton and base, as from the various meanings that we find in the simplex preposition *over*.

5 Extending the system – quantity

I turn next to a set of features that I will characterize roughly as having to do with QUANTITY, by which I mean notions pertaining to duration, internal individuation, and boundaries. Here, I tread carefully on much-traveled ground: the subject of the quantitative characteristics of SUBSTANCES/THINGS/ESSENCES and SITUATIONS has been much discussed in both the philosophical literature and the linguistic literature at least since the 1970s. It is intimately connected with the vast literature on the Vendler (1967) classes of predicates (States, Activities, Accomplishments, and Achievements), and with discussions of telicity, terminativity, delimitedness, and measuring out which have figured prominently in the work of Verkuyl (1972, 1989, 1993, 1999), Dowty (1979), Tenny (1987, 1994), Jackendoff (1991, 1996), Pustejovsky (1991), Smith (1997), Tenny and Pustejovsky (2000), among many others.

In this chapter, I will pursue the idea that the quantitative semantics of lexical nouns and verbs can be characterized by a small set of semantic features, and indeed by the same small set of semantic features. I'm not original here; this is an idea which has had wide currency at least since the 1980s, figuring in such works as Carlson (1981), Bach (1986), and Jackendoff (1991, 1996), among others in the linguistic and philosophical literature. As will become apparent shortly, my account owes a great deal to the work of all of these researchers.

Where I distinguish myself from them is in trying to sort out those quantificational characteristics that are manifested in lexical items from those that arise from subtle interactions of lexical items when composed into higher-order syntactic and semantic units. I will first work out how quantitative features allow us to cross-classify the lexical classes that I have already discussed in previous chapters. I will then compare my system to that of Jackendoff (1991, 1996), which mine resembles in certain respects, but from which it differs in one crucial way, and show how my application of the features relates to higher-level aspects of quantitative meaning such as telicity.

The important point which I wish to make in this chapter is this: only those quantitative aspects of meaning which are relevant to the simplex lexicon should manifest themselves in the derivational system of a language. That is, the system which I am developing makes a prediction that if there are quantitative features that are specifically lexical, as I will argue that there are, then it is these features that should be exploited by derivational morphology, and not quantitative characteristics that appear at higher levels of syntactic organization. I will argue that the derivational system of English indeed does exploit the features that appear to be necessary in characterizing the simplex lexicon, in the form of the verbal prefix *re-* and the nominal suffixes *-ery* and *-age*. I will also raise the issue of inherent inflection (Booij 1996), briefly considering the extent to which the feature system I develop can be extended from derivation to inherent inflections like the plural and the progressive.

5.1   *Quantity features*

I propose that two semantic features are needed to capture the quantificational characteristics of simplex lexical items:

(1)   • **[B]**: This feature stands for "Bounded." It signals the relevance of intrinsic
            spatial or temporal boundaries in a SITUATION or SUBSTANCE/THING/
            ESSENCE. If the feature [B] is absent, the item may be ontologically
            bounded or not, but its boundaries are conceptually and/or linguistically
            irrelevant. If the item bears the feature [+B], it is limited spatially or
            temporally. If it is [−B], it is without intrinsic limits in time or space.
          • **[CI]**: This feature stands for "Composed of Individuals." The feature [CI]
            signals the relevance of spatial or temporal units implied in the meaning of
            a lexical item. If an item is [+CI], it is conceived of as being composed of
            separable similar internal units. If an item is [−CI], then it denotes
            something which is spatially or temporally homogeneous or internally
            undifferentiated.

Quantity features are of relevance to both SUBSTANCES/THINGS/ESSENCES and SITUATIONS. I start with their use in distinguishing kinds of nouns, as this is the less controversial of the applications of these features that I will make.

The distinction between [+B] and [−B] nouns corresponds to the distinction between count and mass nouns, at least when they are singular. Count nouns are SUBSTANCES/THINGS/ESSENCES which are conceived of as being intrinsically bounded, and mass nouns as SUBSTANCES/THINGS/ESSENCES having no intrinsic boundaries. The distinction between [+CI] and [−CI] corresponds to the distinction between items which are not composed of discernible replicable parts (e.g., individual nouns like *person*)[1] and aggregates (e.g., *committee*), that is, conglomerations of similar individuals. Together, these two features can cross-classify four classes of nouns, three of which are regularly represented in the simplex lexicon.[2] The reader will note here that my analysis of types of nouns (or SUBSTANCES/THINGS/ESSENCES) is thus far identical to that proposed by Jackendoff (1991); however, as my use of the features differs from Jackendoff's in its application to SITUATIONS, I will defer a comparison of the two analyses until after I have discussed quantitative characteristics of both nouns and verbs.

(2)   Application of quantitative features to SUBSTANCES/THINGS/ESSENCES
        [+B, −CI]:   singular count nouns   *person, pig, fact*
        [−B, −CI]:   mass nouns   *furniture, water*
        [+B, +CI]:   group nouns   *committee, herd*
        [−B, +CI]:   plural nouns   *cattle, sheep*

Singular count nouns denote substances which are not themselves composed of individuals, but which are intrinsically bounded. Plural count nouns, in contrast, are composed of individuals, but the collective of individuals is inherently without boundaries. Mass nouns are neither individuated nor intrinsically bounded. Group nouns are internally individuated and conceptually unitary.

I believe that the features [B] and [CI] can be of use in characterizing quantitative or aspectual classes among simplex verbs, as they are among simplex nouns, and that these features should be applied in such a way as to elucidate quantitative and temporal characteristics that appear intrinsically in the meanings of simplex verbs no matter what sort of arguments they appear with at higher levels of syntactic/semantic organization (this point will be clearer when we examine the notion of "telicity" in a moment). I propose that the feature [B] be used to encode the distinction between temporally punctual situations and temporally durative ones. [+B] items will be those which have no linguistically significant duration, for example *explode, jump, flash, name*. [−B] items will be those which have linguistically significant duration, for example, *descend, walk, draw, eat, build, push*.

It is crucial first to clarify what I mean by "linguistically significant" or "insignificant" duration. As Engelberg (1999) documents, linguists as early as

1. Note that although individuals may be composed of parts, they are not composed of parts which are inherently similar to one another.
2. I use as examples here plurals which are irregular, and arguably encoded in the simplex lexicon. Of course, the plural affix will provide the features [−B, +CI] as well; see section 5.4.3 for further discussion of the plural.

the middle of the nineteenth century recognized a special linguistic interpretation of the term "punctual." It is clear that in the real world actions always take time – even blinks, sneezes, and explosions can be timed with stopwatches or filmed in slow motion. Indeed, Tenny (1994) takes this as evidence that instantaneous and durative events should not be distinguished.[3]

Nevertheless, events do seem to be distinguished from the point of view of language as being durative or instantaneous, as suggested by familiar facts involving adverbials. It is well known that adverbials like *for an hour* are either wholly infelicitous with linguistically punctual events, or induce an iterative reading that is not intrinsic to the meaning of the verb itself:

(3)   a. *The train arrived for an hour.
       b. *The bomb exploded for an hour.
       c. The prisoner tapped for an hour. (iterative reading)
       d. The student sneezed for an hour. (iterative reading)

(4)   a. We walked for an hour.
       b. They studied the map for an hour.

Verbs like those in (3) are treated as punctual or instantaneous by the language, even if they have some (small) duration in time. In contrast, [−B] events like those in (4) are unexceptional with durative adverbials like *for an hour*. As the distinction between punctual and durative seems to be both lexically based and significant syntactically, I believe myself justified in applying the feature [B] as I have.[4]

The feature [+CI] is meant here, when applied to SITUATIONS, to be the lexical correlate of plurality in nouns. Correspondingly, the feature [−CI] would be the situational correlate of nonplural nouns. Plural nouns denote multiple individuals of the same kind, nonplural nouns single individuals or mass substances. I would like to suggest that the corresponding lexical distinction in SITUATIONS is one of iterativity vs. homogeneity.[5] Some verbs denote events which by their very nature imply repeated actions of the same sort, for example, *totter*, *wiggle*, *pummel*, or *giggle*. By definition, to *totter* or to *wiggle* is to produce repeated motions of a certain sort, to *pummel* is to produce repeated

3. See also Verkuyl (1989) on this point, and Mittwoch (1991) for a defense of the notion of linguistic punctuality.
4. This is not to say that punctual and durative verbs always pattern differently in terms of syntax; as Levin (1999) shows, punctual verbs like *blink* and durative verbs like *eat* can both occur in the reflexive resultative construction.
5. Brinton (1998, 45) likens plurality in nouns not to iterativity, but to serial action, i.e., "an event occurring on a specified number of occasions." But she, like Jackendoff, Vendler, and others, is concerned not with the lexical semantics of verbs, but with the interpretation of verbs in VPs. Her treatment is therefore not immediately relevant to my concerns here.

blows, and to *giggle* to emit repeated small bursts of laughter. Such verbs, I would say, are lexically [+CI]. The vast majority of other verbs would be [−CI]. Verbs such as *walk* or *laugh* or *build*, although perhaps not implying perfectly homogeneous events,[6] are not composed of multiple, repeated, relatively identical actions.

The two quantitative features give rise to the following intrinsic aspectual classes of SITUATIONS:

(5)   Application of quantitative features to SITUATIONS
        [+B, −CI]:   nonrepetitive punctuals[7]   *explode, jump, flash*
        [−B, −CI]:   nonrepetitive duratives   *descend, walk, draw*
        [+B, +CI]:   <logically impossible>
        [−B, +CI]:   repetitive duratives   *totter, pummel, wiggle*

A few comments are in order. Note that the intrinsically iterative verbs like *totter* are also, by their very nature, durative (they are wholly felicitous with adverbials like *for an hour*) (cf. also Brinton 1998, 42). In fact, it would seem that one of the possible classes defined for SITUATIONS by the two features constitutes a logical impossibility. That is, for a verb to be intrinsically [+B, +CI] it would have to denote an event that is at the same time instantaneous/punctual and yet made up of replicable individual events, a combination which does not seem possible. Note also that although I claim that the durative/punctual and iterative/homogeneous distinctions are visible in the simplex lexicon, I believe that they may also be induced at higher levels of syntactic/semantic organization. For example, a normally punctual nonrepetitive verb can be coerced into an iterative reading in a sentence by adding the right kind of adverbial (*The light flashed continuously*). So these distinctions are lexically relevant, but they are not exclusively lexical.

5.2   Comparison to Jackendoff (1991, 1996)

I now compare my interpretation of the features [B] and [CI] to Jackendoff's features [b] and [i]. Jackendoff (1991, 19–20) proposes the two features [b] and [i] to define four classes of nouns: singular count nouns, plural count nouns, group nouns, and mass nouns. He extends the use of these features to events as well. His feature [+/−b] stands for "bounded"; my feature [B] is identical to it,

---

6. See Verkuyl (1993) for an enlightening discussion of homogeneity in events.
7. Of these verbs, those which do not have the feature [+IEPS], that is, those which are not inchoatives or unaccusatives, are the ones that can be coerced into being repetitive by adding a durative adverbial *for an hour* (e.g., *The light flashed for an hour*). These verbs correspond to the class that is referred to as "semelfactive" in other literature (see, for example, Smith [1997]).

both in name and in application within the nominal system. For Jackendoff, as for me, the feature [b] distinguishes nouns with inherent boundaries – singular count nouns and group nouns – from nouns lacking boundaries – mass nouns and plurals. Similarly, at least with respect to the nominal system, my feature [CI] is identical to Jackendoff's feature [+/−i], which stands for "internal structure." Like [CI], Jackendoff's [i] distinguishes plural count nouns and group nouns on the one hand from singular count nouns and mass nouns on the other.

It is in the application of quantitative features to events, however, that my interpretation of [B] and [CI] differs substantially from Jackendoff's interpretation of [b] and [i]. Jackendoff is not concerned with quantificational or aspectual characteristics displayed in the simplex lexicon, but with quantitative meaning manifested at higher levels of organization. Specifically, Jackendoff (1991, 1996) attempts to elucidate the vexed notion of "telicity" in his application of [b] and [i] to situations. I will first try to clarify the ways in which the term "telicity" and related terms like "boundedness," "delimitedness," and "measuring out" have been used in the literature, and then explain Jackendoff's application of the features.

Telicity is an aspectual characteristic of SITUATIONS that has received wide attention in recent years. According to Comrie (1976, 4), a telic situation is "one that involves a process that leads up to a well-defined terminal point." In its strongest form, telicity involves not just the stopping of an event, but the achieving of some final endpoint, goal, result, or change of state (Smith 1997, 3; 42–3). For example, the sentence *I ate the apple* denotes an event that reaches its natural endpoint when the speaker finishes the last bite of apple. Atelic events – for example, the event denoted in a sentence like *I slept* – are ones that have no natural endpoint. They may stop or come to an end, but the stopping point is arbitrary.

Related to the telic/atelic distinction are terms like "terminative/durative" (used by Verkuyl 1972, 1989, 1993, 1999), "delimited/nondelimited" (used by Tenny 1994), and "bounded/unbounded" (used by Jackendoff 1991, 1996). These related terms are often used in a slightly looser way than telic/atelic in that they depend on an event's having a final endpoint in time, but not necessarily an explicit goal, result, or change of state. In this way, they seem to encode – at least at the level of the predicate or the sentence – the durative/punctual distinction that I make with the feature [B]. These cousins of telicity do not by themselves add up to telicity.[8] Thus, a semelfactive verb like *flash* might

8. A problem seemingly endemic to the literature on aspectuality is that the telic/atelic distinction is often used in the looser sense of delimited/nondelimited, terminative/durative, etc. See

be delimited or bounded without being telic, if I understand these definitions correctly.

In order to arrive at the stricter aspectual designation, Tenny adds the notion "measuring out" to "delimited": "Measuring-Out contains two ingredients: a measuring scale associated with an argument, and a temporal bound or delimitedness" (1994, 15). Jackendoff (1991) uses his bounded/unbounded distinction much as Tenny uses delimited/nondelimited, and in Jackendoff (1996) adds the device of "structure-preserving binding" to LCSs to operationalize what Tenny calls "measuring-out."

Telicity in the strict sense clearly is an aspectual property which is not purely or even primarily lexical. As Verkuyl (1972, 1989, 1993, 1999) has shown, whether a sentence denotes a telic or atelic situation can depend on a combination of factors including the type of verb and the quantificational characteristics of the verb's arguments. With the right kind of quantified arguments (e.g., a singular count noun with a definite or indefinite determiner, or a plural with a numeral), the right kind of verb (e.g., *eat*) will deliver a telic reading. But with a bare plural argument, for example, or the wrong kind of verb altogether (e.g., *push*), the resulting sentence will be atelic:

(6)   a. The waiter ate a sandwich.   (telic)
          b. The waiter ate sandwiches.   (atelic)
          c. Waiters ate a sandwich.   (atelic)
          d. Waiters ate sandwiches.   (atelic)

(7)   a. The waiter pushed the cart.   (atelic)
          b. The waiter pushed carts.   (atelic)
          c. Waiters pushed the cart.   (atelic)
          d. Waiters pushed carts.   (atelic)

Telicity, then, is an aspectual characteristic which appears at higher levels of syntactic/semantic composition. Although there must be some lexical contribution to telicity (cf. the difference between *eat* and *push* in [6]–[7]), an issue to which I will return shortly, telicity is not directly a characteristic of verbs in the simplex lexicon, and is therefore not of prime interest to me here.

I can return now to the comparison of my features [B] and [CI] to Jackendoff's [b] and [i]. In contrast to my lexical interpretation of [B] and [CI], Jackendoff (1991, 1996) applies his features to situations as a whole, using [b] to capture the distinction of temporal delimitedness and [i] to capture the

Depraetere (1995), Filip (2000), and Tenny and Pustejovsky (2000) for some enlightening discussion of the history of these terms and of the variations in their applications.

notion of iterated events. He uses the two binary features to classify four kinds of events:

(8)   [+b, −i]   *John ran to the store.*
        [−b, −i]   *John slept.*
        [+b, +i]   *The light flashed until dawn.*
        [−b, +i]   *The light flashed continually.*

In his application, events are [+b] if they refer to a closed period of time (but not necessarily a punctual one), [−b] if they refer to an open-ended period of time. Events receive the feature [+i] if they have a repetitive or iterative interpretation, [−i] if they do not.[9]

My conception of the features clearly owes much to Jackendoff's, but for Jackendoff these features are applied at the level of events, which are manifested syntactically as predicates, or sentences as a whole; Jackendoff explicitly makes no attempt to tease out the semantic properties inherent in lexical items from the semantic properties exhibited at higher levels. Note that with Jackendoff's application of the features, any verb, say *run* or *flash,* can occur in predicates of different sorts, depending on the arguments and adverbial modifiers it co-occurs with. And although Jackendoff might choose to classify a punctual verb such as *flash* as [+b], [+b] does not mean "punctual" per se, as any temporally closed event can be [+b], even if it has duration (e.g., *run to the store*).[10]

My intention here is not to argue against Jackendoff's use of the features [b] and [i], but simply to point out that his aim in using the features is to try to account for the property of telicity, which is an aspectual property appearing at the level of the predicate or the sentence as a whole. My aim in this work is different from Jackendoff's, and therefore my interpretation and application of the features [B] and [CI] is somewhat different.

My goal is not to explain telicity, but to characterize those aspectual distinctions that are manifested at the level of the lexical item, for it is those distinctions, I claim, that are exploited by derivational morphology. That is, by

---

9. See Brinton (1998) for a comparison of Jackendoff to other possible interpretations of aspect and aspectuality at the phrase level.

10. It may also be useful, at least in passing, to note that my system of features has no direct correlate to the much-discussed Vendler classes (States, Activities, Accomplishments, and Achievements), as these classes, like Jackendoff's, are at least in part grounded in the notion of telicity. Because of this, they denote classes of propositions or predicates and not aspects of meaning that are confined to the lexical level. Roughly speaking, however, Vendler's States correspond to [−dynamic] verbs in my system. Vendler's Activities would be [+dynamic] in my system, and durative, but also atelic. Accomplishments and Achievements are also [+dynamic], and both are telic, with the former being durative and the latter punctual.

confining my system to aspectual distinctions which are truly lexical, I derive a prediction: if derivational affixes express notions of quantity or aspect, it is precisely the ones manifested in the simplex lexicon that they should express, rather than higher-level quantitative or aspectual distinctions such as telicity. It is to this prediction that I devote section 5.4.

5.3   *More on telicity*

Before I get to the main point, however, a few last words about telicity. It would be lovely, of course, if my interpretation of the features [B] and [CI] finally solved the mystery of exactly what the lexical contribution of the verb to telicity really is. To the extent that attempts have been made to do this in the past, they have largely been a failure. Verkuyl (1989, 1993), for example, proposes a feature [+ADD TO] which characterizes all and only those verbs which have the potential (given the right kinds of quantified arguments) to give rise in sentences to telic readings. Notionally, the feature [+ADD TO] seems, however, to carry approximately the semantic content of my feature [+dynamic] (1993, 16–17):

> . . . the category ADD TO emerged to refer to the dynamic semantic information distinguishing verbs like *eat*, *walk*, *dance*, *knit*, etc. from verbs like *want*, *hate*, etc. . . . In later work, the abbreviatory feature [+ADD TO] was used to stand for categorial nodes like MOVEMENT, TAKE, ADD TO, etc., to account for the dynamicity expressed by the verb.

For Verkuyl (1993, 20), verbs which are [+ADD TO] involve change. The problem, however, is that some eventive verbs have the potential to deliver telic readings with the right kind of arguments (e.g., *eat*, *build*) and others do not (e.g., *push*). Arguably, all these verbs involve change; certainly none of these verbs is stative, as opposed to dynamic. Verkuyl (1993, 329) is forced to consider verbs like *push* as "a sort of hybrid between [+ADD TO] and [−ADD TO]" without really explaining what makes them hybrids, that is, what in their lexical semantics distinguishes them from real [+ADD TO] verbs like *eat*.[11]

I would like, of course, to do better than this, and perhaps I can do just a bit better. My intention here is not to designate verbs once and for all as telic, but rather to identify those semantic features which give a verb a chance (with the right kind of arguments) to give rise to telic readings. Certainly, verbs must be

11. See Ramchand (1997) and Hay, Kennedy, and Levin (1999) for discussion of similar issues.

[+dynamic] to give rise to a telic reading. Further, verbs that are [+B] (that is, punctual/instantaneous) have a good chance to contribute a telic reading, as they have intrinsic temporal endpoints. But the lexical presence of [+B] is not by itself enough to give rise to full-blown telicity, as telicity involves a goal, result, or change of state in addition to temporal boundedness. The verbs that come closest lexically to fulfilling both criteria (temporal boundedness and intrinsic result/change of state) are verbs which are both [+B] and [+IEPS] in my framework, for example verbs like *explode* or *forget*.

Of course, other verbs can give rise to telic readings. For example, a [+B, −IEPS] verb like *hop* or *jump* can give rise to a telic reading if an explicit goal is added in the form of a [+IEPS] prepositional phrase (e.g., *She hopped to the store*). For that matter, so can a [−B, −IEPS] verb like *walk* (e.g., *She walked to the store*). A [−B, +IEPS] verb like *evaporate* can also give rise to a telic reading, but only if helped along by the right kind of adverbial (e.g., *The water evaporated in an hour*). Perhaps what this suggests is a scale of strength: some lexical features contribute to telicity ([+B], [+IEPS]); the fewer the intrinsic features contributing to telicity, the more help a verb needs from outside to deliver a telic reading.

The most mysterious cases still remain a mystery to me, however, namely verbs like *eat*, *build*, and *push*, all of which my system would classify as durative SIMPLE ACTIVITY verbs. All are [+dynamic] and [−B], and none is marked with the feature [IEPS], as they lack "inferable eventual positions or states." Nevertheless the first two easily give rise to telic readings (with appropriate arguments, but without the help of extra adverbials), whereas the third does not. The difference between *eat* and *build* on the one hand and *push* on the other seems to hinge on the presence of what Tenny (1994 citing Dowty 1991) calls "incremental themes" in *eat* and *build*. "Incremental themes" are themes that are consumed or created bit by bit by the event denoted by the verb. The distinction between verbs with incremental themes and those without suggests the need for further decomposition of lexical meanings, and perhaps the addition of a feature in my system, but as yet I am unsure of what the relevant distinction should be. So at this point, the goal of isolating the lexical contribution to telicity cannot be met. I leave this problem to further research.

Let me stress the main point again, however. The features I have proposed, or properly speaking the particular lexical application of those features, allow us to make a prediction about the sorts of derivational morphology we ought to find. To the extent that the derivational system exploits those features, and does not express higher-level semantic distinctions like telicity, my use of the features is justified. It is to this issue that I now turn.

5.4   *Quantity and affixes*

English is a language which is not particularly rich in aspectual or quantitative derivational affixes. Nevertheless, there are three affixes that are worth exploring in this section. The verbal prefix *re-* is of special interest, as it has a clear effect on the internal temporal interpretation of its verbal bases, and further because it has been explicitly claimed in the literature (Smith 1997) to be a telic prefix. It thus stands as a potential counterexample to the prediction that I made above. The other two affixes are the nominal affixes *-ery* and *-age*, which I mentioned briefly in chapter 1. The reader will remember that at that point I suggested that, in spite of some rather flamboyant polysemy, these affixes be characterized as forming collective nouns, and offered a promissory note to return to their analysis when we had sufficient ammunition in our arsenal to tackle quantitative meanings. We have that ammunition now, and it is time to redeem the promissory note.

5.4.1   *The prefix* "re-"
The prefix *re-* attaches to verbs to indicate a repeated action:

(9)   *rebuild, refreeze, remelt, rename, reassure, reforest, reorient, reascend,
         recapture *reyawn, *reeat, *redance, *reknow, *reflash, *reexplode, *repush*

There are two questions to consider: first, what the semantic contribution of *re-* is, and second, what group of verbs this prefix attaches to. Marchand (1969, 189–90) describes this prefix as follows:

> The prefix is almost only used with transitive verbs, i.e., *re-* does not express mere repetition of an action; it connotes the idea of repetition only with actions connected with an object. And it is with a view to the result of the action performed on an object that *re-* is used. The result of the action is 1) either understood to be imperfect or unattained, and *re-* then denotes repetition with a view to changing or improving the previous inadequate result (as in *rearrange*, *redirect* (a letter), *redistrict* AE, *respell*, *rewrite*) . . . 2) The result of the action or the former state has come undone, and then *re-* reverses the reversal, restores the previous result or state. Examples of this meaning are *recapture, reconvert, reimburse, reinstate, reinvest, repossess, resole*.

Marchand is correct that *re-* attaches most easily to transitive verbs (*rewrite, rerun the race* but not *rerun*). However, it does attach to some intransitives and it does not attach to all transitives. With respect to intransitives, there are a few unaccusative/inchoative verbs to which *re-* can attach (*reascend, redescend, regrow*), although there are also some unaccusatives/inchoatives (**reexplode, *rearrive*) to which *re-* does not attach. As for the transitive verbs, there are clearly some which take *re-* (*rebuild, reuse*) and some which do not (**reeat, *reknow, *repush*). Transitivity alone does not delimit the domain of this prefix. Marchand is right to suggest that the meaning of *re-* involves repetition of an action, but it is not clear in what way and to what extent that action must be "performed on an object."

Smith (1997, 179) suggests that *re-* means "to do over again" but further, and more interestingly for our purposes, characterizes *re-* as a telic prefix:

> The verbal prefix *re-* (to do over again) is telic: it appears in constellations with verbs such as *reopen, reevaluate, reassemble*, etc. Stative, Activity and Semelfactive verbs do not take this prefix: **rebelieve, *reunderstand, *resneeze, *relaugh, *reknock* are impossible, nor do verbs with *re-* appear in atelic constellations.

Smith illustrates by citing the contrast between, for example, **They redanced* and *They redanced the second number*, the first of which seems to be impossible, and the second telic. Nevertheless, it is not clear to me what Smith means when she characterizes *re-* as "telic"; for example, whether she means that *re-* actually makes verbs telic (and therefore that "telic" is part of its semantic contribution to its base), or that *re-* attaches only to telic predicates, adding the meaning "to do again" and presumably maintaining their telicity. Note, for example, that *They danced the second number* is already telic, so *re-* cannot be said to have changed the telicity of the sentence.

In fact, neither of these possibilities can be correct. The prefix *re-* attaches to some verbs like *forest* or *stock* which typically in sentences give rise to atelic readings (e.g., *to forest the hillside (for months) / to stock the shelf (for hours)*). On the other hand, the prefix does not attach to some verbs which typically deliver telic readings (e.g., **reexplode the bomb*). So *re-* cannot be said to select for telicity.

Further, the prefix *re-* does not itself necessarily deliver a telic reading. When attached to a verb that is usually atelic, the sentence with *re-* can remain atelic; sentences like *The logging company reforested the hillside (for months)* or *I restocked the shelf (for hours)* seem as atelic to me as their *re-*less counterparts. Although the addition of the right kind of adverbial (e.g., *in an hour, in a month*) can push these sentences over the edge to a telic reading, they are equally compatible with *for* adverbials. In fact, it seems that *re-* is neutral between telic and atelic readings.

So Smith cannot be correct that *re-* is a telic prefix. Telicity is neither part of its meaning nor an apt characterization of the class of verbs it attaches to. But this is exactly as we would want it to be, given the theory I have developed in this book.

How then to characterize *re-*? Recall that there are two issues: (1) what is the semantic contribution of *re-*, and (2) what class of verbs does *re-* attach to? The first of these questions is the easier one to tackle. In the framework I have developed here, *re-* adds the feature [+CI] to the skeleton of its verbal base. In other words, I propose the following (partial) lexical entry for *re-*:

(10)   *re-*
        [+CI ([   ], <base>)]

In other words, what we mean when we say that *re-* means "to do again" is that *re-* induces an iteration of the action denoted by the verb. It does derivationally what verbs like *totter* or *pummel* do intrinsically. It adds a component of meaning that is independently necessary in the simplex lexicon, one of iterated replicable action.

But it can do this only on certain sorts of verbs. Recall that *re-* attaches both to transitive verbs and to intransitive verbs, but not to all transitive verbs and not to all intransitive verbs. Consider the data in (11):

(11)   **take *re-***   **do not take *re-***
        transitive   *rebuild*   **reeat*
                            reassure   **rebelieve*
                            reforest   **repush*
        intransitive   *reascend*   **reexplode*
                            regrow   **reyawn*

What seems crucial in delimiting the domain of *re-* is first of all that the verbs to which *re-* attaches imply some sort of result and second that the result of the action denoted by the base verb cannot be one that is finite, fixed, or permanent. So, *re-* fails to attach to verbs that have no inherent result (**reyawn*, **reflash*, **repush*). But it also does not attach to verbs which imply a result which cannot be reversed. For example, it is impossible to **reeat the apple* or **reexplode the bomb*. All of these imply events in which the result of the action is depletion or complete consumption of the object argument. But it is possible to *repaint a house* or *reassure the passenger* or *reforest the hillside* as the verbs *paint*, *assure*, and *forest* imply results which are not permanent and irreversible.

In fact, the set of verbs that may be prefixed with *re-* is largely coextensive with the set that may take *un-* with reversative meaning that were discussed in chapter 4. Again, I am unsure at this time how to characterize formally the notion of "nonpermanent or reversible result." Perhaps it will become clearer when we have investigated further the relationship between stage-level properties and individual-level properties (Carlson 1977), but I will not pursue this idea here. I leave open the possibility that there may be another semantic feature to distinguish permanent results from reversible ones. Or it may be that this distinction should not be encoded in the semantic skeleton at all, and ought to be relegated to the body.

My central point, however, is relatively clear. Hard as it is to characterize formally the class of verbs to which *re-* attaches, the rest of the analysis shows that the prediction made by my framework is on the right track. The meaning of *re-* itself can be easily characterized in the feature system I have developed. It is a meaning that occurs independently in the simplex lexicon. And it is apparently no more than passingly related to the aspectual characteristic of telicity, which we have seen is not a semantic feature of the simplex lexicon.

5.4.2   *The suffixes* "-ery" *and* "-age"

In chapter 1, I looked briefly at the suffixes *-ery* and *-age*, which were of interest there as they appeared to be counterexamples to the prediction that individual derivational affixes should give rise to either concrete nouns or abstract nouns, but not both. According to Marchand (1969, 282), the suffix *-ery* (and its allomorph *-ry*) derives from French *-erie*:

> It forms concrete and abstract substantives. The principal semantic groups are today: 1) a collectivity of persons (type *yeomanry*), 2) things taken collectively (type *jewelry*), 3) acting, behavior (especially undesirable) characteristic of – (type *treachery*), 4) place which is connected with – (types *swannery/printery*). With the exception of *swannery*, all types are French.

Marchand also lists a number of senses for *-age* (1969, 234–5), among them "collectivity," "condition, state, rank, office of," and "abode." These affixes thus express a challenging range of polysemy illustrated by the data in (12) and (13):

(12)   *-ery*
        collectives: peasantry, tenantry, jewelry, machinery, crockery, cutlery, pottery
        behavior characteristic of: snobbery, prudery, savagery, archery, midwifery
        place nouns: eatery, brewery, nunnery, piggery, fishery

(13)   *-age*
        collectives: baggage, wreckage, poundage, plumage, spillage
        condition of being, behavior of: brigandage
        place nouns: orphanage, parsonage, hermitage, anchorage

At issue in chapter 1 was not only whether to designate these affixes as concrete or abstract, but also how to account for the odd range of polysemy that they both show. In chapter 1, I suggested that the central meaning of *-ery* and *-age* was a quantitative one. I now return to that deferred analysis and take up again the semantic contribution of these affixes, and the question of their polysemy.

My proposal is that both *-ery* and *-age* are, at their core, affixes which contribute a collective meaning to their bases. Within the featural framework I have developed here, they would add the skeleton in (14) to their nominal bases:

(14)   *-ery, -age*
        [+B, +CI ([   ], <base>)]

My claim, then, is that *-ery* and *-age* make a specific semantic contribution to their bases, and further, that their contribution is quantitative. Both affixes add the features [+B, +CI] to their base, indicating that the derived noun is to be construed as a bounded aggregate or collectivity of individuals related to the base noun. The polysemy of the affixes arises, I suggest, from the way in which that collective reading is construed on particular kinds of base nouns.

For forms like *jewelry*, *machinery*, *peasantry*, *wreckage*, *poundage*, and *mileage* the collective reading is straightforward. Such nouns are derived on the base of nouns that are singular count nouns, most often concrete ones, and therefore the addition of the suffix has the simple effect of changing the quantificational class of the noun, leaving the value of the feature [material] unchanged. Nouns like *jewelry* and *wreckage*, that is, remain concrete (i.e., [+material]), as the affixes *-ery* and *-age* do not change the base designation for materiality, but they do come to denote bounded aggregates of *jewels*, *machines*, *peasants*, or whatever their bases denote. In cases where the base is abstract, such as with measure words like *pound* or *mile*, the *-age* derivative is abstract as well.

The meaning of the "behavior" or "condition" nouns also follows fairly straightforwardly from this same analysis if we assume that "behavior" nouns are formed on a particular type of nominal base – names for types of people, often derogatory ones – and if we assume further that those base nouns come to be construed metonymically.[12] In other words, the "behavior" reading is a natural sense extension from the "collective" reading. So bases like *buffoon*, *midwife*, or *brigand* are taken to stand for "what buffoons, midwives or brigands do," and the attachment of *-ery* or *-age* then denotes the collectivity of those behavioral characteristics of buffoons, midwives, brigands, etc. The derived nouns are abstract not because the affix itself provides the feature [−material], but rather because the bases have already come to be construed as abstractions.

---

12. Note that *-age* attaches to this kind of base only occasionally, and therefore only rarely gives rise to the behavioral meaning. Generally, *-age* is not a particularly productive affix, and many of its derivations have come to have lexicalized meanings.

We turn finally to the use of *-ery* and *-age* to create nouns denoting places. This is perhaps the most divergent of the meanings of these affixes. For *-age*, there are only a few place-name derivations, and it seems fairly difficult to coin new ones. But place names with *-ery* are relatively productive: the word *bagelry* (actually the name of a bagel shop in Durham, NH) is a perfectly natural coinage in the last couple of decades. So we ought not to dismiss these derivatives as aberrations or lexicalized forms. What is perhaps most interesting is that **both** *-age* and *-ery* give rise to place-name derivations, which suggests that there is some natural connection between the collective meaning and the place-name meaning.

What would the intrinsic connection between collectivity and place names be? In the case of *-ery* nouns based on animal names such a connection is not implausible: a *swannery* or *piggery* would be a place where a collectivity of swans or pigs is gathered. As has been pointed out a number of times in the literature on polysemy (e.g., Apresjan 1974, Copestake and Briscoe 1996, Nunberg 1996, Cruse 2000, Tyler and Evans 2001), there is a very common sense extension from a "place" reading to a "collectivity" reading, as where the place name *Seattle* in *Seattle voted Democratic* is taken to mean the collectivity of citizens of the city. What we find with *-ery* and *-age* nouns is precisely the same equivalence (place = collectivity), but with the collective meaning being the primary one, and the place the extension. What I would suggest is that the sense extension involved with this equivalency is in fact bidirectional.[13]

But if we admit that the extension of the collective meaning to place nouns is a relatively natural one, we must still explain why that extension needs to be made in English. Here, I appeal again to the notion of paradigmatic extension, which I introduced in chapter 3. Recall that paradigmatic extension is a process that takes place when there is no particular affix in a language to supply a meaning (see also Booij and Lieber 2004). When a particular affix is lacking, and at the same time there is pragmatic pressure – that is, real-world need – to create a word with that meaning, the needed words are derived by a process of sense extension from the closest productive affixes a language has. It is in fact the case that English has no specific affix which creates place nouns. What I would suggest, then, is that English extends the meaning of the collective-forming affixes for the purpose of creating place nouns.

13. Words like *brewery* and *bakery* might appear to be a problem for this account, as they seem to be place nouns derived from verbs. Marchand points out (1969, 284), however, that they might just as well be derived from agent nouns like *brewer* and *baker*. If we accept *brewer* and *baker* as the bases, the sense extension of the collective meaning to the place meaning is once again possible: *breweries* and *bakeries* are places where there are (generally) *brewers* and *bakers*.

The polysemy of *-ery* and *-age* therefore follows from a combination of the abstract nature of the semantic contribution of the affixes, the interaction of that underspecified skeletal contribution with bases of different sorts, and a sense extension brought about by paradigmatic pressure.

5.4.3 A word about inflection

In the Introduction, I suggested that my main focus in this work would be on processes of lexeme formation, primarily derivation, but also compounding and conversion. I excluded from the scope of this work a detailed discussion of inflection. It is clear, however, that a discussion of quantity features in my framework begs at least a bit of attention to inflectional categories such as the plural and the progressive. I will therefore briefly address these affixes here.

It is obvious that the majority of plural nouns in English are not simplex, but rather are derived by the affixation of *-s* (and its allomorphs). In this framework, the semantic contribution of the plural affix can be characterized simply as the addition of the features [−B, +CI] to the base noun:

(15)   *-s*
         [−B, +CI (<base>)]

Note that I distinguish between the contribution of an inflectional affix like *-s* and a derivational one like *-ery* not in the semantic content of the skeleton – both add quantity features – but in the absence of an argument in the skeleton of the inflection. That is, inflectional word formation differs from derivation in that the former, not being lexeme formation, has no chance to change the referential nature of its base.

As for the progressive, my analysis is only a partial and tentative one. There is an enormous literature on the semantics of progressivity which I cannot hope to do justice to here. In fact much disagreement exists on what progressive *-ing* actually does. Comrie (1976), for example, suggests that the progressive imposes an imperfective viewpoint on a situation, by which a situation is conceptualized, or reconceptualized, so that it can be seen from the inside. Progressivity also involves continuousness for Comrie (1976, 33). Dowty, citing Jespersen 1931 and Bennett and Partee 1972 as precursors, notes that a central part of the meaning of the progressive is that of duration.[14] Smith (1997, 74) notes, "The progressive viewpoint has meanings that do not arise for other types of imperfective. Nuances of activity, dynamism, and vividness are often associated with sentences of this viewpoint."

---

14. Dowty (1979, 146) himself believes that there is an additional component to the meaning of the progressive, a modal one, but I will not pursue this idea here.

I will not attempt a complete analysis of the progressive here, but if duration or continuativity is at least part of the semantic contribution of progressive *-ing*, then I would assume that its lexical representation would contribute (at least) the feature [−B] to its base:

(16)   *-ing*
       [−B (<base>)]

Again, as an inflectional morpheme, *-ing* does not add arguments of its own to the base. The feature [−B] is imposed on whatever quantitative features a base verb has to begin with, changing that verb to durative if it was not already so. So, for example, for punctual verbs like *explode* (*The bomb was exploding*) the action is drawn out to take place over time, and for semelfactive verbs like *flash* (*The light was flashing*) the result is a derived iterative or repetitive meaning. It is obvious that [−B] cannot be the sole contribution of the progressive, though; if it were, then we would expect that already durative verbs (like *eat* or *run*) would be semantically unchanged in the progressive, which is surely not the case. I will leave for future research, however, the nature of this additional contribution of the progressive.

One last word about inflection. In this short foray into the subject of inflection, I do not mean to give the impression that the semantic features that I have developed here can equally well be applied to all inflectional concepts. Rather, I suspect that the features that figure in the simplex lexicon, and that circumscribe the domain and limits of derivational word formation, have a limited application in the semantics of only one area of inflection, what Booij (1996, 2) has dubbed "inherent inflection":

> Inherent inflection is the kind of inflection that is not required by the syntactic context, although it may have syntactic relevance. Examples are the category number for nouns, comparative and superlative degree of the adjective, and tense and aspect for verbs. Other examples of inherent verbal inflection are infinitives and participles. Contextual inflection, on the other hand, is that kind of inflection that is dictated by the syntax, such as person and number markers on verbs that agree with subjects and/or objects, agreement markers for adjectives, and structural case markers on nouns.

Inherent inflection might be expected to capitalize on some of the features relevant for derivational word formation (for example, passive participles might in my terms involve the addition of the feature [−dynamic] to the verbal base), but contextual inflection would involve features of a more syntactic nature, for example case or agreement features.

5.5   *Conclusion*

In this chapter I have proposed two more semantic features, [B] and [CI], that appear to play a role in characterizing quantitative aspects of the simplex lexicon. I have further tried to show that these features are also exploited by the derivational system of English and indeed by a certain part of the inflectional system, that of inherent inflection. The features [B] and [CI] complete the inventory of semantic features I intend to introduce in this work.

Certainly, the inventory of semantic features necessary to characterize the simplex lexicon and the derivational system of English – much less of other languages – is not yet complete. To arrive at a complete system, indeed even to approach one, will require a great deal more work. What I hope to have done so far is merely to present enough of a fragment to suggest the utility of this approach both in describing lexical semantics and in explaining the major issues in the semantics of word formation: polysemy, the multiple-affix question, the issue of zero derivation. In the next chapter I will turn to the one major question I posed at the outset that I have not yet broached, that of semantic mismatches.

6 Combinability and the correspondence between form and meaning

In previous chapters I have begun to develop a framework of representation that allows us to describe affixal semantics, to see the relationship between the semantics of derivation and that of the simplex lexicon, and to address questions of affixal polysemy, zero-affixation, and the existence of multiple synonymous affixes. For the most part, we have looked at the meanings of individual affixes, or at clusters of affixes which share the same meaning. What we have not looked at so far, except in passing, is what happens when we derive complex words by a process of successive affixation.

We have a number of separate issues to consider. One prominent question concerns restrictions on stacking up derivational affixes, specifically, **semantic** restrictions on affixation. To what extent is the attachment of a particular affix dependent on the semantic characteristics of its base? In the course of previous chapters we have mentioned a few such restrictions, and we will revisit them more fully below. Another problem is that of adding up the meanings of successive affixes: assuming that affixes are added to bases (simplex and complex) subject to their semantic restrictions (not to mention phonological and morphological restrictions), can they attach freely and meaningfully? To what extent is the semantics of successive affixation compositional and additive? How do we compute the meanings of words with multiple affixes? Is redundancy allowed? In other words, is there any reason to believe that multiple affixes with the same meaning should not be allowed to attach in the same word?

Such questions in fact lead to the general issue of mismatches between form and meaning, to cases where there seems to be more than one form that expresses the same meaning, and to forms that apparently express no meaning at all. The former case has been referred to in the literature as *overdetermination* (Beard 1995) and it might be linked to what Matthews (1974, 149) terms *extended exponence* in inflection (see also Matthews 1972, Spencer 1991, 51, Carstairs-McCarthy 1992). Here, for clarity, I will refer to it as "derivational redundancy".

The latter might be called the empty-affix question. Issues of extended exponence and empty affixes have been discussed in some depth with respect to
inflection (see Anderson 1992, Stump 2001), but analogous issues have not
been as thoroughly explored with respect to derivation.

I will take up each of these issues in turn. Section 6.1 deals with semantic
restrictions on derivational affixation, and on issues of redundancy. Section 6.2
looks in some detail at cumulativity and recursivity in affixal meanings. The
third section of the chapter turns finally to the issue of other semantic mismatches in derivation and to the empty-affix question, that is, what to do about
words which appear to have either too much or too little in the way of semantic
stuff.

6.1   Semantic restrictions on affixation

Not surprisingly, given the general lack of attention to affixal semantics, there
has been relatively little work done on the semantic restrictions on affixation.
There is, of course, a substantial and interesting literature concerning other
sorts of restrictions on the successive attachment of derivational affixes, and I
will give this literature just a brief review here, primarily for the purpose of
identifying some of the other sorts of mechanisms that have been proposed to
restrict the combinability of affixes. Following this, I will turn to the question
of semantic restrictions on affixation.

6.1.1   Non-semantic approaches to affix ordering
All theories of morphology agree that there are syntactic/categorial restrictions
on affixation. The suffix -*ness*, for example, attaches to adjectives, so we might
expect to find it attached to derived adjectives in -*al* or -*ive*, as well as to
simplex adjectives. But we would not expect to find it attached to simplex
nouns or to nouns derived from -*ity* or -*age*, to simplex verbs or verbs derived
from -*ize*. Of course there are many restrictions on the combining of affixes
beyond the straightforward, purely categorial ones. Not every affix which forms
lexical items of a particular category can serve as base to other affixes which
select that category. For example, -*age* takes nouns (*orphanage*, *mileage*), but
it does not attach to nouns derived with the suffix -*ness* (**happinessage*). So
morphologists have for some time endeavored to find other sorts of restrictions
on the combining of affixes.

Most well known of this work is the sizeable literature on Lexical Phonology and Morphology (Siegel 1974, Kiparsky 1982, Strauss 1982, Halle and
Mohanan 1985, Mohanan 1986, Giegerich 1999, among many others), which

seeks to explain restrictions on the ordering of derivational affixes by postulating that different affixes belong to different strata or levels. According to the Level Ordering hypothesis, the morphology and phonology of a language may be divided into levels or strata which are strictly ordered with respect to one another in the sense that each represents a block in which affixes are attached and relevant phonological rules applied. Affixes on an earlier level are expected to occur inside affixes that belong to a later level, but not vice versa. Phonological rules active on an earlier stratum do not affect words formed by affixation on a later stratum.

I will not review either the positive results or the shortcomings of Lexical Phonology and Morphology; Giegerich (1999) gives an excellent historical overview and analysis. What is important here is merely to point out that the sort of restrictions on affix ordering proposed in this literature are non-semantic in nature: morphemes are grouped into blocks based on their phonological behavior, not on the basis of their meanings.

Related to the tradition of Lexical Phonology and Morphology is the theoretical thread in morphology which seeks to explain affix ordering – at least in English – on the basis of groupings of affixes into native and non-native or [−Latinate] and [+Latinate] classes; see, for example, Selkirk (1982). The general wisdom in theories of this sort is that native affixes are free to attach to non-native ones, but not vice versa.[1] Again, the ordering and co-occurrence of derivational affixes is explained on the basis of a diacritic distinction (albeit one which has some historical basis) without appeal to lexical semantics. In other words, affixes are again partitioned into classes, and restrictions placed on these classes.

Nor do other treatments of affix ordering outside the Lexical Phonology and Morphology tradition have much to say about semantic restrictions on affixation. Fabb (1988) is an important work which attempts to debunk the explanations of affix ordering offered in Lexical Phonology and Morphology. Fabb shows that Lexical Phonology and Morphology would lead us to expect far more affix combinations than we actually find. He suggests instead that English suffixes simply fall into four groups. According to Fabb, the vast majority of suffixes in English are restricted to simplex bases. Other suffixes fall into one of three smaller classes: suffixes that attach to one other suffix, suffixes that attach freely, and suffixes that Fabb deems problematic. The failure of affixes to stack up has nothing to do with their meaning.

---

1. See Giegerich (1999) for an argument that both Level Ordering and the division of affixes into [+Latinate] and [−Latinate] classes are independently needed in English.

Plag (1999) looks at Fabb's generalizations, suggesting first that they are empirically flawed; he finds that many of the affixes that Fabb claims not to attach to complex bases in fact do so. Second, Plag argues that there are more cogent, if also more particularistic, explanations of some of the more empirically solid of Fabb's observations. In fact, Plag turns away from a grouping approach to explaining combinatorial restrictions on affixation, and looks carefully at individual restrictions on affixes – both on what they attach to and on what can attach to them. For example, nominalizers like *-al*, *-ance*, and *-ment* appear to attach only to underived verbs in English, and thus belong to Fabb's first group. Plag, however, explains why they belong to this group: the only productive verb-forming suffixes in English are *-ize* and *-ify*, both of which are always nominalized by adding the suffix *-ation*.

Significantly for our purposes, among current morphologists who have taken up issues of combinability, Plag is virtually alone in acknowledging that the restrictions on the attachment of some affixes must have a semantic basis (1999, 64): "the role of semantic compatibility of suffixes certainly deserves further attention since it seems that in this domain a number of interesting restrictions can be located."[2] We will return to some of Plag's observations shortly.

Before we go on to the issue of semantic restrictions, I mention one last approach to affix ordering. Aronoff and Fuhrhop (2002) attempt to explain the combinations of affixes that do and do not occur in both German and English. For German, they propose that some suffixes are "closing suffixes," by which they mean suffixes that cannot themselves serve as bases for further affixation. For English, they propose what they call the Monosuffix Constraint, which essentially restricts native suffixes to one per word. It is beyond the scope of this chapter to explore whether the monosuffix generalization is actually true for English.[3] I mention Aronoff and Fuhrhop's work mainly to illustrate another restriction that might prevent full combinability of affixes. My point here is that the Monosuffix Constraint is intended to be a purely morphological constraint: there are no apparent phonological, syntactic, or semantic reasons why more than one native affix might not attach to an appropriate base.

What this previous literature has shown us is that there are indeed different sorts of restrictions that limit the combinatorial possibilities of affixes:

2. Carstairs-McCarthy (1992) notes the lack of such investigation of the topic. Booij (2000) mentions some previous work on Dutch.

3. I suspect that it is not. In addition to the universal exception to the constraint that Aronoff and Fuhrhop cite (the affix *-ness* is the one native affix that can combine freely with other native affixes), there are other combinations of native affixes that Aronoff and Fuhrhop seem to have missed (*porterage, baggager, readership, leadership, loverhood, survivorship*).

categorial, phonological, and perhaps purely morphological ones. But their existence should not prevent us from looking for semantic restrictions as well.

6.1.2   *Specific semantic constraints*

In fact, most affixes have semantic restrictions on their attachment. As is well known, and as I mentioned above, much derivational affixation is category-changing. Of course categorial restrictions on affixation are always accompanied by semantic consequences: to say that -*ness* attaches to adjectives is to say something about not only its syntactic selection, but also its semantic selection, as adjectives bear different semantic features from nouns. So to the extent that particular affixes select for particular syntactic categories of bases, they also show concomitant semantic selection.

But affixes which do not change syntactic category also show semantic restrictions. We will survey here some of the ones that have been proposed. For example, in the course of previous chapters, I have suggested semantic restrictions on the attachment of two affixes, the prefixes *re-* and *un-*: both, we saw, select for verbal bases that imply results which are impermanent. For example, we saw that we cannot form verbs like *unyawn or *reswim from verbs that imply no result at all, nor can we create verbs like *unexplode or *rekill from bases whose results are permanent. This generalization seems fairly solid.

The subject of semantic constraints on derivational affixation has generally not received wide attention in the literature, but there are at least two previous works that explore semantic restrictions on specific affixes: Zimmer (1964) on negative prefixes, and Aronoff and Cho (2001) on -*ship*.

Perhaps the best known of the semantic restrictions on affixation – and certainly the one given most attention in generative morphology – is the one mentioned briefly in chapter 4, the putative restriction on attaching negative affixes like *in-*, *un-*, and *non-* to bases which already express negative content. The most comprehensive treatment of this restriction is Zimmer's (1964) (see also Horn 1989/2001). Zimmer traces the observation back to nineteenth-century sources on moral philosophy, and later to Jespersen (1942, 466), who observes: "The same general rule obtains in English as in other languages, that most adjectives with *un-* or *in-* have a depreciatory sense; we have *undue*, *unkind*, *unworthy*, etc., but it is not possible to form similar adjectives from *foolish*, *naughty*, *ugly*, or *wicked*." Zimmer takes on the task of exploring Jespersen's claim more carefully, unpacking both the extent to which *un-* derivatives are depreciatory, and more importantly for our purposes, the extent to which the bases of *un-* affixation really cannot themselves be negative. His conclusion for

English is interestingly equivocal (1964, 44): "As for the particular restriction that primarily concerns us, i.e., that against the use of *un-* with 'negative' bases, it does seem to apply to at least part of the corpus, although the exact delimitation of the part to which it does apply poses some problems." In other words, Zimmer suggests that the generalization is sound for the most part, but not completely sound, and he gives sufficient data to call it into serious question.

Some of Zimmer's counterexamples have indeed drawn the attention of generative morphologists, who have argued that they do not constitute counterexamples at all. For example, Zimmer points out that there are numerous forms like *unblemished, unimpeachable, unerring*, and *unpainful* (1964, 35–6), which have a negative prefix even though their bases seem to have clearly negative semantic content. But such examples have been used in support of the so-called Adjacency Condition in morphology (Siegel 1977, Allen 1978), which claims that only the content of the most recently affixed material is "visible" to successive affixation. As Zimmer himself is aware, all these examples share the same sort of structure, with the semantically negative base being innermost, a suffix attaching to them, and the negative prefix occurring outside the suffix (e.g., [un [[pain]ful]]). According to the Adjacency Condition, the material visible to *un-* is not negative in content because *un-* can "see" only as far down in its base as the previously attached affix, which has only positive semantic content. The Adjacency Condition thus purports to eliminate a large class of the exceptions that Zimmer finds to his generalization.[4]

Nevertheless, as Zimmer points out, it is still not clear that the generalization is entirely robust. There are still numerous attested *un-* derivatives that are not explained by appealing to Adjacency:

(1)   examples from Zimmer (1964, 30, 35–7)

incorrupt	unselfish	uncruel
inculpable	unsordid	unevil
uncorrupt	unvicious	unsick
undegenerate	unvulgar	unsilly
unmalicious	unhostile	unstupid
unobnoxious		

The examples in (1) are arguably derived by affixation of *un-* to simplex bases. Although the vast majority of forms to which negative affixes like *un-* attach are

---

4. We might ask why this would be so. If the semantic interpretation of derivation is compositional, why should the negative prefix see only the semantic content of the most recently attached suffix, and not the composed semantic representation of the complex base?

either positive or neutral in content, not all of them are. Zimmer's generalization seems at best to be a strong tendency, but not a general restriction.[5]

Another semantic restriction on affixation is proposed by Aronoff and Cho (2001) who try to explain an apparent difference between the affixes *-ship* and *-hood* in English. The former, they argue, is restricted to attach only to stage-level nouns, that is, nouns that denote temporary characteristics of their referents. It does not attach to individual-level nouns, that is, those that denote permanent and immutable characteristics of their referents. So we find forms like *deanship*, *friendship*, or *sponsorship* on stage-level bases, but not forms like **parentship*, **nieceship*, or **womanship* on individual-level nouns. The suffix *-hood*, on the other hand, attaches to either stage- or individual-level nouns (*priesthood*, *motherhood*, etc.).

As in the case of Zimmer's generalization, however, it is not clear how robust this restriction is. Plausible counterexamples are not hard to find: Lehnert (1971), for example, lists forms like *uncleship*, *cousinship*, *twinship*, *manship*, and *sonship*, all of which seem to me to be based on individual-level nouns, and in fact to be quite comparable to the examples that Aronoff and Cho rule out. The form *kinship* is also based, as far as I can tell, on an individual noun, and is not in the least exotic. As in the case of the negative prefixes discussed above, we seem to be dealing with a tendency here, rather than a hard-and-fast restriction.

Plag (1999, 76) suggests another semantic restriction on affixation, this time a somewhat more general one: we should not expect to find suffixes that form abstract nouns which attach to other suffixes which form abstract nouns:

> Apart from extra-linguistic mechanisms at work, which may influence the productivity of certain word formation patterns, a look at the meaning of the suffixes reveals that the low rate of suffixed bases may be a consequence of the semantics of *-age*, *-hood*, and *-ism*. Of the nouns that end in a suffix, a large portion are abstract nouns, in which case the stacking of another abstract-noun suffix leads to uninterpretable results. Thus, words like **concentrationhood* or **concentrationage* are hard to interpret, to say the least.

In other words, Plag seems to suggest that affixes like *-age*, *-hood*, and *-ism*, which attach to nouns and do not change syntactic category, might avoid attaching to other nominalizers, because they form abstract nouns. This would be an

---

5. Zimmer also points out that there are quite a few simple adjectives in English that resist the affixation of *un-* or *in-*, even though their content is nicely positive or neutral, among them *short*, *long*, *wide*, *high*, *warm*, and *cold* (1964, 40).

interesting semantic restriction on affixation, but we might want to explore it further and try to make it more precise.

6.1.3   Derivational redundancy

As Plag suggests, it makes perfect sense to assume that an abstract noun-forming suffix should avoid attaching to already abstract nouns: once a word is abstract, what would be the point of making it abstract again? Such a restriction is in fact reminiscent of Zimmer's restriction on negative prefixes: why, generally speaking, would one want to negate an already negative form? The similarity between the two restrictions suggests that we might begin to formulate a more general "redundancy restriction," which we might tentatively state as in (2):

(2)   The Redundancy Restriction
        Affixes do not add semantic content that is already available within a base
        word (simplex or derived).

That is, we might expect that affixes in general would avoid duplicating semantic features that a base word already has. Stated otherwise, we might expect that expressing the same content more than once in a word should be prohibited. But we must be cautious in looking at this restriction: Zimmer suggested in the case of negatives that the restriction was at best a tendency, not always scrupulously adhered to.

Further, it is worth pointing out that some degree of redundancy is not unheard of in inflection, where it is referred to as "extended exponence": Matthews (1974, 149) uses this term to describe cases in which an inflectional category "would have exponents in each of two or more distinct positions." These positions in turn may also express other inflectional categories, so that particular morphemes may not be redundant, but some of the inflectional features they express may be. Indeed, as Stump (2001, 208) points out, an assumption much like the Redundancy Restriction has sometimes been made with respect to inflectional morphology (cf. Kiparsky 1982, Marantz 1984, Anderson 1992), where it is more often than not the case that a given morphosyntactic feature is marked only once in a word. Nevertheless, redundantly marked morphosyntactic features are found, and it is therefore not possible to rule out entirely multiple marking of the same feature.[6]

Let us start our investigation of derivational redundancy by looking in some detail at Plag's case of abstract nouns. The Redundancy Restriction in fact

---

6. Even in a language as inflectionally impoverished as English, double marking is not unknown, either diachronically (*children* is an historical example) or dialectally (e.g., in dialects where the plural of *child* can be *childrens*).

does seem to hold for *-hood*, which typically attaches to personal nouns, either simple (*fatherhood, priesthood*) or derived (*loverhood*), and to animal names, especially names for the young of various species (*kittenhood, puppyhood*). We do not find the suffix *-hood* attached to abstract nouns, either simple or derived. But *-age* and *-ism* are more complicated, and force us to explore our putative restriction further.

First, as I argued in the last chapter, the suffix *-age* is not an abstract noun-forming suffix, as Plag suggests. Rather, the central meaning of *-age* is a quantitative one; I have proposed that *-age* adds the features [+B, +CI] to its base. We can still ask whether it attaches to abstract nouns (simplex or derived), but to test the Redundancy Restriction, we should really look at the quantitative characteristics of the bases it attaches to; specifically, whether it attaches to other nouns with the features [+B, +CI].

The majority of nouns that *-age* favors are personal nouns (e.g., *brigand, orphan*) and concrete nouns (*shrub, leaf*).[7] What is most notable is that the nouns that *-age* attaches to are almost all singular count nouns, that is, nouns which bear the features [+B, −CI]. It attaches to just a few mass nouns, as far as I can tell; Lehnert (1971) lists, for example, *contrabandage, groundage,* and *waterage*. In the system outlined in chapter 5, these bases would bear the features [−B, −CI]. In either case, *-age* changes the quantitative class of its base. And as (2) would predict, *-age* does fail to attach to simplex nouns which are already collective: **crowdage*, **herdage*, or **bunchage* seem very odd. This suggests some support for the Redundancy Restriction.

But perhaps there is more to be said. As Plag points out, *-age* does not usually attach to abstract nouns. Generally, *-age* avoids simplex abstract nouns, although there is one specific class of simple abstract nouns that it attaches to quite productively, namely words for types of measure (*mile, ton, acre, watt,* etc.). This makes good sense: the particular abstract nouns that *-age* chooses are ones that are all singular count nouns which express quantities or units of measure, and in attaching to them, *-age* again changes their quantitative class to collectives of these units.

As for derived abstract nouns, as Plag observes, we generally do not find *-age* attached to them. I would argue, however, that this is not because of the Redundancy Restriction, or because of some general obscurity in their composed meanings – Plag's suggestion – but because of a positive semantic condition on *-age* that we seem to have uncovered, namely that *-age* is most comfortable on singular count nouns, and primarily on concrete ones. The quantitative

---

7. *-age* also attaches to verb stems: e.g., *steerage, breakage, spoilage*.

characteristics of nominalizing affixes like *-ation, -ment, -al*, and *-ance* are a bit unclear. It appears that these affixes have no inherent quantitative characteristics, but merely add the features [−material, dynamic] to their bases. Whatever quantitative characteristics nominalizations have are developed on the basis of lexicalized meanings of words: so *refusal* is a count noun, *satisfaction* a mass noun. Only when a nominalization has been lexicalized with the interpretation of a concrete singular count noun does an *-age* derivation seem even remotely possible. For example, one might contemplate a word like *transmissionage* to denote a collectivity of transmissions, but only where *transmission* means the part of a car. In other words, *-age* fails to attach to nominalized forms because generally they lack the quantitative characteristics to fulfill its positive semantic restrictions.

The case of *-ism* is instructive as well. According to Marchand (1969, 306–7), *-ism* can be characterized as a suffix which forms abstract nouns, in our terms simple (as opposed to processual) abstract nouns, which adds the feature [−material]. If (2) is a correct semantic restriction on affixation, we would expect that *-ism* should not attach to other simple (as opposed to processual) abstract words, either simplex or derived. What we find, however, is that *-ism* is freer in choosing the bases it attaches to than (2) would lead us to expect. It attaches to personal nouns, both simple and derived (*snobbism, cannibalism, refugeeism, reporterism*), to non-personal concrete nouns (*animalism, magnetism*), to abstract processual nouns, many of which are complex (*sutteeism, revisionism, perfectionism, obstructionism*). Note that this lends some support to the formalism I have developed in earlier chapters. As *-ism* bears only the feature [−material], and the last group of nouns is characterized by [−material, dynamic], *-ism* should still effect enough of a semantic change to be felicitous on this group of abstract nouns. The fact that we find an abundance of *-ism* words based on abstract nominalizations in *-ation* suggests that the formalism is on the right track.

The suffix *-ism* does not, as far as I can tell, attach to nouns derived with other [−material] suffixes, for example, *-ity, -ness, -hood*, or *-ship*. Of course, the failure of *-ism* to attach to *-ness, -hood*, and *-ship* might be attributed to Level Ordering, or to the failure of non-native affixes to attach to native affixes – that is, to some of the non-semantic constraints on affix ordering that we mentioned above. Still, these would not explain the failure of *-ism* to attach to *-ity*, whereas the Redundancy Restriction would explain all four cases. So again, we seem to have some evidence for this general restriction.

But once again, it seems that we have a tendency, rather than a hard-and-fast restriction: *-ism* also seems to attach to at least some simple abstract nouns, that is, to nouns that are already characterized by only the feature [−material]: *propagandism, imagism, tokenism, monadism, racism, syllabism, nothingism,* and a few more that can be found in Lehnert (1971). The tentative conclusion to be drawn at this point is that Plag is generally right: forming abstract nouns from abstract nouns tends not to happen. But "generally" is the key word here: there are enough cases where abstract nouns are formed from already abstract nouns that we would want to consider carefully whether there really should be a grammatical constraint on semantic redundancy.

Further investigation of English affixation suggests that redundancy or extended exponence in derivation – although rare – is nevertheless possible. For example, the OED cites a number of examples of double agentives, derived words with combinations of the concrete processual noun-forming suffixes *-er, -ist,* and *-ian* in various orders: *checkerist, consumerist, tympanister, pardonister, collegianer, musicianer, physicianer,* among others. Such cases are rare, often obsolete, and possibly sometimes the result of reanalysis: Marchand (1969, 310) speculates, for example, that *-ister* words might have arisen as a reinterpretation of the French affix *-istre* which occurs in words like *alchemistre* and *choristre.* But the fact remains that the words were coined, and their coinage suggests that a doubling of affixes is possible. Perhaps there is more to be said here as well: note that the majority of forms with two agentive suffixes have *-er* attached outside the other affix. The suffix *-er* is by far the most productive concrete processual noun-forming affix in English. It is possible that its addition to already agentive forms serves to strengthen a perceived weakness in the agentive content of the less productive suffixes *-ian* and *-ist.*

Another example of affixal doubling comes in the case of adjective-forming suffixes. In English one can form relational adjectives from nouns by adding *-ic* (*romantic, analytic*), *-al* (*procedural, coastal*), and *-oid* (*rhomboid, tuberculoid*). All three suffixes would be characterized by the skeletal feature [−dynamic] in the framework I have developed. What is curious is that *-al* can be found in combination with both *-ic* and *-oid*:

(3)   a. arithmetic (ærɪθ'mɛtɪk)   arithmetical
          dramatic   dramatical
          geographic   geographical
       b. alkaloid   alkaloidal
          rhomboid   rhomboidal

While in some pairs, one or another of the two forms has been lexicalized with a special meaning (e.g., *historic* vs. *historical, economic* vs. *economical*), in many cases there appears to be no distinction in meaning at all. The OED lists *arithmetic*, *dramatic*, and *geographic* as respective variants of *arithmetical*, *dramatical*, and *geographical*. Indeed, in its entry on the suffix *-ical*, the OED comments: "Often also the form in *-ic* is restricted to the sense 'of' or 'of the nature of' the subject in question, while that in *-ical* has wider or more transferred senses, including that of 'practically connected' or 'dealing with' the subject. . . . **But in many cases this distinction is, from the nature of the subject, difficult to maintain or entirely inappreciable** [emphasis mine – R.L.]." Similarly, forms like *alkaloid* and *alkaloidal* or *rhomboid* and *rhomboidal* are listed as semantic equivalents. We therefore cannot categorically rule out redundant affixation.

There is yet another kind of violation of redundancy that we have not mentioned so far. While redundancy in affixation seems at least to be discouraged, full-scale repetition of affixes is by no means unheard of. Double diminutives are attested in a number of languages, among them Afrikaans (Schultink 1975), Italian (Scalise 1984), and Zulu (Bauer 1988). Bauer (1988, 196) also cites German forms like *Ur-ur-gross-mutter* "great great grandmother." Muysken (1986, 635) cites a number of derivational affixes in Quechua which can occur more than once in a single word, including causatives, diminutives, and morphemes that he labels as "decisiveness," "many objects," and "action with force." Even in English we can double at least some affixes in a meaningful way; for example, those which allow iterative or scalar readings which can be intensified by repetition. The prefixes *re-* and *over-* are plausible candidates for repetition in English; for example, *to re-rewrite* or *to over-overcompensate* seem fine to me. In all of these cases repetition clearly does not constitute redundancy, although it would be difficult to state a restriction like (2) so that it would rule out one without also ruling out the other.

What are we to make of this? We seem to have ample evidence that the Redundancy Restriction is not quite correct. But there's also clearly something to it: although there are violations of redundancy, there are not terribly many. We can only assume that when violations of Redundancy occur, they are useful. In fact, the notion of usefulness I think suggests a solution to our dilemma. Perhaps the Redundancy Restriction is not a semantic restriction at all, but the effect of general pragmatic conditions on expansion of the lexicon. Here, I take a cue from a comment Marchand makes on the negative case we looked at above. Discussing the putative restriction on attaching negative affixes to negative bases, he remarks (1969, 203): "Natural linguistic instinct would not make the sophisticated detour of negativing a negative to obtain a positive." In other words, Marchand's observation suggests a sort of pragmatic constraint on coinage: negative prefixes might be disfavored on negative bases simply because it's usually not particularly useful to coin such words. To extend the idea somewhat, nothing rules out redundancy, but we would not expect it either unless it proves to be useful.

The evidence we have looked at so far suggests that the restriction on affixation is actually not a semantic one, but rather a pragmatic one. Here we might appeal to Grice's (1975, 1978) felicity principles, specifically to his Maxim of Manner, which enjoins speakers to be perspicuous in their speech. Among other things being perspicuous involves avoiding obscurity and being as brief as possible (Grice 1975, 45–6; cf. also Saeed 1997, 193). We need to be informative when we coin new words; new words need to be useful and to be useful they must be clear. Redundancy is therefore not ruled out – but neither is it particularly favored. Redundancy or even repetition is permitted in deriving words as long as what results is informative. To add extra affixes is otherwise linguistically perverse.

6.1.4   Summary

We have seen in this section that there indeed seem to be semantic restrictions on affixation, for example those that typically accompany syntactic category change, as well as restrictions on *re-* and *un-*, *-age* and *-ship*. An exhaustive analysis of the derivational morphology of English (especially of non-category-changing morphology) would surely turn up more. But a general restriction on redundancy or a prohibition on extended exponence seems not to hold; repeating the same semantic features is possible as long as the result is useful and interpretable. Of course, in saying this I am laying myself open to easy criticism. In appealing to notions like "usefulness" or "interpretability" I seem to be eschewing solid formal explanations for vague functional ones. After all, what makes a word useful and interpretable beyond the fact that a speaker uses it and an interlocutor understands it? But Newmeyer (1999) argues wisely that formal and functional explanations are not antithetical or even mutually exclusive. I will try to show why this is especially true with regard to the lexicon. In the next section I will look further at what makes some complex words useful, and others less useful, and at what makes complex words interpretable.

6.1.5   Addendum: redeeming a promissory note

The careful reader will remember that in chapter 4 I raised the question of how to characterize the skeleton of the prefix *de-*. I argued that denominal and deadjectival forms in *de-* were semantically both causative and privative, and therefore should have the skeleton in (4):

(4)   [+dynamic ([$_{volitional-i}$], [$_j$])]; [+dynamic ([$_i$], [+dynamic,
           +IEPS ([$_j$], [−Loc ([   ])])]), <base>]

At issue was how to represent deverbal *de-*, specifically whether that form of
the prefix should be different from its category-changing sibling, adding only
the feature [−Loc] and not the rest of the causative scaffolding. Certainly, the
skeletal representation that results when *de-* is composed with already causative
verbs like *demilitarize* and *degasify* would look simpler in that case. But we
would also be left with two skeletal variants of *de-*. Nevertheless, in chapter 4
that solution seemed more obvious than the one in which *de-* always adds the
skeleton in (4), whether its base is already causative or not.

   However, in this chapter I have argued that nothing rules out redundancy in
semantic representation, and that redundancy is a pervasive, if not a frequent,
characteristic of derivation. We have no real reason therefore to opt for the solution suggested in chapter 4, where *de-* has two representations. The existence
of semantic redundancy elsewhere in derivation allows us to maintain a unitary
analysis of *de-* here.

6.2   Cumulativity and recursivity: when do complex words cease to be useful?

What in general makes a word useful? The common-sense answer to this question is a sneaky one: surely a useful word identifies some useful conceptual
space. To determine what makes a conceptual space useful, however, is way
beyond the scope of my philosophical abilities; surely a combination of factors
must be involved, both internal – innate to the human mind – and external –
responding to historical and cultural pressures.[8] I will not attempt to answer
this large and interesting question here. But I can narrow down the question to
a point that might permit more fruitful speculation on the topic immediately at
hand. Since the focus of this book has been on the semantics of derivation, we
might simply ask: what makes a derived word useful?

   In some ways the answer here seems deceptively simple. Sometimes, deriving a word allows us to transfer a concept easily expressible in one category to
another category where that concept has no simplex equivalent. At other times,
we derive new words to modify slightly the meanings of already existing lexemes. Assuming that all phonological, morphological, syntactic, and semantic
restrictions on the attachment of affixes are met, we should be able to attach

---

8. What makes Sniglets amusing is that they are typically words that identify some part of conceptual space that is not normally recognized as useful.

affixes freely and recursively as long as their attachment allows us either to transpose a useful concept from one category to another or to augment the meaning of an already existing lexeme. Let me illustrate with some examples.

Consider first the affixes *-ation*, *-ize*, and *-al*. As Plag (1999) has pointed out, verbs in *-ize* are typically nominalized with the suffix *-ation*, so words like *organization* or *hospitalization* are common. The suffix *-ize* in turn can attach to nouns, among them ones derived with *-ation*. Examples include *revolutionize, protectionize, resurrectionize, conversationize, educationize*, among others (examples from Lehnert 1971 and the OED). We therefore have a potential to create a derivational loop between these two affixes. We may add adjective-forming *-al* into the mix as well. This suffix attaches to nouns (*logical, tubal*), and therefore has the potential to attach to *-ation* (e.g., *conventional, gravitational*, etc.). The suffix *-ize* can attach to adjectives as well as to nouns, and among those adjectives are ones in *-al* (e.g., *brutalize, orientalize*). The addition of *-al* gives us the potential for a somewhat larger loop. Let us see what happens when we try to attach these affixes recursively. The examples in (5) are instructive:

(5) a. organ   revolve
        organize   revolution
        organization   revolutionize
        *organizationize   *revolutionization
        *organizationization   *revolutionizationize
     b. confess   convene   profess
        confession   convention   profession
        confessional   conventional   professional
        ??confessionalize conventionalize   professionalize
        *confessionalization ??conventionalization professionalization
        *confessionalizational *conventionalizational ??professionalizational

The judgments on these forms are my own, and I imagine that there might be some disagreement in detail; but I trust that other speakers will find that the examples begin to degrade at some point as we add further affixes.[9]

As the examples in (5a) indicate, with a loop of just two affixes, judgments degrade very rapidly. In fact, it seems as if each affix can be used only once. With a noun like *organ* we can verbalize once and then renominalize; with the verb *revolve* we can nominalize once and then reverbalize. Anything beyond that becomes unlikely, if not downright unacceptable. Further, in both cases,

---

9. A quick Google search yields hits for both the words *confessionalization* (although I cannot figure out what the word is supposed to mean) and *conventionalization*. But as expected there are no hits for *confessionalizational, conventionalizational,* or *professionalizational*.

the first derivational step has become highly lexicalized in English; the relationships between *organ* and *organize* and between *revolve* and *revolution* are quite remote. Thus, when we renominalize *organize* or reverbalize *revolution* we are creating words with rather different meanings from the simplex noun *organ* and verb *revolve* with which we started. Each step constitutes a useful and meaningful transposition. But if we try to go beyond this, further nominalizations and verbalizations make no semantic changes, at least none that are useful or interpretable.

The examples in (5b) show the same pattern, although the deterioration in acceptability is a bit slower. What we see again is that the further along the derivational pattern lexicalization has occurred, the more we can continue to add the same affixes in our loop felicitously, that is, creating useful and interpretable words. So *confess*, *confession*, and *confessional*[10] are all fairly transparent in meaning. *Confessionalize* would mean something like "make confessional," but what exactly would that mean, as compared to *confess*? The word is difficult to interpret (at least in the absence of any context), and therefore questionable. To go further by adding *-ation* and then *-al* to *confessionalize* yields progressively less interpretable words.

Note, in contrast, that *conventionalize*, a word with precisely the same sequence of affixes, is perfectly fine. Because *conventional* has a lexicalized meaning (i.e., "ordinary"), adding *-ize* makes a verb whose meaning is transparent, and transparently different from *convene* – and therefore is useful. Further affixation, however, begins the process of semantic degradation. Similarly with *professional*, which has the lexicalized meaning "businesslike," only here I find the form *professionalize* perfectly natural and interpretable. But with further affixation acceptability begins to deteriorate.

The point here is a simple one. Affixes add semantic material in the form of skeletal features. Transpositional affixes like *-ize*, *-al*, and *-ation* lack semantic bodies and bear very little semantic content. This lack of content limits recursivity. Unless a derived form has undergone lexicalization – which means that the derived word as a whole has acquired corporeal material beyond what the simplex base supplies – at a certain point continued semantic transposition becomes uninformative. Further rounds of affixation are not prohibited; they are simply not useful or interpretable.

On the other hand, with affixes like *re-* and *over-* (also affixes like *pre-*, *post-*, *super-*, *mega-*, and the like), successive affixation continues to be informative, as

10. Here I intend the adjectival form. The noun *confessional* of course does have a lexicalized meaning ("the place where confession occurs"), and if *-ize* is affixed, it might mean "put in a confessional."

it has an intensifying effect. One can *re-retest*[11] or even *re-re-retest* something to express repetition of the activity, or *over-overcompensate* to compensate way too much. Such intensification is perfectly understandable and in fact conversationally useful. Note that in featural terms *re-* is a quantitative affix (it bears the feature [+CI]), and it is therefore not hard to see why augmentation should be possible. I argued in chapter 4 that prepositional affixes like *over-* should be characterized not only by the skeletal feature [+Loc], but also by bodily characteristics specifying the dimension of the reference object, the focus of the object (towards an initial or final point), the axis (vertical, horizontal, depth), and whether contact is implied or not. These bodily characteristics often lend themselves to scalar interpretation, and therefore to intensification or augmentation by repetition. Continued affixation of *over-* and similar prefixes is therefore often useful and perfectly interpretable.

We can therefore say that derivation is cumulative and recursive. Aside from the particular phonological, morphological, syntactic, and semantic restrictions that affect particular affixes, there are no general and purely linguistic limits on derivation. There are, however, pragmatic limits: derived words have to have enough semantic content to be useful. If the semantic content (either skeletal or corporeal) lends itself to intensification, there is in principle no limit on the number of times that affix can be added. For transpositional affixes, where semantic content does not lend itself to intensification, the limits of interpretability are soon reached; unless a derived form has been lexicalized with a specialized meaning, continued transposition soon loses its utility. A transposition of a transposition may be useful up to a point, but pure transposition does not add enough semantic content to be sustained indefinitely.

6.3   *Mismatches*

There are two other kinds of mismatches between form and meaning that we have yet to consider: cases where affixes appear to have no semantic content at all and cases where the semantic content of an affix appears to be eliminated when further affixation occurs. We will look at each of these cases in turn.

6.3.1   *Empty morphs*

Empty morphs are usually discussed in the context of inflectional, rather than derivational, morphology. Anderson (1992, 53–4) defines empty morphs as

---

11. Example heard on National Public Radio's "All Things Considered," May 6, 2002.

"subparts of a form that lack any content whatsoever" and cites as a typical example the theme vowel in Romance conjugations, for example, the *-e-* in French *pens-e-r-ai* "I will think" or the *-i-* in *sent-i-r-ai* "I will feel." The theme vowel in Romance conjugation signals morphological class. The verb *penser* "to think" has the root *pens* and belongs to the second conjugation, which takes *-e-* as its theme vowel. The verb *sentir* "to feel" has the root *sent* and takes *-i-* as its theme vowel. The theme vowel is necessary in certain inflectional environments (e.g., in the infinitive, or before the future morpheme *-r-*), but it bears no meaning of its own.

What is at issue here is whether there are empty morphs in derivation or compounding, and if there are, how such cases might be treated in the present theory. My position will be the following: I have maintained throughout this work that derivation and compounding are means of extending the simplex lexicon, in other words that they are a means of forming new lexemes. As such, these processes should be meaningful. We should no more expect empty morphs in derivation than we should expect meaningless simplex lexical items.[12] There appear to be several cases in English derivation that raise questions about the correctness of this prediction, however.

In English, candidates for empty morphs in derivation are rather rare, and occur primarily in conjunction with Latinate affixes like *-ion*, *-ic*, *-ive*, *-al*, and to some extent *-ory*. Possibilities include the segments listed in (6) (examples are all listed in Lehnert 1971):

(6)   a. *-at-*   orient-at-ion
                victimiz-at-ion
                affect-at-ion
                recommend-at-ive
                retard-at-ive
                laud-at-ive
                lymph-at-ic
                them-at-ic
                idiom-at-ic
                invit-at-ory
                observ-at-ory
                oblig-at-ory

12. There are a few candidates for meaningless simplex items, for example, pleonastic *it* or *there*, but this is certainly a closed class, and we would not expect derivation or compounding to be involved in extending it.

b. *-et-*   theor-et-ic
energ-et-ic
sympath-et-ic

c. *-it-*   repet-it-ion
add-it-ion
defin-it-ion

repet-it-ive
add-it-ive
defin-it-ive

crystall-it-ic
granul-it-ic
pneumon-it-ic

compet-it-ory

d. *-ut-*   revol-ut-ion
resol-ut-ion
dimin-ut-ion
resol-ut-ory
absol-ut-ory

e. *-t-*   schema-t-ic
Asia-t-ic
opera-t-ic

deduc-t-ion
prescrip-t-ion
redemp-t-ion

deduc-t-ive
prescrip-t-ive
redemp-t-ive

f. *-in-*   longitud-in-al
multitud-in-al
offic-in-al

g. *-n-*   bubo-n-ic
Plato-n-ic
Messia-n-ic

h. *-i-*   president-i-al
gerund-i-al
vestig-i-al

i. *-u-*   habit-u-al
sex-u-al
aspect-u-al

j. *-e-*   esophog-e-al
corpor-e-al

In most cases, there is no apparent phonological motivation for the segments added before the suffixes.[13] For example, although it might seem that an -*n*- or a -*t*- might be inserted by phonological rule to separate a vowel-final base from a vowel-initial suffix like -*ic*, there are examples like *heroic* or *algebraic* in which the sequence of two vowels is fine. Further, there is no phonological reason why the inserted consonant should be -*t*- in one case (e.g., *schematic*) but -*n*- in another (*Messianic*). Note also that the choice of additional segments seems to be made once per stem; if a particular stem can occur with more than one of these affixes, the same extension occurs in all the resulting derivatives (*repetition ~ repetitive*; *recommendation ~ recommendative*; *invitation ~ invitatory*). What we have then are phonologically unmotivated, semantically empty segments or sequences of segments – in other words, apparent perfect candidates for empty derivational morphs.

How are we to reconcile such data with the prediction made above that our system allows no semantically empty derivational morphs? The answer is in fact quite simple, and follows from the way in which so-called empty morphs are often treated in the analysis of inflection. For example, it is not unusual in analyses of the French or Latin conjugations to treat the theme-vowel stem (e.g., *pense*) as an arbitrary allomorph of the root (*pens*). It does not particularly matter whether the root and the theme-vowel stem are treated as listed alternants of each other as in Lieber (1980) or Lapointe (2001), or as derived by morphological rule or morphemic function, as would be the case in realizational theories such as Anderson (1992), Aronoff (1994), or Stump (2001). What matters, rather, is that the appearance of the theme vowel is treated as a matter of allomorphy, however allomorphy is executed within a given theory.

I will assume, then, that the Latinate derivational affixes -*ion*, -*ic*, -*ive*, -*al*, and -*ory* have various forms (whether listed or derived by realizational rule of some sort), and that the semantic content of a set of variants (e.g., -*ion*, -*tion*, -*ation*, -*ition*, -*ution*) will be precisely the same. It would also be possible to attribute the allomorphy to the bases rather than to the affixes (so *orient* would have the alternant *orientat*, and *revolv* the alternant *revolu*). Stem allomorphy is needed in any case for Latinate bases such as *receive* (allomorph *recept*) or

---

13. A possible exception here is the -*u*- which Aronoff (1976, 104) derives by morphophonological rule from the final -*v*- of the base by a process of vocalization (roughly [v→ u / l __ + ion]), but even here, a phonological solution is unlikely. With the root *salv* we find -*at-ion*, rather than the *salution* we would expect if *v* regularly became *u* before -*ion*. Also, Raffelsiefen (1996), Orgun and Sprouse (1999), and Plag (1999) all attempt to explain some of the allomorphy found with the suffix -*ize* within Optimality Theory.

destroy (allomorph *destruct*). Nothing in what follows hinges on the choice
between these two analyses, however, so I will leave the issue open.

Another case of empty morphology appears prominently in Germanic languages other than English (e.g., German, Afrikaans, and Dutch), and might be
mentioned here as well. That is, it has been observed frequently that the first
word of a compound or derived word in these languages sometimes occurs with
a "linking element" that is semantically empty (Aronoff 1994, citing Bloomfield 1933 and Botha 1968 as earlier sources). Aronoff and Fuhrhop (2002,
462) list three stem forms for the German noun *Blume* "flower": the inflectional
stem *blume*, the derivational stem *blum*, and the compounding stem *blumen*.
The word *Amerika* has a separate derivational stem *amerikan*. Again, neither
the final *e* in *blume*, the *en* in *blumen*, nor the *n* in *amerikan* bears meaning,
nor are any of the linking elements conditioned phonologically. But they do
not pose any problem for us. Whether we treat the stems as listed elements or
derive them by some sort of morphological function or rule, the issue here is
one of stem allomorphy, and not of semantically empty morphs.

6.3.2   Semantic subtraction

We have one remaining type of semantic mismatch to deal with here, what I
will call, for lack of a better term, semantic subtraction. In a case of semantic subtraction, we find a derivation affix (Y) which attaches to an already
affixed base ([base+X]), yielding a word which structurally has the form
[[base+X]+Y], but semantically seems to consist only of [base+Y]. That is,
the meaning of the affix X plays no role in the interpretation of the derived
word [[base+X]+Y]. At least one example of semantic subtraction has been
noted in Dutch (Booij 1997), and there is one case that we must examine in
English.

Consider the complex words in (7):

(7)   realistic
         surrealistic
         paternalistic
         ritualistic
         linguistic
         feudalistic
         artistic

All of these seem to have the form [[N/A] ist] ic]. The suffix *-ist*, as argued in
earlier chapters, provides the features [+material, dynamic] and forms personal

nouns. The suffix *-ic* adds the feature [−dynamic], yielding relational adjectives. But in the examples in (7) at least, the resulting words do not mean "pertaining to a person associated with <base>," but rather something like "pertaining to <base>." In other words, the meaning of the personal noun-forming suffix *-ist* seems to have been subtracted from the semantic interpretation of the derived word as a whole. Such examples suggest, at least superficially, that we might need to postulate rules of semantic deletion that operate over composed semantic skeletons.

However, before taking the step of adding special, and potentially very powerful, rules of semantic deletion to our theory, it is important to note that the data are more complex than the samples in (7) alone indicate. First, as (8) suggests, there are words in *-ist+ic* that have the expected compositional interpretation:

(8)   novelistic
       nationalistic
       formalistic
       fetishistic
       individualistic
       royalistic

All of these can plausibly be interpreted as "pertaining to a person associated with <base>." Further, some *-istic* derivations seem more closely tied semantically to corresponding bases in *-ism*:

(9)   masochistic
       Buddhistic
       naturalistic
       negativistic
       shamanistic
       sadistic

The OED defines *sadistic*, for example, as "related to sadism." Indeed, Aronoff (1976, 120–1), in discussing examples of this sort, proposes deriving *-istic* forms generally from the corresponding *-ism* forms by a readjustment rule: [m → t / s__ +ic]. But Aronoff himself points out that there are some words in *-istic* for which there is no corresponding *-ism* form (e.g., *artistic*, *linguistic*, and 24 others that Aronoff cites [1976, 118]). Although it is tempting to contemplate that the *-ist* in these *-istic* forms is something other than the familiar personal noun-forming affix, *-ism* does not seem like the best candidate.

Finally, there are a number of *-istic* forms that have no corresponding form in *-ist* at all:

(10)   characteristic
          logistic
          ballistic
          euphemistic
          totemistic
          shamanistic

Aronoff cites a number of other examples as well in which the corresponding -*ist* form is not only not semantically related to the -*istic* form, but not even
a plausible potential (much less existing) word at all.

All of these data taken together – but especially the data in (10) – suggest that
special rules of semantic deletion might not be necessary after all. The forms
in (10) suggest that the sequence -*istic* might in some cases best be analyzed as
an allomorph of -*ic*. As we saw in the previous section, -*ic* is already subject to
extensive allomorphy, with variants like -*ic*, -*nic*, -*tic*, -*atic*, -*etic*, -*itic*. Let us
suppose that -*ic* has the additional allomorph -*istic*, which, like all the others,
simply adds the feature [−dynamic] to the skeleton of its base.

We then have two ways of deriving words in -*istic*. Examples like those in
(10) which have no plausible -*ist* forms, as well as those in (7) in which -*ist* does
not contribute an independent meaning, will be derived by affixation of the -*istic*
allomorph to a nominal or adjectival base. Even examples like those in (9) might
be derived in this way. Examples with obviously compositional meanings like
those in (8), on the other hand, will be derived with the -*ic* allomorph attaching to
the noun or adjective in -*ist*. Some forms could plausibly have both derivations.
For example, the OED defines *artistic* as meaning either "pertaining to the
artist" or as "pertaining to art." The present analysis gives us a way at arriving
at both interpretations.

Our putative case of semantic subtraction thus reduces to another example of
allomorphy, and supports the analysis of Booij (1997). Indeed, Booij reaches
the same conclusion about the derivation of geographical adjectives in Dutch.
He notes, with respect to examples like those in (11), that "the formal base for
coining Dutch geographical adjectives is not the corresponding name of the
country, but the name of the corresponding inhabitant's name":

(11)   country   inhabitative   adjective
          Amerika   Amerikaan   Amerikaan-s
          Israel   Israëliet   Israëlit-isch

Formally, the basis of the geographical adjective seems to be the inhabitative,
but the semantic contribution of apparent affixal material like -*an* or -*iet* seems
to be subtracted from the interpretation of the adjective, just as -*ist* seems to be

subtracted in some of the cases above. Booij argues, however, that lexemes like *Amerika* and *Israël* have separate allomorphs *Amerikaan* and *Israëliet* respectively, the second of which is used in forming both the inhabitative and the adjectival forms. As the adjective is not formed from the inhabitative, we have no issue of semantic subtraction here.

The conclusion I draw from these examples is that semantic subtraction is an apparent, rather than a real, problem. Potential examples of semantic subtraction are not abundant to begin with in English and Dutch at least, and seem amenable to treatment as cases of allomorphy.

6.4   *Conclusion*

In this chapter I have considered several questions concerning the semantic interpretation of complex derived words: the nature of semantic restrictions on affixation, the issue of extended exponence or redundancy in affixation, the extent to which derivational affixes can be attached successively and recursively, and the proper treatment of apparent cases of empty derivational morphs and semantic subtraction in derivation. All of these phenomena receive reasonable explanations within the framework I have described in this book.

Although there may be semantic restrictions on the affixation of particular affixes, like those proposed on *re-* or *un-* in English, there is no general prohibition against semantic redundancy in derivation. Rather we rely on a pragmatic constraint on the usefulness and interpretability of newly coined words, perhaps following from Gricean principles, that discourages redundancy that does not serve a purpose or that leads to uninterpretable words. Extended exponence in derivation is therefore a formal possibility. On the other hand, I argued that both apparent empty morphs and subtractive semantics can be attributed to allomorphy.

The conclusion that I draw is that a theory of lexical semantic representation such as the one I have begun to develop in this book is fully capable of dealing with all the ways in which the correspondence between form and meaning can fail to be one-to-one.

7 Looking back, looking forward

At the beginning of this book, I articulated four questions about the semantics of word formation:

- *The polysemy question*: why are derivational affixes frequently polysemous? Do they have a unitary core of meaning, and if so, what is it?
- *The multiple-affix question*: why does English often have several affixes that perform the same kind of function or create the same kind of derived word?
- *The zero-derivation question*: how do we account for word formation in which there is semantic change without any concomitant formal change?
- *The semantic mismatch question*: why is the correspondence between form and meaning in word formation sometimes not one-to-one?

My goal throughout has been to begin to find answers to these questions. Doing so has necessitated developing a system of lexical semantic representation that allows us to characterize the meanings of simplex lexemes as well as affixes and complex words. In this system I have distinguished the semantic skeleton – that part of the representation that is decompositional, hierarchically arranged, and devoted to those aspects of meaning that have consequences for the syntax – from the semantic body – that part of the representation that is encyclopedic, holistic, and nondecompositional. I have motivated six semantic features [material], [dynamic], [IEPS], [Location], [B], and [CI] which allow us to distinguish major ontological categories of lexemes, as well as basic concepts of time, space, and quantity. And I have articulated a principle of co-indexation that allows parts of complex words to be integrated into single referential units. The system as it stands is only a beginning; it will surely need refining and it will have to be extended beyond the basic six features if it is to provide an adequate account of word formation cross-linguistically.

But even in its fragmentary form, the system has allowed us to frame tentative answers to our guiding questions.

Polysemy in word formation has several sources. On the one hand, derivational affixes frequently, indeed almost always, exhibit what has been called logical or constructional polysemy (Pustejovsky and Boguraev 1996, Copestake and Briscoe 1996): affixes – even purely transpositional ones – have semantic content, but that content is minimal, abstract, and vastly underdetermined. It consists of the same semantic features that define simplex lexical semantic classes, but most frequently without an accompanying body. When the semantically underdetermined affix is combined with the more semantically robust base and deployed in context, the semantic contribution of the affix can be lexicalized in a number of different ways. On the other hand, derivational affixes occasionally give rise to sense extensions, just as simplex lexemes do. Especially when forced by pragmatic circumstance – the lack of an existing affix with the necessary meaning and the need for a word – the meaning of an affix may be stretched (we saw a good example of this in chapter 5 with the extension of the collective affix *-ery* to place names).

The existence of multiple affixes with the same meaning follows from the architecture of the system of lexical semantic representation. The main formal claim that I have made is that affixal meanings are characterized by a small number of semantic features which serve generally to define lexical semantic classes in the simplex lexicon. But whereas simplex lexical items have bodies that distinguish them, affixes frequently do not. The featural system therefore defines a highly circumscribed semantic space into which affixes must fit. For example, in the absence of distinguishing bodily characteristics, noun-forming affixes must fit roughly into four spaces: [+material], [−material], [+material, dynamic], and [−material, dynamic].[1] Given the complex history of English, with borrowed affixes alongside native ones, it is inevitable that there will be some degree of affixal overlap, giving rise to "rival sets" like *-ation, -ment, -al, -ure*, or *-er, -ant*, etc.

How do we account for word formation in which there is semantic change with no concomitant formal change? We saw in chapter 3 that verbs formed by conversion in English show the entire range of semantic patterns exhibited by simplex verbs in English rather than the relative uniformity or circumscribed

---

1. This is, of course, an oversimplification. The more features we add to the system, the larger the semantic space we define.

polysemy that we find with affixes. What this suggests is that conversion is not a process of zero affixation, but rather a process of coinage or relisting: items from the nominal lexicon are simply transferred to the verbal lexicon with no formal change. Entering a new item in the lexicon, however, requires placing it in an existing lexical semantic class – hence the semantic change that accompanies relisting.

In chapter 6 we turned to the issue of semantic mismatches – derivational redundancy, empty morphs, and semantic subtraction. There I argued that nothing prevents derivational redundancy – cases in which a semantic feature is supplied by more than one derivational morpheme in a word – and that derivational redundancy is even occasionally favored by pragmatic circumstance. We tend not to coin words with redundant affixes unless they are useful: affixes like *re-* or *over-* that can express scalar qualities can be repeated to good effect. Affixes may be used recursively as long as the resulting word can be distinguished from its base. As for empty morphs, I argued that the theory I have developed predicts that they should not exist: as derivation, conversion, and compounding involve extension of the simplex lexicon, there should be no morphemes that add to words without changing semantic class. Indeed, as I showed in chapter 6, putative cases of empty morphs in English can all be analyzed as allomorphs either of a stem or of an affix. Similarly, the theory I have developed predicts that there should be no semantic subtraction. And I have argued again that apparent cases in English are better analyzed as cases of allomorphy as well.

In the course of answering our four framing questions, I have looked at a number of case studies of word formation in English: the affixes *-er*, *-ant*, *-ist*, and *-ee*, the verb-forming suffixes *-ize* and *-ify*, privative and negative affixes, the prefixes *over-* and *re-*, and collective suffixes *-ery* and *-age*. In addition, I have considered the semantic interpretation of compounds and verbs formed by conversion. We have therefore covered a fair amount of ground in English word formation.

But of course, there is more to be done. There is a great deal more that needs to be said about English word formation. Among the interesting questions I have not broached are these:

- Scalar effects: it is well known that some adjectives are gradable (*hot*, *wide*) and others are not (*pregnant*, *dead*). How is gradability expressed in our system, and how is it manifested in adjective-forming affixes such as *-ive* (*repulsive*), *-ary* (*dietary*), or *-al* (*logical*)? What role does the distinction between qualitative and relational adjectives play in derivation?

- The individual/stage distinction: it has been shown that the distinction between individual- and stage-level nouns and adjectives is syntactically significant (Carlson 1977, Kratzer 1995), and there is evidence that this distinction plays a role in derivational morphology as well. For example, the affix *ex-* in English seems to favor stage-level bases, as opposed to individual-level ones. So, an *ex-pedestrian* is fine, but an *ex-mother* is less plausible. Our system of lexical semantic representation does not yet have a way of encoding this distinction.

- Scopal effects: just as quantifiers and negatives may have differing scopal effects in a sentential context, some affixes may have varying scope. The affix *ex-* in English is again illustrative: in a phrase like *my ex-car*, the prefix *ex-* can take scope over its base, with the somewhat unlikely interpretation "something which I own which used to be a car (maybe now it's a pile of twisted scrap metal)," but the more likely interpretation is the one in which *ex-* takes scope over the possessive *my*, "a car which I used to own." Similarly, in the phrase *an ex-shortstop for the Redsox*, *ex-* can take scope over the whole phrase giving rise to the meaning "someone who is no longer a shortstop for any team (say, Johnny Pesky)" or only over *the Redsox*, with the meaning "someone who now plays shortstop for some other team (say, Lou Merloni)." We have no way as yet of encoding scope relations of this sort.

- Inflection: at the outset I decided to confine my study to processes of lexeme formation – derivation, compounding, and conversion. It is an obvious question to ask whether the system of lexical semantic representation can or should be extended to inflection. We have seen in passing that some features we have developed are useful in treating what Booij (1996) calls "inherent inflection." Morphemes like the plural *-s* or the progressive *-ing* might be analyzed using the quantity features [B] and [CI]. It is an open question, however, how inflection, inherent and noninherent, will fit into a wider featural system of lexical semantic representation.

These are four areas of English word formation that strike me as interesting, and sure to lead to important modifications and extensions of the system I have begun to develop. No doubt there are others that bear attention as well.

There are many more questions that arise as soon as we move from a consideration of English word formation to a study of word formation in its cross-linguistic context. What sorts of modifications will we need to make to our system to account, for example, for expressive morphology in Romance and Germanic languages, that is, diminutives, augmentatives, and the like, or for classifying morphemes such as those found in Slave (Rice 1998, 658), or for male/female personal nouns in Dutch (Booij 2002, 102)?

I leave all these issues for future research. What I hope to have done in this book is to begin creating a system in which questions like these may be raised, and indeed in which whole new areas of research open up. The system I have developed is surely wrong in details, perhaps even in fundamentals. But I hope to have shown that questions of the semantics of word formation are important ones that can no longer be ignored.

References

Allen, Margaret. 1978. Morphological investigations. PhD dissertation, University of Connecticut, Storrs.

Anderson, Stephen. 1992. *A-Morphous Morphology*. New York and Cambridge: Cambridge University Press.

Andrews, Edna. 1986. A synchronic semantic analysis of de- and un- in American English. *American Speech* 61: 221–32.

Apresjan, Jurij. 1974. Regular polysemy. *Linguistics* 142: 5–32.

Aronoff, Mark. 1976. *Word Formation in Generative Grammar*. Cambridge, MA: MIT Press.

1994. *Morphology By Itself*. Cambridge, MA: MIT Press.

Aronoff, Mark and Sungeun Cho. 2001. The semantics of -*ship* suffixation. *Linguistic Inquiry* 32: 167–73.

Aronoff, Mark and Nanna Fuhrhop. 2002. Restricting suffix combinations in German and English: closing suffixes and the monosuffix constraint. *Natural Language and Linguistic Theory* 20: 451–90.

Baayen, R. Harald. 1989. A corpus-based approach to morphological productivity. PhD dissertation, Free University, Amsterdam.

Baayen, R. Harald and Rochelle Lieber. 1991. Productivity and English derivations: a corpus-based study. *Linguistics* 29: 801–43.

Bach, Emmon. 1986. The algebra of events. *Linguistics and Philosophy* 9: 5–16.

Baker, Mark. 1985. Incorporation: a theory of grammatical function changing. PhD dissertation, Massachusetts Institute of Technology, Cambridge.

1988. *Incorporation: A Theory of Grammatical Function Changing*. Chicago: University of Chicago Press.

1996. *The Polysynthesis Parameter*. Oxford: Oxford University Press.

Barker, Chris. 1998. Episodic -*ee* in English: a thematic role constraint on new word formation. *Language* 74: 695–727.

Bauer, Laurie. 1987. -ee by gum! *American Speech* 62: 315–19.

1988. *Introducing Linguistic Morphology*. Edinburgh: Edinburgh University Press.

1993. More -ee words. *American Speech* 68: 222–4.

2001. *Morphological Productivity*. Cambridge: Cambridge University Press.

Beard, Robert. 1981. *The Indo-European Lexicon: A Full Synchronic Theory.* North Holland Linguistics Series 44. Amsterdam: North Holland.

1991. Decompositional composition: the semantics of scope ambiguities and "bracketing paradoxes." *Natural Language and Linguistic Theory* 9: 195–229.

1993. Simultaneous dual derivational origin. *Language* 69: 716–41.

1995. *Lexeme Morpheme Base Morphology.* New York: SUNY Press.

Bennett, Michael and Barbara Partee. 1972. *Toward the Logic of Tense and Aspect in English.* Bloomington, IN: distributed by Indiana University Linguistics Club.

Bierwisch, Manfred. 1988. On the grammar of local prepositions. In Manfred Bierwisch, W. Motsch, and I. Zimmermann, eds., *Syntax, Semantik, und Lexikon: Rudolf Ruzicka zum 65. Geburtstag.* Berlin: Akademie-Verlag. 1–65.

1989. The semantics of gradation. In Manfred Bierwisch and Ewald Lang, eds., *Dimensional Adjectives: Grammatical Structure and Conceptual Interpretation.* Berlin: Springer-Verlag. 71–267.

1996. How much space gets into language? In Paul Bloom, Mary Peterson, Lynn Nadel, and Merrill Garrett, eds., *Language and Space.* Cambridge, MA: MIT Press. 31–76.

Bloomfield, Leonard. 1933. *Language.* New York: Henry Holt.

Booij, Geert. 1986. Form and meaning in morphology: the case of Dutch "Agent" nouns. *Linguistics* 24: 503–17.

1988. The relation between inheritance and argument-linking: deverbal nouns in Dutch. In Martin Everaert, Arnold Evers, Riny Huybrechts, and Mieke Trommelen, eds., *Morphology and Modularity.* Dordrecht: Foris. 57–74.

1992. Compounding in Dutch. *Rivista di Linguistica* 4(1): 37–60.

1996. Inherent versus contextual inflection and the split morphology hypothesis. In Geert Booij and Jaap van Marle, eds., *Yearbook of Morphology 1995.* Dordrecht: Kluwer Academic Publishers. 1–16.

1997. Allomorphy and the autonomy of morphology. *Folia Linguistica* 31: 25–56.

2000. Paper delivered at the MPI Workshop on Affix Ordering. Max Planck Institute for Psycholinguistics, Nijmegen, January 2000.

2002. *The Morphology of Dutch.* Oxford: Oxford University Press.

Booij, Geert and Rochelle Lieber. 2004. On the paradigmatic nature of affixal semantics in English and Dutch. *Linguistics* 42: 327–57.

Bresnan, Joan and Joni Kannerva. 1989. Locative inversion in Chichewa: a case study of factorization in grammar. *Linguistic Inquiry* 20: 1–50.

Brinton, Laurel. 1998. Aspectuality and countability: a cross-categorial analogy. *English Language and Linguistics* 2 (1): 37–63.

Brugman, Claudia. 1988. *The Story of Over: Polysemy, Semantics and the Structure of the Lexicon.* New York. Garland Press.

Carlson, Gregory. 1977. Reference to kinds in English. PhD dissertation, University of Massachusetts, Amherst.

Carlson, Lauri. 1981. Aspect and quantification. In P. Tedeschi and A. Zaenen, eds., *Syntax and Semantics,* vol. XIV: *Tense and Aspect.* New York: Academic Press. 31–64.

Carstairs-McCarthy, Andrew. 1992. *Current Morphology*. London: Routledge.

Chomsky, Noam. 1970. Remarks on nominalization. In R. Jacobs and P. Rosenbaum, eds., *Readings in English Transformational Grammar*. Waltham, MA: Ginn. 184–221.

Clark, Eve V. and Herbert H. Clark. 1979. When nouns surface as verbs. *Language* 55: 767–811.

Comrie, Bernard. 1976. *Aspect*. Cambridge: Cambridge University Press.

Copestake, Ann and Ted Briscoe. 1996. Semi-productive polysemy and sense extension. In James Pustejovsky and Brad Boguraev, eds., *Lexical Semantics: The Problem of Polysemy*. Oxford: Clarendon Press. 15–68.

Corbin, Danielle. 1987. *Morphologie dérivationnelle et structuration du lexique*. Tübingen: Max Niemeyer Verlag.

Covington, Michael. 1981. *Evidence for Lexicalism: A Critical Review*. Bloomington, IN: distributed by Indiana University Linguistics Club.

Cruse, D. Alan. 1986. *Lexical Semantics*. Cambridge: Cambridge University Press.

2000. Aspects of the micro-structure of word meanings. In Yael Ravin and Claudia Leacock, eds., *Polysemy: Theoretical and Computational Approaches*. Oxford: Oxford University Press. 30–51.

Delancey, Scott. 1984. Notes on agentivity and causation. *Studies in Language* 8(2): 181–213.

1985. Agentivity and syntax. *Papers from the Regional Meetings, Chicago Linguistic Society* 21(2): 1–12.

Dell, Francois and Elisabeth Selkirk. 1978. On a morphologically governed vowel alternation in French. In S. J. Keyser, ed., *Recent Transformational Studies in European Linguistics*. Cambridge, MA: MIT Press. 1–52.

Depraetere, Ilse. 1995. On the necessity of distinguishing between (un)boundedness and (a)telicity. *Linguistics and Philosophy* 18: 1–19.

DiSciullo, Anna Maria and Edwin Williams. 1987. *On the Definition of Word*. Cambridge, MA: MIT Press.

Don, Jan. 1993. Morphological conversion. PhD dissertation, University of Utrecht.

Dowty, David. 1979. *Word Meaning and Montague Grammar: The Semantics of Verbs and Times in Generative Semantics and Montague's PTQ*. Dordrecht: Reidel.

1991. Thematic proto-roles and argument selection. *Language* 67: 574–619.

Ducrot, O. 1973. *La Preuve et le Dire*. Paris: Maison Mame.

Engelberg, Stefan. 1999. "Punctuality" and verb semantics. *Proceedings of the 23rd Annual Penn Linguistics Colloquium* 6(1): 127–40.

Fabb, Nigel. 1988. English suffixation is constrained only by selectional restrictions. *Natural Language and Linguistic Theory* 6: 527–39.

Filip, Hana. 2000. The quantization puzzle. In Carol Tenny and James Pustejovsky, eds., *Events as Grammatical Objects: The Converging Perspectives of Lexical Semantics and Syntax*. Stanford, CA: CSLI Publications. 39–96.

Fodor, Jerry. 1998. *Concepts: Where Cognitive Science Went Wrong*. Oxford: Oxford University Press.

Giegerich, Heinz. 1999. *Lexical Strata in English: Morphological Causes, Phonological Effects*. Cambridge: Cambridge University Press.

Gillon, Brendan. 1992. Toward a common semantics for English count and mass nouns. *Linguistics and Philosophy* 15: 597–639.

Grice, H. Paul. 1975. Logic and conversation. In Peter Cole and Jerry Morgan, eds., *Syntax and Semantics*, vol. III: *Speech Acts*. New York: Academic Press. 43–58.

1978. Further notes on logic and conversation. In Peter Cole, ed., *Syntax and Semantics*, vol. IX: *Pragmatics*. New York: Academic Press. 113–28.

Grimshaw, Jane. 1990. *Argument Structure*. Cambridge, MA: MIT Press.

Hale, Kenneth and Samuel J. Keyser. 2002. *Prolegomena to a Theory of Argument Structure*. Cambridge, MA: MIT Press.

Halle, Morris and K. P. Mohanan. 1985. Segmental phonology of Modern English. *Linguistic Inquiry* 16: 57–116.

Hay, Jennifer, Christopher Kennedy, and Beth Levin. 1999. Scalar structure underlies telicity in "degree achievements." *Proceedings of SALT 9*: 127–44.

Heyvaert, Liesbet. 2001. Deverbal -*er* suffixation as morphological equivalent of the clausal subject-finite unit. Catholic University of Leuven, Belgium. Preprint 176.

Higginbotham, James. 1985. On semantics. *Linguistic Inquiry* 16: 547–94.

Hockett, Charles. 1954. Two models of grammatical description. *Word* 10: 210–34.

Horn, Laurence. 1989/2001. *A Natural History of Negation*. Chicago: University of Chicago Press; reprinted 2001 by CSLI Publications, Stanford, CA.

2002. Uncovering the un-word: a study in lexical pragmatics. *Sophia Linguistica* 49: 1–64.

Jackendoff, Ray. 1972. *Semantic Interpretation in Generative Grammar*. Cambridge, MA: MIT Press.

1983. *Semantics and Cognition*. Cambridge, MA: MIT Press.

1987. The status of thematic relations in linguistic theory. *Linguistic Inquiry* 18: 369–412.

1990. *Semantic Structures*. Cambridge, MA: MIT Press.

1991. Parts and boundaries. *Cognition* 41: 9–45.

1996a. The proper treatment of measuring out, telicity, and perhaps even quantification in English. *Natural Language and Linguistic Theory* 14: 305–54.

1996b. The architecture of the linguistic-spatial interface. In Paul Bloom, Mary Peterson, Lynn Nadel, and Merrill Garrett, eds., *Language and Space*. Cambridge, MA: MIT Press. 1–30.

Jaeggli, Osvaldo. 1986. Passive. *Linguistic Inquiry* 17: 587–622.

Jespersen, Otto. 1931. *A Modern English Grammar on Historical Principles*. Part IV: Syntax. London: George Allen and Unwin; reprinted 1965.

1942. *A Modern English Grammar on Historical Principles*. Part VI: Morphology. Copenhagen: Einar Munksgaard.

Kiparsky, Paul. 1982. From cyclic phonology to lexical phonology. In H. van der Hulst and N. Smith, eds., *The Structure of Phonological Representations*. Dordrecht: Foris. 131–75.

Kratzer, Angelika. 1995. Stage-level and individual-level predicates. In Gregory N. Carlson and Francis Jeffry Pelletier, eds., *The Generic Book*. Chicago: University of Chicago Press. 125–75.

Lakoff, George. 1987. *Women, Fire, and Dangerous Things.* Chicago: University of Chicago Press.

Landau, Barbara. 1996. Multiple geometric representations of objects in languages and language learners. In Paul Bloom, Mary Peterson, Lynn Nadel, and Merrill Garrett, eds., *Language and Space.* Cambridge, MA: MIT Press. 317–64.

Landman, Fred. 1989. Groups I, II. *Linguistics and Philosophy* 12: 559–605, 723–44.

1996. Plurality. In Shalom Lappin, ed., *The Handbook of Contemporary Semantic Theory.* Oxford: Blackwell. 425–58.

Lapointe, Steven. 2001. Stem selection and OT. In Geert Booij and Jaap van Marle, eds., *Yearbook of Morphology 1999.* Dordrecht: Kluwer Academic Publishers. 263–98.

Lasersohn, Peter. 1995. *Plurality, Conjunction and Events.* Dordrecht: Kluwer Academic Publishers.

Lees, Robert. 1963. *The Grammar of English Nominalizations.* The Hague: Mouton.

Lehnert, Martin. 1971. *Reverse Dictionary of Present-Day English.* Leipzig: VEB Verlag Enzyklopädie.

Levi, Judith. 1978. *The Syntax of Complex Nominals.* New York: Academic Press.

Levin, Beth. 1993. *English Verb Classes and Alternations: A Preliminary Investigation.* Chicago: University of Chicago Press.

1999. Objecthood: an event structure perspective. *Proceedings of the Chicago Linguistic Society* 35(1): 223–47.

Levin, Beth and Malka Rappaport. 1986. The formation of adjectival passives. *Linguistic Inquiry* 17: 623–61.

1988. Non-event *-er* nominals: a probe into argument structure. *Linguistics* 26: 1067–83.

Levin, Beth and Malka Rappaport Hovav. 1995. *Unaccusativity.* Cambridge, MA: MIT Press.

Lieber, Rochelle. 1980. On the organization of the lexicon. PhD dissertation, Massachusetts Institute of Technology, Cambridge, MA. [Published by Indiana University Linguistics Club, 1981 and Garland Press, 1990.]

1981. Morphological conversion within a restrictive theory of the lexicon. In M. Moortgat, H. van der Hulst, and T. Hoekstra, eds., *The Scope of Lexical Rules.* Dordrecht: Foris. 161–200.

1983. Argument linking and compounds in English. *Linguistic Inquiry* 14: 251–86.

1992a. *Deconstructing Morphology: Word Formation in Syntactic Theory.* Chicago: University of Chicago Press.

1992b. Compounding in English. *Rivista di Linguistica* 4(1): 79–96.

1998. The suffix *-ize* in English: implications for morphology. In Steven G. Lapointe, Diane K. Brentari, and Patrick M. Farrell, eds., *Morphology and Its Relation to Phonology and Syntax.* Stanford, CA: CSLI Publications, 12–34.

Lieber, Rochelle and Harald Baayen. 1997. A semantic principle of auxiliary selection in Dutch. *Natural Language and Linguistic Theory* 15: 789–845.

1999. Nominalizations in a calculus of lexical semantic representations. In Geert Booij and Jaap van Marle, eds., *Yearbook of Morphology 1998.* Dordrecht: Kluwer Academic Publishers. 175–98.

Lyons, John. 1977. *Semantics.* Cambridge: Cambridge University Press.

Marantz, Alec. 1984. *On the Nature of Grammatical Relations*. Cambridge, MA: MIT Press.

Marchand, Hans. 1969. *The Categories and Types of Present-Day English Word Formation. A Synchronic-Diachronic Approach.* Munich: Beck.

Matthews, P. 1972. *Inflectional Morphology*. Cambridge: Cambridge University Press.

1974. *Morphology*. Cambridge: Cambridge University Press.

Maynor, Natalie. 1979. The morpheme un: *American Speech* 54: 310–11.

Mittwoch, Anita. 1991. In defense of Vendler's achievements. *Belgian Journal of Linguistics* 6: 71–86.

Mohanan, K. P. 1986. *The Theory of Lexical Phonology*. Dordrecht: Reidel.

Mohanan, Tara and K. P. Mohanan. 1999. On representations in grammatical semantics. In Tara Mohanan and Lionel Wee, eds., *Grammatical Semantics: Evidence for Structure in Meaning*. Stanford, CA: CSLI Publications. 23–76.

Muysken, Pieter. 1986. Approaches to affix order. *Linguistics* 24: 629–43.

Newmeyer, Frederick. 1999. *Language Form and Language Function*. Cambridge, MA: MIT Press.

2002. Optimality and functionality: a critique of functionally-based optimality theoretic syntax. *Natural Language and Linguistic Theory* 20: 43–80.

Nunberg, Geoffrey. 1996. Transfers of meaning. In James Pustejovsky and Brad Boguraev, eds., *Lexical Semantics, The Problem of Polysemy*. Oxford: Clarendon Press. 109–32.

Orgun, Cemil Orhan and Ronald Sprouse. 1999. From MPARSE to CONTROL: deriving ungrammaticality. *Phonology* 16(2): 191–225.

Panther, Klaus-Uwe and Linda Thornburg. 1998. The polysemy of the derivational *-er* suffix in English. Paper delivered at the Cognitive Morphology Workshop, Ghent, Belgium, July, 1998.

Pinker, Steven. 1989. *Learnability and Cognition*. Cambridge, MA: MIT Press.

Plag, Ingo. 1999. *Morphological Productivity: Structural Constraints in English Derivation*. Berlin: Mouton de Gruyter.

Pustejovsky, James. 1991. The syntax of event structure. *Cognition* 41: 47–81.

1995. *The Generative Lexicon*. Cambridge, MA: MIT Press.

Pustejovsky, James and Brad Boguraev. 1996. Introduction: lexical semantics in context. In James Pustejovsky and Brad Boguraev, eds., *Lexical Semantics: The Problem of Polysemy*. Oxford: Clarendon Press. 1–14.

Quirk, Randolph, Sidney Greenbaum, Geoffrey Leech, and Jan Svartvik. 1972. *A Grammar of Contemporary English*. London: Longman.

Raffelsiefen, Renate. 1996. Gaps in word formation. In Ursula Kleinhenz, ed., *Interfaces in Phonology*. Berlin: Academie-Verlag. 194–209.

Ramchand, Gillian. 1997. *Aspect and Predication*. Oxford: Clarendon Press.

Rappaport Hovav, Malka and Beth Levin. 1992. -ER nominals: implications for the theory of argument structure. In T. Stowell and E.Wehrli, eds., *Syntax and Semantics*, vol. XXVI: *Syntax and the Lexicon*. New York: Academic Press. 127–53.

1996. Two types of derived accomplishments. In Miriam Butt and Tracy H. King, eds., *Proceedings of the First LFG Conference*. Grenoble: RANK Xerox. 375–88.

1998. Building verb meanings. In M. Butt and W. Geuder, eds., *The Projection of Arguments: Lexical and Compositional Factors*. Stanford, CSLI Publications. 97–134.

Rice, Keren. 1998. Slave (Northern Athapaskan). In Andrew Spencer and Arnold Zwicky, eds., *The Handbook of Morphology*. Oxford: Blackwell. 648–89.

Richardson, John. 1985. Agenthood and case. *Papers from the Regional Meetings, Chicago Linguistic Society* 21(2): 241–51.

Roeper, Thomas. 1988. Compound syntax and head movement. *Yearbook of Morphology* 1: 187–228.

Roeper, Thomas and Muffy Siegel. 1978. A lexical transformation for verbal compounds. *Linguistic Inquiry* 9: 197–260.

Ryder, Mary Ellen. 1999. Bankers and blue-chippers: an account of *-er* formations in present-day English. *English Language and Linguistics* 3: 269–97.

Saeed, John. 1997. *Semantics*. Oxford: Blackwell.

Sapir, Edward. 1944. *Grading: A Study in Semantics*; reprinted in D. Mandelbaum, ed., *Selected Writings*. Berkeley: University of California Press 1951. 122–49.

Scalise, Sergio. 1984. *Generative Morphology*. Dordrecht: Foris.

Schein, Barry. 1993. *Plurals and Events*. Cambridge, MA: MIT Press.

Schultink, Henk. 1975. Output conditions in word formation? In *Ut Videam: Contributions to an Understanding of Linguistics*. Lisse: Peter De Ridder Press. 263–72.

Schwarzschild, Roger. 1992. Types of plural individuals. *Linguistics and Philosophy* 15: 641–75.

1996. *Pluralities*. Dordrecht: Kluwer Academic Press.

Selkirk, Elisabeth. 1982. *The Syntax of Words*. Cambridge, MA: MIT Press.

Siegel, Dorothy. 1974. Topics in English morphology. PhD dissertation, Massachusetts Institute of Technology, Cambridge, MA.

1977. The adjacency condition and the theory of morphology. *Proceedings of NELS* 8. Amherst, MA: GLSA. 189–97.

Smith, Carlotta. 1997. *The Parameter of Aspect* (2nd edition). Dordrecht: Kluwer Academic Publishers.

Spencer, Andrew. 1991. *Morphological Theory*. Oxford: Blackwell.

Sproat, Richard. 1985. On deriving the lexicon. PhD dissertation, Massachusetts Institute of Technology, Cambridge, MA.

Strauss, Steven. 1982. On "Relatedness Paradoxes" and Related Paradoxes. *Linguistic Inquiry* 13: 694–700.

Stump, Gregory. 2001. *Inflectional Morphology: A Theory of Paradigm Structure*. Cambridge: Cambridge University Press.

Szymanek, Bogdan. 1988. *Categories and Categorization in Morphology*. Lublin: Catholic University Press.

Talmy, Leonard. 1985. Lexicalization patterns: semantic structure in lexical forms. In Timothy Shopen, ed., *Language Typology and Syntactic Description*, vol. III: *Grammatical Categories and the Lexicon*. Cambridge: Cambridge University Press. 57–149.

2000. *Toward a Cognitive Semantics*. Cambridge, MA: MIT Press.

Tenny, Carol. 1987. Grammaticalizing aspect and affectedness. PhD dissertation, Massachusetts Institute of Technology, Cambridge, MA.

1994. *Aspectual Roles and the Syntax-Semantics Interface*. Dordrecht: Kluwer Academic Publishers.

Tenny, Carol and James Pustejovsky. 2000. A history of events in linguistic theory. In Carol Tenny and James Pustejovsky, eds., *Events as Grammatical Objects: The Converging Perspectives of Lexical Semantics and Syntax*. Stanford, CA: CSLI Publications. 3–38.

Tyler, Andrea and Vyvyan Evans. 2001. Reconsidering prepositional polysemy networks: the case of *over*. *Language* 77(4): 724–65.

Van Valin, Robert and Randy LaPolla. 1997. *Syntax: Structure, Meaning and Function*. Cambridge: Cambridge University Press.

Vendler, Zeno. 1967. *Linguistics in Philosophy*. Ithaca, NY: Cornell University Press.

Verkuyl, Henk. 1972. *On the Compositional Nature of the Aspects*. Dordrecht: Reidel.

1989. Aspectual classes and aspectual composition. *Linguistics and Philosophy* 12: 39–94.

1993. *A Theory of Aspectuality*. Cambridge: Cambridge University Press.

1999. *Aspectual Issues: Studies on Time and Quantity*. Stanford, CA: CSLI Publications.

Wierzbicka, Anna. 1972. *Semantic Primitives*. Linguistische Forschungen. No. 22. Frankfurt: Athenäum.

1980. *Lingua Mentalis: The Semantics of Natural Language*. Sydney: Academic Press.

1985. *Lexicography and Conceptual Analysis*. Ann Arbor: Karoma.

1988. *The Semantics of Grammar*. Amsterdam: John Benjamins.

1996. *Semantics: Primes and Universals*. Oxford: Oxford University Press.

Williams, Edwin. 1981. Argument structure and morphology. *Linguistic Review* 1: 81–114.

Zimmer, Karl. 1964. *Affixal Negation in English and Other Languages*. Supplement to *Word*, Monograph No. 5.

Index